TAKEN

Experiences of Forced Adoption

KAREN CONSTANTINE

Published by Pram Publications

prampublications.com

ISBN: 978-1-0685543-0-8

Book design by Chris Constantine

Printed in the UK by Solopress, Southend-on-Sea

**Front cover photograph supplied with kind permission of
Jill Killington and Ian Pritchard**

Jill Killington lost her son, Ian, to adoption in 1968, at a time when forced adoptions of young single women's babies were commonplace. Mothers had to sign legal papers to the effect that it would be unlawful to ever have any further contact with their children.

Jill later married her husband, Richard, and they have two children together, now in their forties.

However, with changes in adoption policy, Jill placed her name on the National Contact Register in 1985 when Ian was eighteen years old, and when he was twenty-six he made contact. They have now been reunited for thirty years, and both are pro-active in supporting the cause for an adoption apology, and support those who have had similar life experiences, having often been asked to give interviews in the media and press. Their stories have touched the hearts of many of the hundreds of thousands of other birth families and their children who were so cruelly parted.

I am grateful to both Jill and Ian for their kind permission to use this photograph of them.

To the Movement for an Adoption Apology and
in memory of its co-founder, Veronica Smith.

Acknowledgements

I first spoke to Veronica Smith who founded the Movement for an Adoption Apology (MAA) in August 2023, after we had exchanged emails about my intention to write this book. To say she was warm and encouraging would be an understatement. Subsequently, I met her properly at the TUC Women's Conference at Congress House in March 2024 where MAA had taken a stall to promote their cause to the women in the trades union movement. Our paths crossed again on 1 June 2024 at a MAA members' and supporters' day in central London. At eighty-three years old, she remained utterly committed to the need to obtain a formal apology, which she told me she desperately wanted to receive in her lifetime. The need for that wasn't lost on me – many MAA women have expressed the same.

On 29 June 2024, Veronica passed away. Her obituaries in *The Telegraph*, *The Guardian*, *The Sydney Morning Herald* and elsewhere are testament to the importance of her shared mission, and celebrate her indomitable spirit, highlighting how she was 'railroaded' into giving up her daughter, Rachel (with whom, thanks to hiring a private detective, she was reunited in 2004). Veronica said, "I honestly felt if I'd have murdered someone it might have been more acceptable." Most, if not all, women who were forced to part with their babies feel the same.

Veronica's unexpected death illustrates that a formal apology from the Government cannot come swiftly enough, and she isn't the first to die without public acknowledgement of the immeasurable wrongs perpetrated against her. If *Taken: Experiences of Forced Adoption* moves us even one step closer to a formal apology and reparations for women whilst they are still alive, it will have been a privilege to write it.

I am beyond grateful to those people who so bravely and openly shared their experiences of forced adoption, their thoughts, feelings, and personal records with me. Often, they were opening up for the first time, talking about complicated and traumatic memories. It took tremendous courage to trust me, and I thank all my interviewees from the very bottom of my heart for the privilege of being able to hear and now share your histories. I hope I have done your courage, strength, resilience and heartache justice. This book is for you: these are your words, your experiences, your lives captured on these pages. This is an anthology of your reality that has, I believe, been purposefully hidden from public consciousness for too many decades.

Huge thanks also to Diana Defries who now runs MAA, Jeannot Farmer, author of *No More Standing in the Shadows – Treating the Wounds of Historic Forced Adoption*, and Ann Keen, previously MP for Brentford and Isleworth who herself experienced forced adoption, losing her only child. To Dr Michael Lambert, Research Fellow, Lancaster University Medical School whose support was inspirational. To my beta readers: Christine and Jenny; to my inspirational friends: author Sarah Pat O'Brien, Jane Hetherington, MBACP (Accred), Dr Avi Ben-Zeev, Marcella Marx, Phillipa Stock and Farha Quadri for their encouragement. Also, to my friends for their support and tolerance, especially when I refused to socialise, requiring solitude to focus. Thanks too to *Chartist Magazine* for printing my first article on the subject, and BBC Radio Kent political reporter, Michael Keogh, and BBC South East *Sunday Politics* for their skillful highlighting of this issue. And I am beyond grateful to my talented and supportive editor, Tracey McEvoy, who I was lucky to meet at The Margate Bookie in 2023. To all those who so generously and courageously contributed, assisted and supported me on this journey, I am indebted to you.

I would also like to make special mention of Chris, my partner, who has supported me emotionally and practically every minute of every day since I first met him many years ago, and to my daughters, Daisy and Lillian for their love, support and effervescence. Last but not least, my sons: Daniel, you were the making of me, and Aaron – forever missed – both dearly loved.

Contents

A Birthmother's Catechism

How did you let him go?

With black ink and legalese

How did you let him go?

It'd be another year before I could vote

How did you let him go?

With altruism, tears, and self-loathing

How did you let him go?

A nurse brought pills for drying up breast milk

How did you let him go?

Who hangs a birdhouse from a sapling?

Carrie Etter, *Imagined Sons*

Foreword

'It's for the best'. This phrase was so often used to me, but 'best' for who?

In 1966 at the age of seventeen, I was sent away to a Swansea mother and baby home from Flintshire. My parents thought it would be for the best if I could have the baby adopted, get on with my life, and my baby have a different opportunity. It was terrifying.

After giving birth to my baby, I was told I should remember the pain, they didn't give me any pain relief because I was a 'bad girl', and it mustn't happen to me again. I remember being stitched and the doctor slapping my leg to keep still.

Taken punches the reader with hard facts, truth and emotion that hurts. This book is even more evidence of why the State needs to be accountable for the damage caused to mothers, their children and families. Many of us live with the consequences to this day, I know that I do. It is of great importance that we have an apology from the UK Government. Only a government can apologise for society's attitude to us all at the time, but not only society, the governments of the time were very aware of what was happening. I have been judged by different generations who say, "How could you give your baby away?" I can now answer, "I didn't – my son was taken, taken by the State."

I trained to be a nurse in 1976 to make sure that I could influence dignity, respect and compassionate care for all. You will read how young terrified women were not given this care. The stigma stays with me; I know it will never leave me.

As a former Labour MP and Health Minister, I have requested that our Prime Minister, Sir Keir Starmer will meet with MAA and discuss a way forward. It is essential this happens soon. Karen has put the case for justice in a very human way. It is truly astonishing how many people are affected by adoption, equally astonishing as to how few know the facts around forced adoption. This has to change.

Ann Keen, October 2024

Ann Keen is a former Labour Health Minister, who served as Member of Parliament for Brentford and Isleworth from 1997 to 2010. She became Parliamentary Private Secretary for Gordon Brown and later, Parliamentary Under-Secretary of State for Health Services from 2007 to 2010. Keen led an independent commission on the future of nursing and midwifery. She is a visiting professor at the University of East London in Politics, Health, and Inequality.

Introduction

When people have been wronged, it is vital to the journey of healing that what happened and the pain it caused are acknowledged. In addition to mattering to those most affected, delivering an apology can be a moment of community knowledge building. We will only avoid future errors if we truly face and learn from the past.

Jeannot Farmer,
No More Standing in the Shadows – Treating the Wounds of Historic Forced Adoption

I, like many other young, unmarried pregnant women, endured incarceration in a Catholic-run mother and baby home at fifteen years of age in 1978. The experience both haunted and shamed me throughout my adult life. Why was I suddenly sent away from home? Why was my formal education abruptly truncated? Why was I forced to work alone in the on-site laundry? Why was there no support to keep my baby?

It wasn't until 2017, in my mid-fifties, that I began to confront the intense and lifelong impact of the months I'd spent in a mother and baby home against my will. Only then, did I begin to address and work through the shame I was still carrying. Despite these experiences, I was profoundly fortunate in keeping my baby son, Daniel. Until I undertook this research, I hadn't realised how rare that was for 'deviant' girls like me. I found out that my aunt's sister-in-law had suffered a similar fate, becoming pregnant when unmarried, and her baby had been taken from her. Evidently, my aunt did not want to see history repeated.

I'm immeasurably indebted to my late aunt Wyn, as I believe she was instrumental in fomenting the circumstances, which allowed me to keep my son, thereby avoiding a fate that many mothers described to me as being 'worse than death'. That fate was forced adoption. As I researched and documented my own history, I became aware of a vast number of women, *up to half a million*, who hadn't been as fortunate.

They, and their now adult children, all too often suffered the devastating and life-long impact of being forcibly separated soon after childbirth.

I came to understand how babies were adopted against their mothers' wills; that, in reality, the mothers had no real choice, and even less say in the future of their babies – because babies were a *commodity* and forced adoption was a *lucrative and efficient business* – and both the church and state benefited from this cruel, socially accepted practice.

Nonetheless, I remained perplexed as to why I was able to keep my baby when the other girls and women in my home were not. What happened to them after they had their babies taken from them? Not least the PFI or Pregnant From Ireland (the term used by so-called welfare agencies), one of whom was the young mother who befriended and guided me as she fought to revoke the *coerced* agreement to have her baby son adopted. Was she successful? I will never know what became of her, or the others and their children.

I have spent my working life defending people as a trades union officer, holding some high-profile influential roles, including National Officer for Equality for the GMB Union, and although I have no midwifery training, I was Head of the South for the Royal College of Midwives. I've been a member of the Labour Party since I was nineteen and spent eight years from 2015 representing Labour Party members on the South East Regional Executive and the National Policy Forum. Since 4 May 2017, I've been the somewhat outspoken Labour County Councillor for the seaside town of Ramsgate, well-known for its wonderful coast, chalk cliffs and unique Royal Harbour. A friendly place, marred by political neglect and ever-more unpalatable metrics of deprivation that are wholly out of step with the rest of leafy, well-heeled Kent.

I abhor injustice (in part due to my experience of being a young unmarried mother in the seventies and eighties) and have spent my working life fighting for equality and challenging the status quo.

It isn't hyperbole to state that historic forced adoptions are among the UK's greatest examples of social injustice, the most extraordinary public scandal that has yet to be adequately addressed by those in power. I hope the frank personal narratives and often barbaric experiences in this book help to bring attention to these issues and promote the change and redress that is so long overdue, not least the *formal apology* owed to many women and their children, which the Conservative government should have issued during their time in office, but also meaningful and practical *reparations*.

When I discovered how many women and children had been subject to historic forced adoptions, and knowing a general election would be forthcoming, I vowed to use all my energy, political will and connections in my last year of elected office to push for action from the incoming government. I started by attending the Labour Party Conference in 2023, seeking a meeting with Helen Hayes MP, then Shadow Secretary of State for Education, who kindly agreed to meet with me; we have corresponded and met several times as this book has developed.

Following the General Election in July 2024, Janet Daby MP was appointed as Parliamentary Under-Secretary of State (Minister for Children and Families). I pressed for a formal meeting with her, which I finally secured, attending the DfE, Department for Education, on 15 October 2024. I met with Minister Daby, and two advisors, Emma Davies, the Deputy Director for Adoption, Kinship and Alternatives to Care, and Tom Waters, Special Advisor to the Rt Hon Bridget Phillipson MP, Secretary of State for Education and Minister for Women and Equalities.

During our thirty-minute meeting, I again outlined MAA's case for an apology and explained the findings of my own research. It was an opportunity to strongly emphasise to this new team, the need for a timely formal apology and to outline the support measures that should be brought forward. I acknowledged and agreed that the in-coming government have a great deal to do, however I couldn't refrain from responding to the potential barriers to action being put forward, by pointing out, "There is little that is worse than the trauma of a woman having her baby forcibly taken for adoption – either for her, or the baby." Especially given the numbers of women and adult adoptees involved. I suggested that the Minister and her team should meet with MAA, as a fact-finding opportunity for the Minister, and in an effort to build trust and collaboration, to begin to move forward. To date no such meeting has been arranged.

This isn't an academic book. It's my attempt to give a voice and increased visibility to the lived experiences of historic forced adoption, and to galvanise support for the much-needed apology and reparations.

I hope you will understand why I have used pseudonyms where contributors have requested this, and obscured other identifying details. I have otherwise kept to first names, used with permission. A number of people only felt comfortable sharing their experiences due to the passage of time, knowing that after many decades no hurt or upset was likely to be caused.

A note of caution. For many, this book may well be a troubling and disconcerting read, whether or not you have lived experience of forced adoption. Collecting these personal testimonies and rendering them onto the page has been moving and at times emotionally challenging for me. Jeannot Farmer in her work *No More Standing in the Shadows – Treating the Wounds of Historic Forced Adoption* has some words of wisdom, which I'll highlight here:

> For those of you who find this reading matter difficult, I urge you to put it down, have a cup of tea and come back to it, if and when it feels right.

About historic forced adoption

Until relatively recently, the Catholic Church and other religious bodies, including the Salvation Army and the Church of England, supported by the State, all ran homes for *fallen women* (i.e. unmarried pregnant women and girls) supported by social workers, moral welfare workers, and clinicians. They worked in concert to supply pregnant women and girls into the homes, ensuring a plentiful supply of babies for waiting adoptive parents. These often austere and isolated places were also known as Magdalene Laundries in Ireland and Northern Ireland.

Mother and baby homes first appeared in England in 1891; by 1968 there were 172 homes, mainly run by religious bodies. In the 1960s, mother and baby homes catered for between 11,000 and 12,000 unmarried mothers annually. The number of mothers 'giving up their children' peaked in 1968 when 16,164 adoption orders were granted. By the mid-eighties, most homes had closed.

The women and girls in these homes all too often experienced significant neglect, were also forced into unpaid manual work within the homes, received poor antenatal care and inhumane mistreatment during labour and postpartum. This way, these women who were made to feel extreme shame, who were very often utterly shunned and *othered* by their families (and their own mothers in particular), excluded from church and community, separated from workplaces and education, without access to *any* support, were forced – *coerced* – into surrendering their babies for adoption. Both adoption and residency in the mother and baby homes were monetised by way of *fees* and/or *donations* to the Church; in some circumstances, the State paid. According to the interviews I conducted, versions of these practices were still in place into the 1980s.

Poor treatment of women and their children in Irish mother and baby homes was well-known. The now infamous Irish home, Tuam, is notable. The *Final Report of the Commission into Mother and Baby Homes* in January 2021, shockingly confirmed that of the 3,251 children born in or admitted to the home, 802 died and were furtively buried in mass graves and septic tanks. Tuam and other homes essentially operated as large factories, best described as 'shame industrial complexes'. After the appalling treatment of women and their babies at Tuam was revealed, the Bon Secours Sisters (the order of nuns who ran the home) issued a public apology for the 'disrespectful and unacceptable' way in which the victims were buried (BBC News, 2021). In fact, there were no burial records for the 802 children who died at Tuam. The Bessborough home had a scandalously high infant mortality rate, the highest in Ireland. Three-quarters of children born there died before their first birthday.

The mother and baby homes, which usually operated with minimal transparency, often failing to gain proper consent from their residents, also offered a potentially ideal environment in which to conduct experimental procedures. Vaccine trials were running in several Irish children's homes and children's hospitals. One woman I interviewed for background and context, shared first-hand knowledge of these vaccine trials and the challenges of obtaining the truth from either the State or Church. It's reasonable to believe that these and other homes' practices were known and feared. People do talk. With these appalling examples and this history of abuse, it's little wonder that women in Britain latterly feared that they may have been unwitting guinea pigs when it came to unconsented treatment to prevent lactation. It's entirely plausible. And as we have seen in the recent infected blood scandal, 30,000 people were infected with HIV and hepatitis C after being given infected blood products in the 1970s and 1980s – children were *used* as guinea pigs in clinical trials. The empirical evidence of antenatal care – or rather the lack of it – and the cruelty of forcing mothers to labour, without medical intervention to relieve pain and suffering, possibly overseen by unqualified staff, must have had an impact on infant mortality and health. Research into this area urgently needs to be undertaken.

Like me, you're probably wondering how this situation could have evolved in Ireland, and then have been so successfully transposed to England, Wales, Scotland and Northern Ireland. It's Atwood-like in its dystopian vision.

My life, as I have volunteered, has been a political one, and the answer to this is political. Ireland has been formed in a very particular way; the Irish Republic rose after 800 years of oppression by the English. The Irish Free State was established in 1922 and, from then until 1937, Irish society was largely socially permissive. Sharon Lawless details the cultural and political change that prepared the ground for the brutality in mother and baby homes in Theresa Hiney Tinggal's book, *Against All Odds*:

> Ireland had an unassailable Church and State partnership, that persists to this day. From 1937 onwards, women were suppressed, contraception was made illegal … Eamon de Valera, an ultra-conservative politician and eventual Taoiseach, and Archbishop John McQuaid made sure Ireland was white, Catholic-controlled and a blemish-free country. Sex before marriage was a big no-no and, even worse, the evidence of sex before marriage: pregnancy. Women in this condition were ostracised and shamed, resulting in thousands of women and children, having no choice, but to go into the now infamous mother and baby homes.

It wasn't only an irrepressible coalition of the patriarchal, ecumenical and the patriotic – but also an institutionalised zeal to make money. How those women earned their place 'through arduous and relentless work' is now well-documented. Indeed, it was my own teenage experience and the experience of many – in fact most – of the mothers who contributed to this book.

Consider also that the Catholic doctrine commands procreation. If a Catholic man failed in this obligation, he was deemed a failure. Infertility wasn't spoken about, let alone treated. This created a market that lasted decades and fallen women tumbled into it, as Theresa Hiney Tinggal writes in *Against All Odds*:

> The pregnant woman was referred by social worker, doctor, priest, or another well-connected family friend. She was assured her pregnancy would be covered up so that no future employer or husband would ever know she was 'damaged goods'. The fee was paid for her time in the home.

Private maternity nursing homes were common at the time, often established in large homes, and could easily cater for both respectable married women and the immoral unmarried. The powerful network of medical, legal, political, and religious actors were then easily able to steer women in, and to make a profit disguised as providing a socially and morally necessary service. Expansion into other countries was then established. An unknown number of babies were adopted around the world using these forced adoption techniques.

Recently, illegal adoptions, where babies were sold directly, have also come to light. Jill's story is notable. She doesn't understand how she could have been sold for twelve shillings in Deal Magistrates' Court. Again, we need to look towards Ireland to find the genesis.

There were couples in Ireland who, for a variety of reasons, could not legally adopt. They didn't pass the required health board examination for reasons listed as 'advanced years, alcoholism, mental health issues, or violence'. If they let a local doctor or priest know of their need and could pay the fee, often a baby would be found. The couple would then be guided as to how to best manage the situation of suddenly acquiring an infant. Somehow, the 'adoptive' parents simply became the 'natural' parents. No one would know the difference if the secret was kept. The Irish Government apologised for these practices in 2021.

The UK Government accepts that during the 1950s, 1960s and 1970s evidence shows that more than 215,000 unmarried mothers were coerced into surrendering their illegitimate babies for adoption. Others estimate the number of women impacted by this practice may be more than double this figure, such as Howe, Sawbridge and Hinings writing in *Half a Million Women: Mothers who lose their children by adoption*. The exact figure is impossible to ascertain, as this issue has been swept so firmly under the carpet; we do not have sufficient research.

This removal of babies from their often young, almost always unmarried mothers wasn't an unfortunate historic blip. It wasn't the result of a singular catastrophic event like Ceauşescu's orphan crisis, which saw more than fifteen thousand orphans with physical or mental disabilities, and those unwanted by their parents left to suffer and die in state orphanages – images that rightly outraged the world in 1989.

Very rarely did historic forced adoptions occur because those infants were *actually* unwanted and therefore freely available for adoption. There was never a surfeit of unwanted or abandoned babies requiring loving care and adoption by grateful and good alternative parents. That is one of the pervasive myths still in play.

Nor was it a temporary social policy; forced adoption practices started in the 1950s and echoes of the practice persist today. It was, in fact, a mass transfer of humans; often from a working-class girl or woman to middle-class parents, a trade in both shame and misery; forced adoption happened to all sorts of women and occurred in all parts of the UK on an industrial scale.

Stereotypes abounded, useful to perpetrate myths that supported the practice. The unmarried mothers were *bad girls,* who were *morally lax, unintelligent* girls who *asked for trouble, fast girls* who couldn't keep their legs closed, *loose women* with no *shame* and no *self-control. Degenerate* women whose shameful behaviour demanded an intervention. The forced adoption system that was put into place was designed to teach them shame. To instil shame. From being exiled, to being forced to work, to enduring labour without pain relief, to receiving medical procedures without consent. The harsh treatment was baked-in so that you would never forget your shame. Never forget your sin.

Many of the women I interviewed reported frequently being called names: *one of those girls, slut, whore* within their family or community, and even worse, inside the mother and baby home by the staff and sisters whilst receiving antenatal care and, contemptibly, during labour. Once they'd had their babies, the name-calling and public shaming often continued. Over the decades they endured a double dose of shame: the humiliation of getting pregnant out-of-wedlock, and second, when society's attitude to unmarried mothers changed and softened, the women were judged for supposedly not caring about their babies and giving them away.

Women told me that the notes they acquired, decades later through SARs (Subject Access Requests), displayed the same tone of judgmental vindictiveness. Several women said to me that had their child acquired these notes – and many adoptees sought files to establish contact – that they were sufficiently off-putting to prevent reunion ever being successful.

The brutality and hostility displayed to these women was quite astounding, with little regard given to the trauma that separation caused for both parties: for the mother to forcibly lose her child, and for the child to be separated from its mother. As adoption psychotherapist, Paul Sunderland says, 'The trauma is remembered but can't be recalled.' Little wonder, he contends, 'adoptees are massively over-represented in therapy.'

My aim in researching and writing *Taken: Experiences of Forced Adoption* is to document and acknowledge the all-too-often lifelong and unspoken trauma, which is at the heart of the experience of this group.

Adoption apology and redress

The scales of justice are now slowly, inexorably tipping in favour of those women and their now adult children, against whom one of the twenty-first century's major social injustices has been perpetrated. Until relatively recently, forced adoption was conveniently overlooked and minimised as an unfortunate practice, belonging to a bygone age, rather than the formal *social policy* it was. The widespread practice of forced adoption rendered these women's lives a never-ending anguish; women who for *shame's sake*, with no choice, let alone informed consent, had their babies taken from them. Indeed, it is challenging in this era of human rights and social support to imagine how social coercion could have been so impactful.

The experiences detailed here are an invitation to stand in the shoes of these women and their adult children, within that particular and abusive, social, historic and cultural context. *There was no choice*. What can be done to one generation of people can be repeated against another as we witness elsewhere in the world. Progress can be wound backwards. Human Rights Watch detail terrifyingly the erosion of women's and girls' rights and liberties in Afghanistan, describing these recent changes as a 'gender apartheid'. In America, the US Supreme Court overturned Roe v. Wade in June 2022; this ruling 'dissolved' federal protections on reproductive rights, also causing outrage, concern and fear about the erosion of women's and girls' rights.

In September 2021, Harriet Harman then QC and MP, launched a Parliamentary Inquiry into the 'right to family life'. She chaired the Joint Committee on Human Rights (JCHR), which sought to understand the experiences of unmarried women whose children were adopted between 1949 and 1976. She said:

> Everyone has the right to family life. The Joint Committee on Human Rights will look at whether the right to family life of young unmarried mothers and their children was respected in the 1950s, 60s and 70s. We have launched this inquiry to understand the realities of what the adoption process was like at that time and hear the experiences of those who went through it. The adoptions took place decades ago, but the pain and suffering remains today.

Following that JCHR Inquiry on the right to family life, an unequivocal instruction was sent to the British Government. The final report, published in July 2022, called upon the Government to issue a *formal apology* and to provide support measures to all the unmarried mothers who had their babies taken for adoption. It also outlined what more needed to be done to support those dealing with the long-term impacts of historic forced adoption. The Government was urged, based on the inquiry, to improve access to counselling and to remove barriers to accessing adoption documents.

Some of those I interviewed attended the inquiry to give evidence and were hopeful that they were at last being heard. The importance of a formal apology cannot be overstated. It would mean that it was understood and accepted that there was no choice but to opt for adoption. Many women I interviewed said they *feared* going to their graves with this unresolved, and that it would bring them some much needed peace of mind. Sadly, this was not the case for Veronica Smith who died in 2024, after enduring decades of sadness and trauma, and energetically campaigning for the apology she and many others deserved. That apology is vital and now significantly overdue.

The then-Conservative government's tardy response came in March 2023. Months overdue, it stated:

> The government agrees with the Committee that the treatment of women and their children in adoption practices during this period

was wrong and should not have happened. Whilst we do not think it is appropriate for a formal government apology to be given, since the state did not actively support these practices, we do wish to say we are sorry on behalf of society to all those affected.

So, sorry it wasn't us and we will not accept responsibility!

Dr Michael Lambert, who has researched this area extensively, has proven the state's hand in these abhorrent practices. On 4 March 2023 in response to the JCHR findings, he wrote to MAA:

I find the government's claims that 'the state did not actively support these practices' ahistorical, unfounded, and against a significant weight of academic opinion. Instead, they blame limited oversight of activities by local authorities and voluntary organisations corrected by the 1976 Act. This is untrue.

1. Although the 1949 and 1976 Acts bookend the inquiry, the 1943 Ministry of Health circular 2866 is the key document. It placed upon local authorities a duty to provide a certain range of 'services' for unmarried mothers and their children as part of wartime efforts to maximise participation in the workforce. In 1943 policy preference was still for mother and child to be kept together despite the growing influence of the adoption lobby as Jenny Keating has written about. This was not out of a sense of justice but because it was felt that mothers should carry their shame with them. Between 1943 and 1949 this changed with closed forced adoption becoming the norm. Guidance given in the circular was becoming detached from local practice and funding with local authority services and voluntary organisations, notably moral welfare associations. The 1949 Act amended this element, yet most local authority funding for adoptions – both to homes and for individual mothers – was undertaken under circular 2866. The circular gave local authorities funding for this purpose, covering portions of fixed (home) and variable (cases) costs, although there was discretion

between them. In short, central government not only actively supported, but determined and shaped forced adoption practices.

Clearly, Dr Lambert proves state involvement.

The Conservative government therefore has consistently continued to fail the women and people involved. The Minister at that time, Nadhim Zahawi, not only chose not to issue a formal apology but also repeatedly declined to meet with those impacted. This inaction is despite both the Scottish and Welsh administrations' attempts to grasp the nettle and comply with the instruction to issue an apology. MAA has been relentless and determined in continuing to push the issue.

Some of those lobbying for these actions are now elderly and are simply too tired or frail to continue the fight for justice that they so bravely and determinedly started. They have already carried a heavy burden with stoic dignity. For others, the Conservative government's recalcitrant attitude in refusing to issue a formal apology has encouraged them to feel militant. The refusal to issue an apology has emboldened them; they now refuse to be silenced or to be 'fobbed off'. They demand justice – and will continue to do all they can to obtain it, as will a great many adult adoptees.

For context, the UK Government is an outlier. The Irish Government issued its formal apology on 13 January 2021, and the Scottish and Welsh Parliaments issued formal apologies for historic forced adoption practices on 22 March 2023 and 25 April 2023 respectively, adhering to the recommendations made by the JCHR following the Parliamentary Inquiry. However, many now see these apologies as tokenistic, failing to include the campaigning organisations involved, failing to address the issues and lacking pace. In Scotland, there is growing concern and unease from the mothers who campaigned for an apology about the power of the adoption lobby, and concern that the UK Government may drag its feet.

Jeannot Farmer outlines this in *No More Standing in the Shadows – Treating the Wounds of Historic Forced Adoption*:

> It was a recurring feature of my research to be told that changes in political leadership led to stalling or reversals of policy developments on forced adoption … I lost count of the number of interviewees who told me that dramatic political events on the day of the apology had dominated the news cycle, and that the expected boost to community awareness of the issue was lost and has never been regained.

Governments around the world including Australia, Denmark, Belgium and latterly Bangladesh, have also taken steps to apologise, to acknowledge the pain and scale of the suffering and to ease access to vital support. It is hoped that Canada will also soon issue an apology.

At a time when many other mass injustices have rightly achieved prominence and political leverage: the Horizon Post Office scandal, the infected blood scandal, Women Against State Pension Inequality (WASPI) campaign, Justice4Grenfell, Windrush, and the Hillsborough Justice Campaign and others, all form part of the growing number of social movements demanding rectification of historic injustices. All are now located in the burgeoning Justice Sector. All these campaigns, and more, are in the public eye and are becoming seared into popular consciousness. But by its very nature, forced adoption is an intimate, personal miscarriage of justice. Some of those impacted have therefore shunned the spotlight, choosing not to speak out publicly, providing all the more reason to champion this cause. Isn't it also now time that the media glare and weight of social opinion supported the call for action on forced adoptions? It is no less a scandal, no less an historic social injustice, no less an injury … and we still have bodies to count … as Judy's story about baby Stephen will attest.

All hopes for an apology and redress are now pinned on Sir Keir Starmer, Prime Minister. The Former Director of Public Prosecutions at the Crown Prosecution Service can at least be expected to comprehend the illegality of these historic practices, in addition to the social, personal, financial and emotional injury endured. It is hoped that he will, as Prime Minister, issue a formal apology without delay.

Further actions and reparations should follow, and quickly, given the age profile of both mothers and adult children.

Personal experiences

In order to understand the widespread practice of historic forced adoption, I interviewed women who were sent into these homes during the late 1950s, through to the early 1980s, and their now adult children. Between June 2023 and August 2024, I conducted in-depth interviews with more than thirty people from across England and some who lived further afield in the United States and Australia, where they had migrated in the intervening decades. I interviewed mothers and their daughters and sons who are in reunion, both successfully and painfully failed. I detail the experience of the adult daughter of a deceased man who was himself unhappily adopted, as she searches to understand her father's past, uncovering the long-term intergenerational impact of forced adoption. I interviewed Stephen, the husband of a woman who took her own life, decades after her son died, due to his gross maltreatment and neglect in St Monica's mother and baby home; after a lifetime of pain and trauma she was simply unable to endure the pain of her experiences any longer.

One woman explained how she clearly recalled her parents being far more concerned with what other people thought than her own welfare. That was a frequent theme – maintaining the family reputation was often paramount. I also interviewed women who didn't go into a mother and baby home, but even so, the sucker tentacles of this culture, this malpractice, this dehumanising industry, snatched their babies from them. Not to mention my conversations with women who were adopted themselves, who went on to have their own babies taken from them through forced adoption. The widespread practice of taking babies from unmarried women, who were vilified as unfit and morally deficient, was persuasive and profitable, and cloaked in secrecy and shame. These frank interviews and explicit experiences hold a mirror to British society and seek to give voice to the voiceless.

The impact of this practice isn't restricted to the mother and the infant, the hurt caused has also been to brothers and sisters, grandparents and partners. The emotional harm, the ripple effect, unfurls across families and communities and down the generations. Nor was the pain of that relinquishment ever short-term. There is no woman that I interviewed that 'got over' losing her baby, as she was so often assured would be the case. Rather she suffered and suffered and suffered … Always wondering what happened to her child, not knowing whether her child was dead or alive. Or whether the child had a good adoption? Or whether her child was happy or not? The agony of not knowing is tremendous. Likewise, adopted people told me of the long-term trauma they experienced, and of how they would walk past strangers on the street and wonder, 'Is that my mum? Is that my brother or sister?' They frequently expressed the need to meet somebody who looked like them and told of their delight when they finally did meet a family member or saw themselves reflected in their own offspring. They also needed to know their medical history. It is hard to imagine the agony and harm of that lack of knowledge. Not all the women were abandoned by the men with whom they had become pregnant, indeed some maintained those relationships, marrying after the adoption. Many of those involved in the forced adoption business conveniently forgot that the girls and women often suffered a double blow: the loss of a loved one and then the loss of their baby.

In undertaking these interviews, I developed a particular approach that eschewed prior research into the backgrounds of my interviewees. In today's age of hyperconnectivity, where it seems everybody has a profile on Facebook or WhatsApp, I deliberately chose not to 'check them out' on social media. I preferred a more open, unfettered approach, without even the image of a person to influence my perception about their personality or anything that would imply what their life story might be. There was something about the anonymity of this approach that appealed to me. As a writer, I've treated every person with the utmost respect, and only when they described themselves and their own circumstances, did I commit those words to the page.

I have given a great deal of thought as to what language to use. We know that words are value-laden, and as the discourse on the need for a formal adoption apology gathers pace, and the specifics of the formal apology and reparations are decided, the matter of language, and which words to use, will continue to be debated. It is my view that language is fluid and changes over time. I have endeavoured to be inclusive and respectful to all those affected and involved in this debate.

I am sharing my interviews verbatim and it's possible that some of the language my interviewees and I used was in common usage and acceptable at the time of these historic events and now, decades later, some of which may be considered inappropriate. If I have inadvertently caused any offence, it is not my intention and I apologise.

It has been useful to read the introduction to the Joint Committee on Human Rights report on *The Violation of Family Life: Adoption of Children of Unmarried Women 1949-1976* published 15 July 2022. The language used in this document seems a good fit for this book, and I have endeavoured to adhere to these guidelines as far as possible:

> 7. We became increasingly aware of the great sensitivity regarding the use of language during the course of the inquiry. Throughout this report we use the terms "birth mother" and "birth father" and "adoptive mother" and "adoptive father" only in order to be able to distinguish between biological and adoptive parents, though we are aware that the term "birth mother" is anathema to those women, who prefer simply to be described as they are, that is, mothers. We also use the term "adopted person" as an acknowledgement of the ages of those who were adopted

as babies during the period of the inquiry. We hope from the context of our report it is clear where we refer to minors, and those who are adults.

8. We also share the strong antipathy to the allegation that they "gave up" their babies for adoption, which perpetuates the fiction that the mothers had a choice. In this report, we use the term "put up for adoption".

Karen

"My legacy to my son – intergenerational trauma. Unrecognised and unresolved, my struggle became his."

I have skin in the game. My experience of being in a mother and baby home in 1978, aged fifteen, was as formative as it was traumatic. I was taken without my agreement or warning from my family home in Stoke-on-Trent, and deposited miles away in St Paul's mother and baby home in Coleshill, Birmingham. It was an austere annexe of Father Hudson's Homes and my incarceration abruptly terminated family connections, friendships, and my formal education. The Catholic Church, effectively in *loco parentis*, overlooked the fact I had passed the eleven-plus, was a good student attending a grammar school, anticipating O-level examination success, and replaced my education with laundry room duties.

Bafflingly, my weight was the first item noted in the report, which was provided to me via my SAR, decades later. I was apparently the only woman to ever contact the home to make this request. At nine stone, and six months pregnant, I was deemed 'chubby'. My IQ was 'assessed' (average in case you're wondering), as was that of the 'PF' (putative father) – a wholly demeaning term used frequently in homes to underscore the 'lax morals' of those that *got themselves* pregnant; the implication that such girls and women were entirely responsible for their condition and worse, may not always have been certain of their baby's father. This was a thinly disguised eugenic assessment, ostensibly taken so that the baby could be carefully placed, skillfully matched, to just the right family. That was fiction, as adoptive parents were often allowed and encouraged to freely choose their baby – the way most people choose a dog.

While living in St Paul's, I was forced to attend daily mass and undertake heavy manual work, which I did in isolation in the on-site laundry. I received inadequate antenatal care, no preparation for birth and suffered the distress of my roommate going into painful labour in the bedroom we were required to share. She, too, was completely unprepared for birth. We were all deliberately uninformed. As I listened helplessly, baffled by her screaming, I knew I was next. This, it seems, was part of my lesson. We *should* suffer so as not to repeat our mistakes and get *ourselves* pregnant again.

The person responsible for my well-being in the home is incongruously listed in my SAR, as both my priest *and* my social worker. This conflation of roles and responsibilities was riven with conflict since he attempted to coerce me daily into 'giving my baby up' for adoption. With no agency, no rights, and no advocate, and left with no options, I duly signed some of the adoption papers under duress. I was coerced. Forced. How else can it be described?

The SAR also revealed a weekly fee of £20, paid to St Paul's by my family to meet my residency costs. That's approximately £143 today. This was, the notes explain, a discounted rate from the standard £30 per week. It was demanded, despite my family's evident poverty. I had two younger siblings, and both my parents had insecure and low earnings. The SAR notes my family could not afford to run a car and therefore couldn't easily visit me in the home. My mother, then a part-time carer, mostly worked nights at the old people's home (also run by the Church) as the rates of pay for night work were marginally higher, and she could better combine work with childcare. My self-employed stepfather, a gardener, was subject to the vagaries of both seasonal work and a declining urban labour market; a tight economy meant less work for him, and he was, I realised decades later, also a chronic alcoholic. The SAR reveals that Staffordshire County Council, my local authority, declined to meet the Church's invoice. This, further research revealed, was despite me already being known to social services. And my research has revealed that in some cases, the local authority did indeed pay the bill. However, that didn't mean my needs (and later those of my child), or my family's impoverished circumstances disappeared. Nor did the response from either the local authority or the Church itself consider or balance my needs with those of my siblings, let alone assess my family's parlous finances. The State showed its hand by ignoring my plight and that of my family. It was aware of my fate. The whole family had to suffer.

When it became evident that I wouldn't let them take my infant, I was eventually returned to my family the day before my due date to have my baby in the local maternity hospital. There was no assessment of my home circumstances, frequently marred by domestic abuse, and overcrowded (six people in a very small two-bedroomed house). No ongoing assistance was offered. Once the highly valued commodity – the baby – was removed from the equation, the Church's interest, involvement, and responsibility ceased entirely. The pressures this suddenly and inevitably placed on my already struggling family were immense and irreparable (and avoidable) damage was inflicted on family relationships. The subsequent hardship and difficulties my son and I endured, in the years before I found my feet, cannot be minimised.

These compelling experiences of vulnerable young girls and young women like me in the 1950s through to the 1980s: unmarried, pregnant, who were mandated and channelled – one way or another – into these homes, forms an intriguing hidden history. Unlike high-profile stories about homes such as Tuam and Bessborough, much of England's own recent forced adoption history remains undocumented and unspoken. Many people experience surprise and horror when they realise these 'things' happened here in England, Wales and Scotland. More than simply an account of our shared experiences over the decades, *Taken: Experiences of Forced Adoption* is also a call to action. It's time for political accountability.

After a delivery that can best be described as neglectful but thankfully straightforward, my son Daniel left my teenage body and entered this world on 15 July 1978. He was put wet, hot and pulsing with life onto my tummy. He lifted his beautiful inquisitive head and blinked his eyes. 'I'm here!' If I hadn't *already been in love* with him, the bond would have cemented there and then. I don't think it was my imagination, but everyone immediately loved him. Nonetheless … he was born a 'bastard', a pejorative phrase that was still in use in the 1970s and beyond.

> The bastard, like the prostitute, thief and beggar, belongs to that motley crowd of disreputable social types which society has generally resented, always endured. He is a living symbol of social irregularity.
>
> Kingsley Davis, *'Illegitimacy and the Social Structure'*, 1939

I never thought being born a bastard could be a problem. But it was drilled into me that having chosen to keep my baby, I had ruined two lives. His and my own. Having been forcefully instructed that I should give him up to someone 'better', because I was bad and not good enough – a concept that I wholeheartedly came to believe – I had no idea that *he* also might be considered not good enough.

A schoolgirl mum in a grammar school uniform, I frequently met undisguised hostility. It *never* occurred to me that Daniel may have experienced something similar. I assumed he charmed everyone as much as he charmed me. The expression 'ignorance is bliss' is apt.

I always told anyone who was interested that having my son was the making of me, and he absolutely was, but only much later in life did I start to wonder how hard it was for him.

In 2019, Lemn Sissay's book *My Name is Why* was published and, having listened to Sissay discussing his experiences on the radio, my son Daniel wrote the following Facebook post:

> Beautiful podcast with Lemn Sissay, his story resonated, with aftershocks of 'that could have been my story'. If only things were slightly different in 1978, and my mum had let me go when all the authorities were telling her that was her only choice. My mum never let me go. I don't remember those times, but at 41 after listening to this, I understand why she started fighting at fifteen and how lucky I am to be Dan and not Lemn.

My son is right, perhaps he can't fully remember the trauma of his early years, none of us can, but he and I were often met with a baffling degree of hostility and belittling, bordering at times on hate. We were both universally othered, and this came from all quarters, including family, community and the local authority. It has only been through conducting these interviews that I have begun to formulate an understanding of the trauma surrounding being born illegitimate, a bastard, to a young unmarried mother. I'm still working out what to do … This is my legacy to my son: intergenerational trauma, unrecognised and unresolved. My struggle became his. I never recovered. I never shed that cast of shame. Although I did eventually 'find my feet', by securing a decently paid career, I was always an outcast within my family and in wider society. I never felt I was good enough, after being told so often I wasn't at such a formative age. That sense of shame was always an anchor holding me back, the stigma a constant and, until recently, unrecognised burden.

Those experiences in the home, the continual hectoring to give the baby to a proper mother, a more deserving mother, to a moral mother, became the standards against which I continually judged myself and felt I'd failed. Little wonder that three years after having Daniel, I rushed headlong into a disastrous marriage at eighteen, mistakenly assuming it would afford me the cloak of respectability. Baby number two quickly followed. As I became a young single mother, the disapproval increased, and the hostility intensified. Perversely, my stint in care had left me more, not less vulnerable. The pernicious moral washing did nothing but render trauma.

Linda

*"I actually thought I had a choice about the adoption,
but they had someone lined up straight away ..."*

I meet Linda for a coffee on the south coast at a convenient spot halfway between our two homes. She is waiting for me outside the agreed café as I pull up. I can immediately tell from her demeanour that she is feeling anxious about our meeting; she looks uncomfortable, diminutive and pensive. We shake hands and she confirms that she is indeed apprehensive.

She's a friendly, warm woman and I hope I can reassure her. As we settle down to talk, huddled over our coffees, she explains she was born in 1961 and went into a mother and baby home, pregnant, aged seventeen in 1979. Her baby was taken for adoption shortly after birth. Linda explains that she started to look for her adopted daughter in 2010.

Linda tells me about her life. "It's not easy, I suffer with anxiety – post-traumatic stress. I trained to be a mental health nurse when I was twenty-nine, and I didn't click that was a choice I made precisely because I was traumatised. Now I look back and see that I was a strong woman." Linda explains she hasn't had the best relationships with men and realises retrospectively she was looking for love to replace the love she lost. She spent a lot of time blocking out her early life, blocking out the forced adoption.

Reflecting on her life as a girl, she explains the difficult dynamic between her parents and that she didn't really remember cuddles from her mum, whilst she did her best to make sure her dad had a smile on his face. Her mum had suffered since childhood with poor mental health, which persisted her whole life. She wasn't really available to Linda and her dad wasn't an empathetic type and was also in the army, which meant the family moved around. Linda believes her education suffered as a result. As a child, Linda also believed some of the problems in her family were her responsibility. As a result, she grew up feeling guilty.

"When I was sixteen, my mum and dad finally got divorced and we were on the move yet again, this time into a cramped flat. I started college and around that time, I had a big bust-up with my boyfriend. He was my first boyfriend. At the same time, I also had a huge argument with Mum. I hadn't seen my dad for a while. It was an upsetting time for us all. I was in turmoil.

"As a result, I went out on my own to a pub where I thought I would know people. It turned out none of my friends were there. But there was one boy, who I vaguely knew as he was a friend of my boyfriend. I had a couple of ciders and because I wasn't a drinker, quickly became drunk. I was out of my head. My boyfriend's friend persuaded me to go back to his bedsit, where he raped me. I was unconscious and he took full advantage. When I awoke the next morning, I nearly had a heart attack. I was so scared. I tried to get out, but the door was locked. He wouldn't let me out, but I turned around and said to him, 'You know what you did!' He denied it. I walked miles home.

"It was only five months later that I told my mother what happened to me, and that as a result, I was pregnant. I didn't tell anybody else about it because I thought people would blame me for what happened. It was non-consensual. I didn't even know what I was doing. I spent ages wondering how he even got my skin-tight jeans off. I was very prudish at that age. It was awful for my mother. She was already very unwell and taking large numbers of anti-depressants and I knew I had added an extra burden.

"Then when I was at college one day, one of my friends said to me, 'My mum reckons you're pregnant?' That's when I had to acknowledge that I was pregnant. I told my mum in a café; she then took me home and started to make some phone calls asking me what I wanted to do and I said I didn't know. Because it was a rape. My mum contacted the boy's father and he suggested that we, the boy that raped me and myself, should get married. I was hysterical saying, 'You don't know what he did.' Then I ended up in London at an abortion clinic, but I simply couldn't go through with it."

I pushed Linda as gently as I could to try to better understand why, given the circumstances, she wouldn't want an abortion. Linda became very upset and simply said, "She was my baby. I just couldn't do it."

Linda adds, "I didn't really know what sex was, and there was certainly no information about what abortion was." This made informed decision-making extremely difficult. How could she decide, not least when the trauma of rape was overlooked and minimised?

Linda then revealed something very significant. "Prior to this, my boyfriend kept asking me to have sex with him and I would say no, 'I'm not even sixteen yet', and I'd fend him off because I wasn't really interested in sleeping with him. Then when I was sixteen, I kind of had to have sex with him, but I didn't enjoy it and didn't want to have sex with him again after that, and so I continued to say no. When my boyfriend found out about the rape, he said, 'Oh, we were always rivals growing up. He always wants everything of mine. He always used to steal my toys when I was little …' and he dropped a bombshell. 'He came straight round to my house and told me what he done to you.' I couldn't believe it."

Linda tells me she was a 'good girl', and this episode in her life destroyed her as a person. Through tears, she tells me, "All of a sudden, I had become this terrible person and I couldn't even look my family in the eye anymore. I was a Brownie, then a Sea Cadet and had ambitions to join the Wrens." Linda had a clear identity that was rooted in her self-perception of being an archetypal good girl and having the approval of her family. The rape obviously had a profoundly damaging impact. She says to this day, fifty years later, "I still can't wear a low top."

After it was clear to her mother that Linda wouldn't have an abortion, she was sent to the Salvation Army's mother and baby home in Colchester.

"I couldn't decide about my future. I was very well-behaved in the home; I dressed immaculately and wore my hair pulled back neat and tight. I did a lot of housework. I followed my rota, doing the cooking and cleaning. There was one girl in there who had a baby and a couple of girls waiting to have babies. I know I only looked about twelve years old. I actually thought I had a choice about the adoption and I wanted to wait until the baby was born.

"I had visits from a social worker who kept asking me, 'What are you going to do?' and I replied, 'I don't know what I'm going to do,' and she said, 'How are you going to manage? How are you going to look after it?' I would just shake my head.

"The only other visitors were my mum and boyfriend. He and I were still going out together. He would come every Saturday. He had the idea that I would give the baby up and that I could continue to go out with him. He supported me in his way, but he didn't want me to have the baby. And at the time I thought I was so lucky that he was 'standing by me'.

"What I didn't know, was they – the Salvation Army – had somebody lined up ready to take my baby before I even went into the mother and baby home."

We discussed the birth of Linda's baby. Her daughter was placed on a drip of sugar water after a while because she was starting to struggle. Linda didn't know what to expect or what to do in the hospital on her own. When Linda's mother came to visit, Linda was very uncomfortable because she didn't want her mother to be there; she didn't want to create a further burden on her.

"The staff in the hospital shouted at me, 'Stop making a fuss.' My mind wasn't present – I was going through the motions, but I wasn't really there. I thought my God, I don't know what's going on, or what they're doing, and I remember the nurse saying, 'She's just a child herself,' as my baby was delivered. And one of the nurses didn't realise I was from the mother and baby home, and she brought the baby over to me to hold and to nurse, and then someone else came and took her off me.

"I was exhausted. I was put into a room to have some rest and I went to sleep. I haven't got many memories. But I can remember my boyfriend being there, holding her and somebody taking a photograph of her. And then something suddenly changed – it was like, oh! I was moved into a side room and my baby was taken away from me and put into the nursery. That night, I sneaked out and I went to get my baby. I fed her with a bottle and then I took her back to my room and my bed. Somebody must've informed the social worker because the next morning, the door flew open and the social worker came in saying, 'What do you think you're doing? You're not supposed to be doing that. You'll develop feelings. There are parents waiting for that baby.' She then said, 'Give me that baby,' ripped her out of my arms and marched out, and that was the last time I saw her. After that, I was just crying and crying and crying …

"Then I went to an office with my mum to sign some papers and I was still crying, and my mum said to me, 'How can you let these lovely people down? You'll never be able to look after her, you're too young, you won't have any money. No way can you look after her, you won't even have anywhere to live. This couple have already adopted a little boy and they want a sister for him. They've got a lovely family. They're both teachers, you cannot do what they can do.' Then my boyfriend arrived, and I spoke to him explaining, 'I want to keep my baby,' and he said, 'Well, I'm off if you do!' So, then I knew I would have no one.

"Later, I married my boyfriend, I was nothing after the adoption. I was a spot. A nothing. I don't think my soul was in my body.

"I didn't go back to the mother and baby home after the birth. Instead, my family arranged for an auntie to collect me directly from the hospital. At the time, I was kind of under the control of other people, even to the extent of asking them what I should wear. I'd lost all sense of agency.

"I think they didn't want me to go back to the mother and baby home in case somebody I knew told me I had got some rights. They just wanted to get me back down to the family home as quickly as possible. I felt like a prisoner in the back of the car, I cried all the way home. No one said a single word to me."

Returning home wasn't easy. Linda was in a heightened emotional state and, to all intents and purposes, grieving. She'd been away for a while and her older sibling wasn't keen to accommodate Linda's needs; she didn't like her getting preferential treatment. This precipitated a family argument and Linda's sister stormed out. I can't help but reflect on the terrible bind that Linda's mother must have been in, in great need herself, let alone providing support for her understandably emotionally fragile daughter, and at the same time, her other daughter's needs were possibly being overlooked.

Years later, it transpired that Linda's older sister had been pregnant herself and was planning to get married at the same time as Linda went into the home. The calamitous events with Linda overshadowed her own plans, and because of the events in the family, she decided to have an abortion. She later challenged Linda saying, 'Why couldn't you have just gone and got an abortion?' It's not difficult to understand how Linda's sister might have felt left out and not as important as Linda, while she was going through difficulties herself. Linda describes her sister as traumatised.

Linda continues, "I spent the next six months being really depressed. Cleaning the flat. Cleaning. Just cleaning the flat with my boyfriend coming around. From the day I told my mum I was pregnant, my whole life changed to no career, no college, no education, no job. I was also put on antidepressants and told to get out to work. The only work I could get was in a sewing machine factory and I hated sewing, but I had to earn money, so I did it, but I did also go to night school.

"My boyfriend and myself became engaged. His mother was very controlling. In fact, when the engagement ring arrived from the catalogue, *she* opened the box and *she* gave it to me. I didn't even have a romantic proposal. It was as if I didn't matter, and I still think that now. Although I'm doing a lot of work on myself, I've always ended up going for damaged or broken men.

"My husband was in the army, and we were posted to Cyprus. I was very alone there, so I joined the wives' club, which was very difficult, because it was full of women with their babies, and I didn't understand why I felt these horrible feelings. I remember one night I was drinking with some girls, and it all came out – the whole saga. And I felt bad for having told my story. Then the wives' club got involved. Of course, what I really wanted was to have more children. I couldn't wait. So, I had my first baby and then my second, but I've changed how I say that now; I say I had my second and third babies."

I explain to Linda that many women it seems, who had their babies taken away through forced adoption, then went on to form relationships, primarily so that they could have another baby to replace the one that had been taken.

Linda agrees and continues, "My husband didn't really give a shit about me. By that time, I was domesticated, well-trained; I had low expectations because I didn't think I was worth anything, and then I ran off with another soldier because I was chasing love."

Life went on to be disruptive and challenging for Linda. "I was a single mum and my children were getting older. I wondered whether I should tell them about their adopted sister. I tried to register with Norcap, the tracing service, but it was £175 to get going and even the guidance book was twelve pounds. I couldn't afford that."

"I began ardently seeking my first daughter nine years ago. My partner at the time said he didn't want me to. So, we had to separate. It transpired my daughter was in London, although I'd been told she could've been anywhere in the country. When we did eventually meet each other, it was just so natural. We took our time to catch up with each other. We were both emotional, but we followed the guidance and we did it properly. The thing was every time I saw her, I felt very depressed afterwards but that is lessening now. Both my daughters are very supportive and empathic."

Reflecting on her life journey, Linda says, "I was so proud of myself when I became a nurse, and I could be *somebody* not just a woman who had a baby out-of-wedlock." Linda is a very happy mother and grandmother of two "perfect" twin girls. She shows me a photograph of the girls; her daughters and granddaughters all bear a striking resemblance to Linda. All peas in a pod and totally beautiful. I can relate to her sense of pride.

Linda tells me that her adopted daughter has a view on the process. She explains that when they finally made contact through the agency, it transpired that shortly afterwards her daughter's adoptive mother died. This was obviously very sad for her daughter, but she also took a philosophical view and imagined that her other mother was now seeking contact with her because her "heavenly mother" was pulling strings up in heaven, looking over her protectively.

Linda believes an apology from the Government is very important. "I have survived. But my mum died when I was twenty-two. I think what happened to me, and what she had to do for me – for all the right reasons from her perspective – finished her off. She went into hospital and didn't come out. She was on masses of medication for her mental health, and then she had heart failure. I didn't see her before she died. I think she couldn't live with it."

Linda decided she would live her life the opposite way to her mother and had a very wild and free time with her two daughters, travelling, living in the woods in a camper, being part of an 'outsider' community.

Since reuniting with her daughter, Linda found out about MAA. She's been following their requests to email her local MP to press the UK Government to issue an apology.

Following our meeting, I asked Linda if I could use the emails she'd submitted to her local MP, at the time, Natalie Elphicke.

"Yes, that's fine. Not getting a reply from the email left a so familiar feeling of 'not being heard, cut off and being silenced', which for me equated with not being worthy! I am worthy, however."

There was something poignant about her permission and about the emails themselves, which Linda allowed me to reproduce.

Date: 3 October 2022 at 12:10:23 BST
To: natalie.elphicke.mp@parliament.uk
Subject: Movement For Adoption Apology UK

Dear Natalie,

I would like to draw your attention to the above titled Movement, which has had some News coverage this year. I would very much like to discuss this with you and the findings of "The Enquiry by The Joint Committee of Human rights". Entitled "The Violation of Family Life, Adoption of children of unmarried Women. 1949-1976" (although this did not end in 1976).

JULY 2022

The Movement hopes for a public apology to all affected Women and their lost Children. I had my child taken from me Two days after Birth following 4 months of residing away from my family in a Mother and Baby Home.

I will not go into what I went through or how this has affected me Then and Now in this email but most of us have untreated PTSD, difficulty with relationships and Low self Esteem, and that's the tip of the iceberg.

By Voting Yes For the Apology means some kind of Validation of what has happened to us and how we were treated but mostly for Closure.

I am not unaware of any other Women in the Dover and Deal area, who may have been affected and it is possible you may already have had correspondence from others regarding this very difficult subject.

I was lucky! I was able to legally find my daughter in 2015. Thank you for reading this request, it has not been easy to write.

I look forward to hearing from you.

Yours Sincerely,

Linda, Recently retired CPN

Date: 5 July 2023 at 18:23:14 BST
To: natalie.elphicke.mp@parliament.uk
Subject: Apology for forced adoptions

Dear Natalie

MAA – Movement for an Adoption Apology

As you may be aware that between December 2021 and July 2022, the Joint Committee on Human Rights held an Inquiry on 'The right to family life: adoption of children of unmarried women, 1949-1976', during which those affected, both mothers and (now adult) children, and academics with expert knowledge of the issues gave evidence on those events.

At the conclusion of the Inquiry, the JCHR issued a report entitled "The Violation of Family Life", in which they concluded that extensive harm has left thousands with trauma and an enduring sense of shame. They called for an official public apology with measures to support all those still affected today.

This year, devolved governments in Scotland and Wales each issued a public, formal, heartfelt apology for injustices endured by young mothers and their children, to be accompanied by practical support measures in each country. They acknowledged that it is the state that is morally responsible for setting standards and protecting people. Yet to date, Westminster has responded only with a document that denies the facts, which has been deeply hurtful to all affected.

MAA has today written to the Prime Minister to ask him to reconsider issuing a formal public apology for the harmful and damaging historic adoption practices which took place during the three decades following the second World War.

A copy of that letter and its appendices is available via [link redacted].

As you are my MP, I would appreciate your support for the MAA campaign for an unqualified formal, public apology acknowledging the undeniable central role of Government in forced adoption practices for unmarried mothers and their children in England and Wales from 1949 to 1976.

There have been numerous retrospective government apologies for injustices that took place long ago. The JCHR Parliamentary Inquiry has shown that those affected were the victims of a terrible lifelong injustice, and all of us would like this to be recognised and remedied within our lifetimes.

Therefore, I would like your support in asking the UK Government to issue a formal apology, modelled on that given in Australia in 2013, to meet the JCHR recommendations and to help as many people as possible.

With your assistance, we may all find a measure of peace.

Your sincerely,

Linda (Survivor). Please help our cause, I have emailed you before but had no reply. Please reach into your heart ♥.

Linda never received a response. She wrote to me after our meeting saying:

> It was good to meet you. I'm ok, it did stir the feelings up a little but I am now able to smooth them down more easily. Time is a healer. It's such an amazing task you have taken on with the anthology, best wishes and strength.

I know Linda would very much like therapeutic support, but she isn't able to access what she needs. The availability of tailored support services is poor and is also prohibitively expensive; only a formal apology and reparations that address these fundamental needs will suffice. I wonder, given the change in government in 2024, whether Linda's new MP, Mike Tapp, will show more willingness to respond.

Sally

"It doesn't matter how many children you go on to have, you will never get over the one that you lost."

Sally, who wishes to be anonymous, tells me she's now fifty-eight, and in 1982, at seventeen, she found herself pregnant, and like so many others before her, she was unable to keep her baby. She had no option other than to go into a mother and baby home.

Sally had herself been adopted at birth along with her younger brother. Sally, who is bright and bubbly, knows a great deal about adoption from the perspective of being adopted and having her baby taken from her for adoption.

Sally tells me her story. "I was born into care and then I was adopted. From three to almost ten years old I lived with my adoptive parents in East London. Then my adoptive mum was diagnosed with cancer. She knew she was going to die so she put myself and my adoptive brother who is five years younger than me into a convent-run care home. She felt my adoptive father would not be able to cope with us on his own.

"When I was ten, we were returned to again live with our adoptive father, and although I can remember there were some concerns that he was neglectful, I was just so happy to be back home. I think my dad wanted my brother home more than he wanted me. In 1983 when I was seventeen, I became pregnant, and five months later my father called a social worker and she put me into a mother and baby home in Dollis Hill in London. My dad only came to see me once. I had no plans to have my baby adopted, but I didn't really know what I was going to do. The whole thing was horrendous. I did love the idea of having a 'family', but I didn't have money and I didn't have a home. There was no counselling available to me. I was simply told I should give up my child and that I could always have another one. It was so sad.

"I had all my baby's things. I didn't know where any support would come from, but I did think and hope that there would be something to help me. I really wanted some words of hope to keep my baby and some practical advice.

"They said, to avoid strengthening the bond between my baby and myself, that they would take him as soon as he was born. I remember going into the Whittington Hospital on a rainy day; I was put with all the other mothers who had their babies – whilst I didn't have mine." Sally becomes very emotional at this juncture, and it's clear recalling the painful memories is hard for her. It's not difficult to understand why, but the sense of Sally seeking answers and support back then, and doing all she could, remains resonant.

Gathering her composure she continues, "I felt like I didn't have a voice. I was only seventeen and a half. I was grown-up but not. I just wanted somebody to say, 'Look you can have some help', so that I could decide. I remember running into a church very late at night, overcome with emotion trying to find a priest. I wanted to say, 'I want to keep my baby, but I don't know how, can you help me?' I was desperately trying to find a way to keep him.

"Anyway, they took him, and I didn't know where they were taking him to, but a week later I informed them that I wanted him back. He was brought back to me in the mother and baby home and I kept him for a week or two, but I just didn't know what to do. I could just about change his nappy. Nobody showed me how to look after a baby. Then the social worker came back and said if I'd changed my mind, I'd got six weeks to make a decision. I really felt that I had no choice and that there were no other options. The social worker brought all the forms for me to sign, but also kept telling me that I could have another baby …"

Unsurprisingly, the social worker was instrumental in Sally's life and this very difficult decision. Up until that point, her life had been governed by the intervention of social services, so when the social worker said, 'You haven't got anything. You haven't got money. You haven't got a house. You haven't got any friends,' Sally drew the inevitable conclusion that she had no alternative other than adoption.

Sally presses on. "When the time came, I took him to a room in the home …" She breaks down at this point saying, "It's just so hard, it's just so hard …" She goes on, "It was all over then – they just wanted me to sign the papers and get on with my life. After they took him from me, they put me back into a children's home in Enfield. When I reached eighteen, they found me a one-bedroom flat. They helped me a little bit to get it set up, but four months after that, I was raped in that flat. The case went to the Old Bailey. A lot of things happened – and they were really bad things. Even though I was quite strong, I was vulnerable, because of being in a children's home and not really having family, and not really having anybody to properly support me."

Sally believes the love she missed out on as a child led her to make poor choices as an adult, ultimately leading her to become pregnant. Very regretfully, without any support, and in complete emotional turmoil, she had no option but to have her son adopted.

"My son found me about ten years ago, but he's so angry with me. I've only seen him twice. I missed out not only on seeing his life but his two children. And the loss continues. When you have your baby adopted, you always wonder how they are getting on with their other parents. You wonder if he's well and happy. Is he getting on okay? You just want to see your baby. I did go on to have more children and, of course, he missed out on his siblings.

"He is still angry with me. He said he wouldn't have minded if I'd had mental health issues, or if I was a drug addict; he would then understand why I hadn't kept him. He says he knows other people whose mothers did keep them …"

He doesn't know about the mistreatment that Sally endured, neither her rape in the aftermath of his adoption, nor her battle to trace her own birth mother and father. Of course, he doesn't know the context, and how women like Sally were shamed and coerced, and with no real choice and no support, they had to surrender their babies. Successive governments have preferred the false narrative that women had choice, and women supported the damaging myth, by not challenging it.

Sally's son's assumptions underscore why the narrative needs to change, and why the truth needs to be exposed, and the mothers I interviewed would benefit themselves from the historic reality being properly understood. A formal apology would underline the simple fact that the women did not have any options other than adoption and would perhaps foster a sense of empathy rather than negative judgment.

Would Sally get an apology? Her circumstances are out of scope of the Parliamentary Inquiry, which dealt with forced adoptions between 1949 and 1976, so should an apology be forthcoming, it wouldn't, strictly speaking, be to her or her son. But even so, I wondered what a formal apology would mean to her.

On this point Sally was expansive. "You go through a lot of self-blame and guilt, wishing things had never happened and that you kept the baby. An apology would recognise all of that, everything we went through. But it would *never* bring back all of the memories and the relationship you could've had with that child. Also, that child has never seen his mother or parents or siblings, so it's just a massive loss on all sides. In reality, there was no reason for this to happen. The child wasn't abused or anything, I just happened to have been in a children's home.

"It doesn't matter how many children you go on to have, you will never get over the one that you lost. It's so sad because he is so lovely. It's such a shame that he doesn't want to have a relationship with me. I think about him every day. I feel like I was robbed and never given a chance. It was cruel. I mean after a baby, you're extremely vulnerable anyway, and I was exploited and manipulated."

"You were Sally," I say. It's all I can do to agree. By now my research has uncovered a very clear and very abusive pattern. Once a young unmarried mother found herself on the adoption train, she wasn't getting off with her baby in her arms.

Sally's experiences led her to work with children in care. She wanted to make sure that they had the voice she never had. Later, she became a mental health nurse because she wanted to continue to help people. She knows that the statistical outcomes for children who have been in care are very poor – they disproportionally end up on drugs or in prison. I think Sally is a credit to herself, and it's wonderful that she's gone into a caring profession utilising all her lived experience. I don't know how many people would be able to accomplish all that she has.

Lately, she tells me, she has started to write a book about her life, but concludes, "I wouldn't want to go through all of that again, although I know it has shaped my character."

I asked her if her childhood and spells in care failed to equip her to deal with the complexities she faced, not only in stating that she wanted to keep her baby, but also in working out ways she could have done so without any assistance.

Sally is very clear. "Those women were forced into adoption, and were seen as *bad* women, but in fact, it was a death every day. Even now it never ends. Even if there was an apology, it wouldn't make up for the loss. And we are still hidden. Nobody is researching us – and what else can we do? It's important that people speak out and it's important that lessons are learned. But what has changed? Probably adoption is more open now, but I don't know how it can be much different. Now, as a perinatal nurse specialising in midwifery, I'm finding more and more that the children of mothers with learning disabilities have often been put up for adoption – this really concerns me. It's horrendous; it seems to be happening to the more vulnerable. *It's all about support.* If you've got support, you've got a voice. You've got an advocate. But if you're on your own … Sometimes, I find if a mother is younger, she'll be put into an assessment unit and stay with a family and she'll be observed."

Sally talks about raising her children since the adoption of her son. Her second child was born three years after the adoption. She reckons that her children have done pretty well, benefiting from a solid education and moving into a variety of professions. On reflection, she doesn't think she could've been that much of a risk to her firstborn, as her parenting skills seem to have paid dividends. She believes she's been a good role model. She says, "They've always seen me studying, and I've always worked hard. Just because you're vulnerable doesn't mean you can't keep your child; doesn't mean you can't love your child. If you're given the right tools and support then I think a high percentage of women would be able to raise their babies. They would be fine bringing them up."

Sally continues, "The thing was, I used to look after my little brother in the children's home and then when we went home. My adoptive father didn't have any boundaries, so I was basically a mini-mother already."

I ask Sally about her adoption and whether she had traced her birth mother.

"Yes, I found my mum about twenty years ago. I've only met her three times. She has a family of her own. She didn't really want to know me, explaining that because she didn't see me crawl or break my first tooth, she didn't feel connected to me. She just didn't want to take it on really. Which is a shame. I always kept in contact with her though, asking her how she was etc. For instance, once I asked her how she was and she told me she'd had breast cancer and a mastectomy. That prompted me to quickly get to a hospital to be checked, and they found that I did have pre-cancerous cells. Had I not kept in touch I would not have known." This lack of medical history is a known serious risk for children who have been adopted.

"I also met my father; he was in America, and I visited him about three times. I was actually with both my dads, biological and non-biological, when they died. My biological father died when I was quite young."

Last but not least, Sally tells me she would love to meet up with women like herself to share their life experiences but wonders, "How are we going to find each other through all this secrecy and shame?"

Monica

"Why didn't the girls of my era fight? That makes me feel guiltier. We were so downtrodden. I don't think I ever got over the stigma."

Monica is now seventy-six, and tells me, "I got pregnant when I was sixteen. I didn't tell my parents until I was a little over five months. I was actually petrified of telling them, as they were very strict, and after I told them, I was booked straight away into a mother and baby home. I went into a Church of England home in Harrow on 15 of December 1965. My baby was due in January."

Monica continues, "I had a boyfriend and I got pregnant; his parents were very annoyed, and he didn't want to know. My parents told me I wasn't to see him anymore. So, I went into the home and when my baby was about a month old, he [her boyfriend] emigrated to Australia as one of the 'Ten Pound Poms' along with two of our mutual friends. They are all still out there, and I'm still in contact with our friends.

"This part of my life was a huge disappointment to me. My baby, a boy, was born in the February. Whilst in the home we attended the local maternity training hospital, which was dreadful. We were always put in front of people our own age, and it always came up somehow that we were unmarried. Some of the nurses were quite nasty. They treated us very differently from the other mothers-to-be. For instance, after birth, we were put in a separate section of the maternity ward altogether. They always brought it up. 'So, you're not keeping your baby?' It was awful. I stayed in the hospital for ten days, which was normal practice then, and went back to the home after the birth. I didn't surrender my baby until he was eleven weeks old."

I ask Monica about looking after her baby in the home; in particular, I'm curious to know if she breastfed him.

"No, you had the injection to take the milk away, and you bottle-fed them." I'm intrigued by this, as in some situations it seems breastfeeding was mandatory and in other places, the practice was to prevent lactation. I want to know if this process was properly consented to.

Monica tells me, "You were simply told what you were having done to you – there was no choice in anything – that's what you did." Concerns have been raised about both the ethics of the consenting process and the drugs employed to stop lactation. In her memoir, *Taken*, Michelle Pearson raises the alarm that Diethylstibestrol (also known as Stilbestrol and Desplex) were administered to stop lactation, drugs now linked to infertility, cancer and early menopause, not only in the women who were prescribed them but also in their daughters and granddaughters. After my own failed attempts to breastfeed my son, I clearly recall taking whatever was handed to me without question.

I asked Monica about her son's birth.

"I'd been lifting milk crates that morning and I had to go into hospital to be induced because he was late. I went on the bus with the mother and baby home's maternity nurse, and we had to make a detour so she could post her Valentine's Day card. It's so silly the things you remember. She left me at the hospital." Monica found this funny.

Like almost all the women I interviewed, Monica was forced to work. She went on to say, "The nurse was so compassionate towards us. There was another nurse in a church army uniform who was evil – *evil* – even wearing her church army badge. She was bossy; she didn't like us talking and she kept us busy. We had to clean all the stairs, scrub the passages down on our hands and knees. There was a mothers' room for eight or nine nursing mothers, and then about the same number again on the top floor, which was women waiting – expectant mothers. About twenty of us in total. We didn't have antenatal at the hospital. We had it at the home.

"I've got nice memories of the girls in there. You all felt for each other, and all wished the other girl well when it was her turn to go into hospital. I've kept all of my cards. We always sent the girls that had gone into hospital a card, because we didn't want to feel any of us girls were left out. So, we made a special effort so they looked like the other mums. We were treated oddly, but we had our cards up!" Several women mentioned the dissonance they experienced in hospital, where they watched husbands visiting newly delivered wives with wistfully noted flowers, balloons and cards. Celebration was all around except for the 'shameless' single mums.

I asked Monica how they were treated in the maternity hospital. She clarified: "We had our babies all of the time by the side of our bed; they were all bottle-fed. The other mothers were shown how to look after baby and given support to breastfeed. That's when some of the nurses would make a quip, 'Well, here's your bottle because you're not breastfeeding yours, are you?' said in such a nasty way. But usually, somebody else was in there from the home, either just going in or just coming out, so you would crossover and not be completely on your own. The home had quite a turnover.

"Most of the babies were being adopted, but some women did keep their babies. We were in the nursery one night, probably in the dark, probably hanging out of the window having a secret cigarette. One girl was telling us that the boyfriend didn't want to know. Well … blimey, the next day he actually knocked on the door. Two weeks after that, she was going home with him. She wasn't having hers adopted – she'd been rescued. It was lovely, we all celebrated. We were so pleased for her, but we dreaded when it was our time to leave, packing up and bathing them for the last time. I was quite happy to stay in the home. I think I kept my baby boy for so long because girls were 'in fashion' and adoptive parents preferred girls.

"We were so naïve; we seemed to be rushed along with everything. I suppose we were a different generation who obediently did as we were told. You were made to feel so shameful, but you just carried on with it. I came back into the nursery one day after being out to the local town, and I saw somebody holding my boy. I said something and he turned around and smiled, recognising my voice. And the Sister was in there and I was told to prepare to leave the following morning and that my baby would be found foster parents. I persuaded friends to come and collect me so I could take him to the foster mother. I handed him over. He was asleep and then I had to return home. When I went home, it was never mentioned again. I returned to my job. That was it, and then I had to pay the foster fees until September."

In today's context, Monica's story is barely believable. First, forced into a mother and baby home, forced to surrender her baby to a foster mother, forced out of the home and back into the parental home. She was then required to work to pay the foster mother for the months it took to place her baby into permanent adoptive care. Monica's baby was finally adopted in November at nine months old. She had no choice but to work.

Monica's testimony exposes the myth that girls could have their babies and then simply get on with their lives. The truth is a great many suffered Post-Traumatic Stress Disorder (PTSD) and other trauma responses. Many report complex trauma-related memory loss. Describing the years after as 'slow disintegration', they didn't heal and the body did not forget the trauma of loss, as Bessel van der Kolk explains in his book *The Body Keeps Score*.

"I used to ring the foster mother every week to see how he was. It was heartbreaking. I took a long time to get over it. In fact, I never got over it at all. You suffer mentally. I suffered mentally for forty-eight years. I couldn't believe it when he actually found me …"

Monica describes life after having her son adopted. "I had such black moods. I felt so guilty. And I worried all the time. Was he okay? Is he happy? Was he loved? I constantly looked at people his age – all the time. I couldn't help it." To this end, Monica informed me that in one job, she would surreptitiously check the company records to see if anybody had the same birth date as her son. I had the sense from her that she felt he could be anywhere, and she maintained a state of hypervigilance for decades.

"Every time somebody strange walks past, about his age, I would think to myself, is this him? Is he coming to find me? It was awful."

Monica got married in 1974 and had another son in 1978. But she says, "I ended up a single mother because my marriage failed – and the guilt I felt about that! That I couldn't do it then, but I'm doing it now, I mean being a single parent. It made me feel very mixed up. I could never talk to my family, but my close friends helped me through my dark days.

"I did keep in contact with my roommate Barbara. We went into the home at the same time and we had our babies together. She left before me, shortly after six weeks. We stayed friends right until she recently passed away. We kept each other going – very much so."

I asked Monica if Barbara had contacted her child and Monica explained, "No, her husband threw all her papers away and she wasn't allowed any contact and was forbidden to try to trace her baby."

Monica explained that she and Barbara shared a room together. "We just clicked. I miss her so much. If you like, she was my memory; we shared so much in those six weeks that we had our babies. There was nobody else that I could talk about that experience with. It was comforting. We used to discuss what had happened to us together because it was an awful place and nobody wanted to be in there. I was so glad I had Barbara and she had me. Her parents were the same as mine. 'Give your baby up and then just carry on as if nothing had happened,' they said."

Monica goes on to explain to me how when Barbara became ill with terminal cancer, she asked Monica to take the only surviving records she had of her son, six small photographs, which together the pair had connived to have taken all those years ago. They couldn't have known then that these would be their only record of their children as babies. Barbara said she wanted Monica to have the photographs in case her son ever came looking for her after her death.

Monica said, "She managed to hide these from her husband. My son, when he turned up, had no pictures of himself as a baby, and he was delighted when I could show him the six pictures taken whilst we were in the home." Monica has now registered Barbara's details with the Adoption Society tracing service, in case Barbara's son ever does want to try to trace his birth mother.

It wasn't just the parents of women that forbade women to speak of, reminisce, or search for their long-lost babies. It was often their life partner too. Often women would be quick to form partnerships or marry in an attempt to recreate the family that had been taken from them. Young and vulnerable, many found themselves in relationships with coercive, controlling men. At the same time, many men bought into the myth that the women should just get on with the rest of their lives. That the unfortunate event should be left in the past. Women were unable to talk about their terrible loss to anyone, increasing their sense of isolation.

Monica first tried to find her son in the nineties when she went to the Adoption Society. She was told that he was still living at the same address and that she could write to his parents, but they had been in Australia for more than fifteen years by then.

"What was the agency doing when they asked me to write a letter to addresses where the child was no longer resident? I can't tell you what it was like to see his folder on the desk. It was the realisation that yes, he is there. Seeing this lady bring his file into the room – with his and my life contained within it. It was unbearable. I decided against making contact at that time because, although I had lost my father, my mother was still alive and I didn't want to have to continue to hide it under the carpet if I did find him. My mother was elderly, in her late eighties, so I said to myself I would wait until both my parents had gone because I knew if I found him, I would want to absolutely shout for joy. And you have to bear in mind that my parents and my brother never mentioned it ever again. Not once."

Monica adds context to how much shame her mother felt when her daughter became pregnant. "She used to do my washing and hang my clothes out on the line, even though I was in the mother and baby home! That how strong the shame was. When I called my mother to tell her I had to return home from the hostel, she said to me, 'Don't be upset, but your dad won't be very pleased to have you back. He won't like it at all.' I walked into my kitchen and I hadn't been in there since December. My uncle was there, and he said, 'Hello, girl. I haven't seen you for a long time?' So, I responded, 'I've just been down the road to get some cigarettes.' And that was it. I carried on as if nothing had happened even though I had handed my baby over just an hour before. I was forced to carry on. Stiff upper lip. Awful. Awful. Awful. I brought shame onto my family, and I was made to feel shameful. And that's how I remained.

"It was by attending MAA meetings that I realised some of the women had their own folders. This prompted me to apply for mine, which I was entitled to, but I couldn't apply for my child's information. I simply couldn't believe what they had written. He would never have looked for me because of what they said. They said we were so poor. We definitely weren't. They said my mother had to work to supplement the income. That we couldn't afford to feed another mouth. That wasn't the case at all. The truth was my parents didn't want me to keep my child. It was all written to present a view that there was no alternative to his adoption.

"Why don't they tell the truth? It upset me so much and, thank goodness, he hadn't replied to find my information. It was rubbish. My parents were well off. The record should have read I brought shame to the family and my parents didn't want to know. Why wasn't that recorded? I didn't want to get rid of my baby. There was nobody to help me. I was told never to tell anybody. Years later, my aunts and uncles said, 'Why didn't you tell us?' Well, easy to say twenty or thirty years after the event. What would've happened if I'd told them when I was seventeen?"

It feels like the records were determined to illustrate the dire circumstances of both the mother and her family – making clear the inalienable, unquestionable unsuitability of the woman to raise her own baby. This is a theme that turned up in almost every set of records and this massaging of the truth has universally caused upset and hurt, and angered those accessing their records. It's as if the lack of accuracy doesn't matter for this cohort of women, in the same way that the lack of rights and autonomy of the individual women – the mothers – didn't matter.

"One day," Monica tells me, "I had a bicycle stolen from the shed in the garden and the police came round about the bike and asked me if I wanted counselling. I stood there and I was shaking. I was rigid and unable to say anything. Did I want counselling because I'd lost a bike? Nobody ever asked me if I wanted any counselling over losing my baby! I found that so terrible, I found it so hard. Nobody has ever asked me how I was, but a policeman asked me if I wanted counselling over a bike."

At this stage, Monica is very distressed. It's obvious that this still shakes her and it's hard not to feel aligned with her sense of gross injustice.

"I've been robbed of a baby and offered no support – in fact, I'm expected to continue as if nothing has happened.

"I went through a long period of time after losing my son, where I simply couldn't go out socially – years in fact. A friend of mine suggested I speak to somebody about this 'because you're always making arrangements and then breaking them.' And I did go and see somebody, and they said that I felt guilty for enjoying myself because I was so wracked with guilt. She suggested I should come clean and just not make any arrangements, but instead wait until I really wanted to do things. But I did feel guilty for enjoying myself, along with the shame I felt. It took a very long time to get back into having any sort of youngster's life. I didn't want to know anybody really …

"When he found me, it was as if it all lifted. I did listen to people expressing similar sentiments on the *Long Lost Family* TV programme, where people are often reunited and they seem to experience the same thing. It's like that weight is lifted. It's absolutely right – the mere fact you can say *sorry* to them – takes the guilt away. It's so hard to explain, but you've carried such guilt for so long. I am so lucky that I've got the opportunity. I can die tomorrow! That's how I feel now. I didn't want to take all that guilt to my grave; I just wanted to know – needed to know – that he was okay."

Monica explained to me how her son had established contact with her. "It's been ten years since we were reunited. He applied for my birth certificate in 2013. He tried to find me ten years before that; he had my name, but it had a detail recorded incorrectly, the wrong birth date, a digit wrong. Then he applied to a researcher in 2013 on the *Long Lost Family* TV programme. Out of the blue, she contacted me in November 2013, asking if I wanted to make contact with my son. I felt absolutely on cloud nine. When I saw his name, I simply couldn't believe it. I was straight on the phone to say that I wanted to meet. We had to communicate through the researcher for a couple of months and we wrote a few letters which were vetted; then we were allowed to video call and in March he came over – he was living in Australia. We spent a week together. Then he moved here for a short period of time.

"He'd been living in Australia since he was seven. I remember being told that the adoptive parents had lost babies and had miscarriages, and then they had my baby and then managed to have two babies of their own. He is very close to his siblings and his mum and dad. He hasn't told his mum and dad about me and the longer it's gone on the more difficult it is to do that – they would be so upset now to find out he has been in contact with me for these ten years." Reunion often throws up issues like this, and the secrecy continues with people choosing not to inform all those involved of reconnections.

"I do feel very lucky to have had this contact because I know many women won't have had that happen to them, and I do feel very lucky to have left my guilt behind. He's such a lovely boy, and he's such a lovely person with such lovely ways. He looks like my other son; they could've been brought up together and you wouldn't have known that they weren't brothers. They walk the same way, they've got the same shape, they have my family's genes. We talk every Sunday – it's such an easy conversation. We talk about everything and nothing.

"Because he's forgiven me, he doesn't hold any malice towards me at all. He said he wasn't looking for another family. He just wanted to know where he came from. He said that he thought I'd had it much worse than he had, which made me feel good. Because if he had experienced a bad adoption, I would have felt even more terrible. I'm so lucky that I've met my baby and that he's had a good life, but there are so many people who don't ever find out. Like Barbara …"

I'm sure that if the culture was more honest and transparent about how we treated both young, unmarried mothers and their babies during the fifties, sixties, seventies, and even into the eighties, then many more people – including those people directly impacted by the prevailing practices would be more accepting. It is understandable that people may experience complex and often tumultuous emotions upon finding their biological mothers. For many, they have scant knowledge, or no knowledge of the conditions into which they were born, and it is difficult to create a vivid picture of what life was like at that time.

Forced adoption in the UK is a topic that's hardly been covered in popular culture, and few people can imagine that this practice was so deeply embedded in British culture, and so recent. We are accustomed to seeing stories set in Ireland, including *Philomena* and *The Magdalene Sisters*, but it's frustrating that we rarely see depictions of British-based forced adoption.

Even for me, it's hard to stop and absorb the reality of what's being disclosed to me. That women simply had no choice. Upon finding themselves unmarried and pregnant – save for the man concerned offering to marry them – the alternative was that the State or the Church would intervene to ensure that ultimately the baby was taken. Those women had no control over their lives, their bodies, nor their children. Something almost impossible to conceive in the mid-2020s. Almost.

Monica and I discussed the need for an adoption apology.

"I'd like someone to say sorry to me, for putting you through all of that," Monica says, "for making you part with your baby. Especially these days, I do feel bitter, because there are girls who are unmarried and they've got their children, and nobody thinks anything of it. They have three or four with different partners – they get help with housing. Nobody said to me do you want to keep your baby? We were 'put down'. We had so many visitors to the home. I don't know where they were from, whether they were from the council or from the Church. They were all well dressed, all looking down their nose at us, and saying, 'Oh you're not keeping your child?' But you couldn't say – it's not what I want.

"I want an apology for all that. For me being changed so much. For me losing my child. For somebody to say sorry – that's all I want."

"What would that mean?" I asked.

"I just want an apology for the forty-eight years of hell that I went through, preferably from a man, like my MP Oliver Dowden; he didn't want to know, saying it wasn't really his department."

At this stage, Monica is upset and, unsurprisingly, crying. And I note how common it is even after the passage of many decades, even after being successfully reunited with those long-lost babies, how extremely painful the matter still is, and how very close to the surface those emotions are.

However well-regulated they have been, it doesn't take much to bring them to the surface.

"You do get upset because it's so different today and they don't know how lucky they are. It is as it should be. We were made to feel such shame."

Monica reminisces about the church at the top of Harrow on the Hill, overlooking Harrow School, and talks about the grotesque and huge house that the mother and baby home was in, and how years later, she and Barbara would return to look at the house from time to time.

"Even though the home has been turned into flats, we could still see the tree where we'd hang out the washing … We used to go to that church and climb that really steep hill, but we always had to make sure we were the last in and the first out, so that everybody saw us … That was shaming.

"For about two years when I returned to work, some of the other women were terrible – so cruel. Before I went, they made me maternity dresses and knitted baby clothes for me, but when I got back they were horrible. They shunned me. My boss kept my job open for me. I had to go back to work to pay the foster parent. I was so hurt. They said such spiteful things. Until another woman started, and they said something nasty to me one morning, and she told them off. Afterwards, she told me she'd just had a little girl adopted privately. She was thirteen years older than me. We stayed friends for fifty years. I nursed her when she was dying. She'd been let down too.

"All the time I was at work, waiting for the adoption to be final, I was waiting for something to happen, that a miracle would happen, that the adoption would fail. It's the not knowing that is so dreadful. When they can give me counselling for losing a bike, but they can't say sorry for taking my baby."

I could only reply to Monica that it was injury on every level.

Monica concludes, "It was mental torture. You couldn't even get anywhere to live if you've got a child. You couldn't even get a job if you'd got a child. What was the true cost of this practice? How many women were forced back to work to pay for fostering fees? Why didn't the girls of my era fight? That makes me feel guiltier. We were so downtrodden. I don't think I ever got over the stigma, by not rebelling. When you see girls today – they do what they want to do. They've got more balls, which we've never had. We did what we were told to do. You went along with the idea of adoption being the best – the only outcome – hoping that you wouldn't have to. And I'd think to myself that's it, my girl, but I didn't fight back. We never demanded anything; we didn't answer back. We were just put in our place. That's the guilt that I carry. Now I have been able to speak with lots of women and they were also being forced down that path. It was like an industry. There was no way they weren't going to get what they wanted, and what they wanted was your baby. It wouldn't matter who you are, or how strong you were, or how much you fought. *Unless you got a man."*

I asked Monica about the impact on her relationships within the family.

"My older brother didn't speak to me for ten years. Then, his daughter had a child before she got married. I told him I would go to the wedding but that I wouldn't stay. When he asked me why, I explained, 'I couldn't get over the day your grandson was born, you were pouring champagne, but nobody popped corks when I had my baby. And yet your daughter is unmarried. It's no different.' He tried to placate me saying, 'It's water under the bridge,' but it's not like that for me. Our mum said never to mention it again so we didn't, and I said to him, 'So you never did.'"

Monica wondered if other families were very different, or if it was just hers. "That's part of the problem with these hidden histories, you can't see yourself replicated in other *perfect* families. It's all very much hidden, feeding into the trope of it's you, not them. We weren't far away from being put into the asylums. I can actually remember that, unmarried mothers sent into asylums."

I had a question about suicidal feelings, which I put to Monica. Had she, like others I had interviewed, experienced suicidal ideation?

"Yes. Absolutely. I heard him crying at night for a long, long time. I was in a terrible way after."

I'm struck by the way so many women internalised their distress. Unable to voice their trauma, they suffered quietly and frequently alone. The value of women being enabled to share their experiences cannot be underestimated.

"Before Barbara died, she asked me to write our story and I did make a start, but then when my son turned up, I didn't feel the same afterwards; the pain has lessened, and I don't feel as bitter. I can't get back into the writing in the same way. Barbara was my rock. She was the only one that I shared memories of him with, along with my work friend. We helped each other because you couldn't get help anywhere else."

I think Monica's final comments reflect the loneliness and isolation of the historic forced adoption era. A formal apology and reparations may go some way towards addressing this. It seems vital to open a national dialogue and to demonstrate changed attitudes and to demonstrate compassion and empathy. That would help to allay the burden of carrying shame for all these decades.

Diana

*"They were clearly more concerned with what
other people thought than about my welfare."*

Diana runs the Movement for an Adoption Apology (MAA) website and is a key activist, often appearing in the media, undertaking interviews about her lived experience of forced adoption. She is passionate about the MAA, determined to ensure that there is a wider understanding of the injustices perpetrated, and keen to involve people to secure the much-anticipated formal apology and redress.

Our conversation began by focusing on our shared experience of shame encountered during our teenage years, induced by being 'sent away to', 'going into', or being otherwise 'interred into' a Catholic mother and baby home. There were significant parallels between us up to the point of childbirth, and we both recognised how those experiences had a significantly damaging impact on our nascent sense of control and derailed our developing sense of autonomy – a vital milestone in adolescent development. All young people need to be able to develop a sense of self and to be able to set their own boundaries. Diana's trajectory through the mother and baby home system, arguably thwarted her fledgling autonomy, perhaps resulting in lifelong psychological damage and trauma.

Diana describes autonomy as: "The ability to decide your own path, your own way forward. If people have run roughshod over you when you're very young, it's extremely hard to do that …" She goes on to explain the impact, "I've had to relearn things later in life once the blinkers fully fell off." No easy feat.

These experiences left her with a lifelong blighted imprint. In common with other women and girls banished into homes, that sense of being subject to shame, forced to feel guilt, and treated in that culturally and historically specific manner, laid down a pattern that has existed for the rest of her life. Diana expands, "It changes your attitude about what you're entitled to, and you believe you should do things. For instance, if somebody confronts you, women like me, who have been treated in this way, are less confrontational, less able to stand up for themselves, and are worried about being seen as being wrong. Or inappropriate. You are somehow rendered 'less than'. The repercussions are huge."

Diana's story begins in 1973: she's fifteen when she meets her boyfriend – but he's not a boy, in fact, he's a man, and according to contemporary standards, too old to be appropriately interested in her, let alone be romantically involved with a naïve teen. Today, we might determine she was being groomed.

There's a certain ease to believing it is simple cause and effect, when a young woman – a girl in reality – falls madly in love or is willingly and consensually seduced, or otherwise hapless, and this is what renders her pregnant. We can then agree it's her own fault. It was bound to happen; she should've been more careful … The truth is often, perhaps always, far from this. Women and young girls are often duped, forced, and involuntarily the victims of unethical – patriarchal – men. It takes two to tango right?

Cause and effect in fact often begins in childhood. The way we are treated as children may well render us more vulnerable as teenagers and young adults. Diana says, "I was the least favourite child in my family. I wasn't the pink-cheeked, curly-haired cherub my parents wanted." Or maybe the child is, like others in this book (ironically) an adopted or looked-after child, or is being brought up in an abusive family, or an abusive oppressive community.

Other factors are also in play. Many second-wave feminists argued that the UK had a sexist, paedophilic, and racist culture throughout the sixties and seventies, and even a cursory examination of popular culture shows girls and young women as sexually desirable, and available, and depicts men as being unable to 'hold back'. Song lyrics depict scenes where girls have to run, and where schoolgirls can't be resisted … Exactly how young were the girls they were singing about? Girls were depicted as easy prey. Those girls who felt unloved and uncared for – all the more so.

Diana continues, "I didn't think I mattered. I didn't think my parents minded if I lived or died. They weren't cruel: they fed me, they clothed me, but they weren't nice people. I just wasn't loved. So, when somebody comes along and pays you compliments … it's so easy as an unworldly fifteen-year-old to get swept off your feet. I thought this was wonderful! I was convinced this was the man of my dreams. I wasn't mature for my age and I tended to live in my own little world. I was really vulnerable, and I didn't know it. I met him through my Saturday job when I was caught in the rain after a day's work and he offered me a lift home. The relationship progressed very quickly. I was very caught up in the relationship, felt he really liked me and that I was important – all the red flags that we'd now spot from a thousand yards with a blindfold on. I didn't realise what he was doing, or how quickly he was taking things forward. He told me he was divorced, he told me where he lived. He told me all sorts of things that I later realised were untrue. But I believed him and I was caught up in the romance, but really it was quite abusive. We went out together for eighteen months.

"At the beginning of 1974, when I was sixteen, I started to feel really ill. I didn't want to think about what it might be, so I put it to the back of my mind, but I had severe morning sickness, possibly hyperemesis gravidarum. I soon learned to throw up with absolutely no noise. No one at home noticed. My parents had no idea that I was even going out with anyone.

"One day he asked me if I was pregnant. I told him no, of course not, but I was really struggling with it. Then he started to see me less often, and I didn't really know how to handle that. I think he knew that I really was pregnant and he was perhaps thinking I would do something about it or just wake up. I got to about five months and I was sitting in his car chatting and he said, 'You are, aren't you?' and I said, 'Yeah, I think I am.' Then he put his hand on my abdomen, adding, 'Oh well, that's it then.' I never saw him again. I think I went into some kind of shock because I honestly thought, in that romanticised view and being terribly naïve with very limited life experience, it would be ok.

"I went to try to find him at the address he had given me, but he wasn't there, and the people living there were cagey and wouldn't tell me where he was. I had a phone number for him, but he wouldn't answer. I couldn't track him down. I was on my own. I still pretended it wasn't happening. I sat my O-levels, finished my school year and started a summer holiday job and just carried on … By this stage, I started to develop pregnancy-related back pain, which was so bad I was dragging my leg, and I still had the sickness.

"My parents weren't interested in me in any way, but one morning my mother asked, 'What's wrong with you?' Then she took me to see somebody. I don't know who it was, but I do remember lying on this examination table, and him saying after a cursory examination, 'How long have you been like this?' I wasn't sure what he meant. I said I didn't know. He then said, 'Stay there,' and he went off and spoke with my parents. He came back in the room saying, 'Okay you can go,' and after that, nobody actually spoke to me. That was one of the signature themes of the whole experience from then on. Nobody spoke to me. They spoke to my parents. They spoke to my mother. They spoke amongst themselves.

They didn't speak to me. It was a feeling of being excluded from your own fate.

"Once we were at home, there was a big shouting match, where my parents said that the doctor, or whatever he was, had told them he thought I was pregnant. And I thought to myself, this is my opportunity. I'd spent months, sitting at the top of the stairs crying, wondering how I could tell my parents, and so I replied, 'Yes, I must be.'

"Then it got even worse. They called me terrible names using swear words I hadn't even heard until then. My mother said if I'd told her sooner, I could've had an abortion, and then the conversation turned to what would the neighbours say, and that they couldn't tell my grandparents. They were clearly more concerned with what other people thought than about my welfare.

"We then went to the family GP and he greeted me by saying, 'I hear you've been a naughty girl!' The rest of the appointment was spent with him talking to my mother and me staring at my feet.

"Mum also took me to see the headmistress of my Catholic grammar school. She gave the headmistress a litany of woe whilst I sat there, wishing the ground would open up and swallow me. My mother clarified the circumstances explaining, 'The baby is going to be adopted.' The headmistress looked directly at me and asked, 'Is that what you want?' She was the only person who asked me what I wanted and because my mother was there, I felt dumbstruck. I couldn't say anything. If she'd asked me without my mother being present, I would've said, 'I don't know what I want. I'm terrified. Because I don't know how to control my out-of-control body or my out-of-control life.' So, this woman in a habit, who probably had never had an intimate relationship, is asking me a question that I wanted to answer but couldn't in front of my mother.

"I was almost eight months at this stage when my mother whisked me away from London to Nazareth House mother and baby home in Southampton run by The Sisters of Mercy. It was a huge three-storey period property. She didn't speak to me for the entire journey. It seemed so far away and completely alien to me. I'd never lived away from home. We went from the railway station to the home by taxi – I don't like to call it a home because it was in fact a prison. The cab stopped outside, in front of huge curved double doors; it was very ecclesiastical. I remember going in, no one spoke to me and I was put in a room with another girl right at the top of the house. Many years later, it dawned on me why I'd been put in that room with that particular young woman … I have Anglo-Indian heritage – a look that isn't Caucasian. The woman I shared the room with was from Bolivia. We were the two brown girls stashed away in the attic … although I didn't see that perspective at the time.

"My stay there was relatively short and awful. All the nuns who ran the home treated us as if we were a nuisance. The beds were rickety, and the furniture was mismatched as if bought in jumble sales and second-hand stores. The walls were all painted that weird clinical green. There was this feeling of an institution. The bathrooms were sort of separate booths, very odd. Not domestic or homely at all. On our floor, there was a fire door that opened onto an ironwork balcony and staircase, which descended three floors. I say this because it was part of my suicide ideation. I used to stand there and think about jumping off. As you do when you're sixteen and desperate."

Diana says this in such a matter-of-fact way and has clearly retained every detail. The way in which she references suicide ideation alerts me; it's becoming a common thread, and I resolve to gently ask those I am interviewing about this. She recalls other features of the home. "On the ground floor, there was a grand staircase with dark wooden panels. It was very sombre with a stone floor. The entrance hall was particularly large, and there was this weird chalet thing and I didn't know what it was for. There were kitchens at the back of the home with great big Belfast sinks where we all had to do washing of various kinds. Because of my age, I was expected to do academic work, and my school remained supportive throughout and sent coursework for me to complete. I thought this was very good of them. There was also a room where girls like me who were still at school could do their schoolwork. "We didn't have to do hands and knees scrubbing the floor stuff, but we were certainly kept busy. I was expected to do a lot of dusting even when there was no dust. From 1974 things had moved on ..."

I assume that this is the impact of the 1974 Adoption Act, which created a legal framework that conferred more, even if still limited, rights on young women caught in the mother and baby home forced adoption circus. Nevertheless, the prevailing assumption was adoption – the surrender of one's baby – was the optimum outcome for both baby, mother, and the wider family and, of course, the prospective adoptive parents. And coercion is applied in its various guises, as we've seen elsewhere. It was key to the Church, moral welfare organisations, and social services succeeding in their primary objective – a supply of babies to more deserving, *better* people.

Diana continues her description of Nazareth mother and baby home, "On the ground floor, there was a dining area comprised of two areas separated by a wooden grille. One part was where we all ate, sitting around a long table, eating slop, and adjacent, through the white-painted lattice, was where the nuns gathered and ate. While they had vegetables, salads and fresh fruit, we would have unnamed meat, swimming in gravy, served with lots of mash or bread – all fillers. It was almost like we were being fattened up for the kill. Just given carbs, not very nutritious.

"One afternoon shortly before I gave birth, I went for a walk. They said I wasn't supposed to go out, but I managed to get out anyway. They didn't keep the door locked. I think it was because of the fire regulations. Whilst walking, I passed by some offices and noticed they were Social Security offices, so I memorised the number. When I got back to the home, I phoned them to enquire if I was entitled to anything. I was told, 'No, you're not entitled to anything, you're too young.' Then they slammed down the phone. I think I was entitled to some assistance, but nobody would tell me.

"Whilst in the home, I was assigned someone who told me she was 'my' social worker. It wasn't until just a few years ago I discovered she worked for the adoption agency. She would just turn up and say you need to sign this or sign that … I would sign anything because I felt so browbeaten and, on at least one occasion, I remember her dictating to me what I had to say because I didn't know what to do. I just felt completely trapped.

"We had very little antenatal preparation, except for one time in the pseudo-school class. The teacher asked, 'Do you know what's going to happen when you give birth?' The other girl who was only about thirteen and I looked at her and shook our heads, so she gave us a very cursory explanation, which was absolutely terrifying. She showed us pictures in a book and said, 'Now you know that's where the baby comes out.'

"I was out on one of my walks and I started to get these weird abdominal cramps and I know this sounds odd, but I didn't make the connection between that pain and going into labour. When I came back to the home, I didn't tell anyone, but in the middle of the night I started to feel really bad, so I went to the loo and that is when my waters broke. Only then did I realise what was happening. I went and knocked on the door in the forbidden corridor where all the nuns slept. One opened the door and asked, 'What do you want?' I replied that I thought I was in labour and she told me not to be ridiculous and to go back to bed! At that point, I was hit by a contraction and my knees buckled, and she conceded, 'Oh, well … maybe come in then.' I was taken through to a different room where there was an examination couch. I remember she didn't wear any gloves or anything like that, she just popped me on the examination couch and gave me an internal examination to see if I was in labour. I question to this day whether any of these people had any medical qualifications that entitled them to do any of the things that they did?

"They decided to call an ambulance and I had a small bag packed, then I was sent to the hospital on my own. It was very scary.

"One member of staff in the hospital was really sweet. She gave me some reassurance, but she was the only one who spoke to me, the rest of them talked around me. I was taken through to what I assumed was the delivery room, and I was lying on a high table in the middle of the room like a piece of meat on a slab. The table was very high, above waist height, and it was really hard. I was having a problem with my back and was extremely uncomfortable. I wanted to sit up but the nurse kept pushing me back, holding me down with her hands on my shoulders.

"Of course, now I realise I wanted gravity to help me and that the need to sit up was logical. Then I recall them coming in with some scissors, which I now know are episiotomy scissors and she said, 'I'm going to help the baby.' She didn't actually explain what she was going to do; there was this sound like scissors cutting through velvet. I can remember feeling a huge shock and then obviously it was easier for the baby to come out, but nobody cared about me. And I can remember feeling so out of my body that I just wasn't part of what was going on.

"My daughter was born at 4.15 a.m. and, after they made sure the placenta had come away, they got somebody in to stitch me up, which was done quickly. Still, nobody spoke to me. Nobody spoke to me during the birth other than to say we're going to help the baby. One of the nurses picked my baby up and said, 'Oh this baby is flagged for adoption, I'll take her away.' And I started screaming. I shouted, 'No, no, bring her back to me.'

"The nurse came back, and I thought she was going to hand my baby to me, but she didn't. She passed by me and walked to the other side of the room and put her in some sort of basket thing. After that, they all left the room and I was left there until eight o'clock, with my baby crying on the other side of the room, and I couldn't reach her. I couldn't move because I was too weak. I'd just been left there. I called out to my daughter as much as I could to let her know I was there, but I couldn't get to her. I just couldn't. I was terrified of ripping my stitches if I tried to get off the table and I couldn't get my stomach muscles to work. I was so high up, I thought I'd fall and break something.

"And my baby kept crying and crying. Then after a couple of hours, I just completely lost my voice, and she stopped; I thought she'd died. And I just lay there wishing I would die. Eventually, a nurse popped her head into the room and said, 'Oh I didn't know there was anyone in here!' all chirpy. All I could croak was 'Please help!' I don't remember being moved, but I was taken into a side room with my daughter, but still, at no point had I held my baby. The whole thing was really strange, designed to keep us from making contact. The whole thing was brutal. Like torture. Then at around midday a nurse came to check on me and said, 'Oh, my God, they haven't even cleaned you up!'

"I was in there for about five days and one of the worst bits was visiting hours when you were on your own in a little area of misery and everybody else is celebrating. They get balloons, cards and all those visitors smiling, laughing and congratulating them, saying things like, 'She's so beautiful.' But those of us that had fallen from the righteous way, we were just left. It was miserable and then we went back into the home."

During her stay in hospital, Diana was involuntarily given medication, which she had been informed was for postnatal pain, but was actually administered to stop lactation. In the hospital, they provided nappies, formula, etc., but once back in the home, Diana was told her parents hadn't paid sufficient fees for her and her baby, so she had to buy everything for her baby … from the chalet in the entrance hall.

My own memories echo Diana's experience, but they differ in one particularly significant way. Whilst Diana's baby was going to be taken from her, I somehow held on to my son. While I was in hospital receiving postnatal care for two weeks, known as 'lying-in', I recall feeling particularly liberated and equal to the other mothers on the ward, at being able to walk to the ward store cupboard and take out whatever *I* judged was needed for myself and my baby. This included a two-part plastic bowl, which was used to 'top and tail' baby. My recollections of this time remain vivid. The images, smell and noise of the maternity unit persist in my memory.

I can still remember being skilfully and non-judgmentally taught how to care for my baby, in a gentle yet authoritative way, by expert uniformed midwives, whom I could both trust and seek to emulate. I was, for instance, shown how to fill both parts of the two-part bowl with lukewarm water and then take cotton wool balls and use these, soaked in tepid fresh water, to clean each of his eyes, moving from the inner corner to the outer part of the eye, and to repeat with a fresh ball. (I was instructed never to skimp on the number of cotton wool balls used, and that baby's cleanliness was paramount …) This ensured no infection could be inadvertently spread.

Then I was told to use the other half of the bowl to clean my baby's bottom. Top and tail! I was also shown patiently how to put nappies on; indeed, I was even given a choice of techniques. I was shown carefully how to dress my baby in a Babygro and a matinee jacket. I recall with fondness, being guided with such proficiency, not to accidentally catch my baby's delicate fingers in any clothes, but instead to push my hand gently up into the small sleeve and then to hold baby's tiny, impossibly delicate hand, covering the fingers, and then to feed the hand down through the sleeve. This way I would never accidentally rip off his minuscule fingers. Something that might come naturally to others, or be considered simple common sense, but needed to be demonstrated to me, as I'd never held a newborn baby before.

Bathing baby was another important lesson, an elbow dipped into the water to judge the temperature. It was all demonstrated without a hint of condescension or judgment; questions and supervised practice were encouraged. This instruction instilled a logical and methodical approach to the practical business of looking after a baby. It made me feel so confident, that I became confident. Confident and capable mothering and parenting in turn gives rise to a calmer baby. It's exactly the right sort of virtuous circle.

How different from the brutality Diana and her daughter endured.

Diana explains what happened once she was discharged from hospital.

"My 'social worker' turned up with paperwork. Technically, I was under the age of majority, so should have had a parent or guardian with me to sign that I consented. No way should anyone have been dictating content to me, but she did, she also co-signed as a witness. I don't know how that was acceptable? I had my seventeenth birthday in the home and then a few days later my mother took me back to Ladbroke Grove, which is where the Crusade of Rescue, now called The Children's Society was based. I actually held my daughter on the train journey back; it was the longest time I'd been able to hold her. I just kept looking at her and thinking, this is my daughter. It was like it hadn't dawned on me until then. I'd had her for twelve days and somehow the penny hadn't dropped. I think I'd been so disconnected from her by all the shenanigans. I didn't want to let her go …

"At the Crusade of Rescue, we stood in the reception area and a woman appeared in a white coat, a stethoscope and pearls, and she simply said, 'It's time,' and held her arms out. It didn't dawn on me what she wanted, so I just stood there and suddenly the thought hit me. She wants my baby! I was standing there, thinking I can't, I can't, I can't. My mother reached across and said, 'Oh, for goodness' sake,' and she yanked my daughter out of my arms and gave her to the woman. I remember her walking away, turning around saying, 'Say bye-bye,' holding one of my baby's hands up to wave at me. Then my knees started to give way; my daughter made a sound I'd never heard her make, not a hungry or nappy cry. A really horrible howling, which I've never forgotten."

Diana talked about her poor relationship with her mother and I wondered how many mothers had inflicted this punishing treatment on their daughters because they were less than whole themselves in some way.

These babies were their grandchildren. How had they become so hardened towards the anguish of their daughters and the loss of a grandchild?

I asked Diana how she had contacted her daughter.

"When she was approaching fifteen, I decided I was going to phone the Crusade of Rescue to find out if she was okay because I didn't know if she was dead or alive. That's very hard to live with. I called and told them my name and explained I was just trying to find out if she was okay, that I didn't want to make waves, and I didn't want to try and contact her – I just wanted to know if she's alright. The person who answered the phone didn't miss a beat, didn't even pause, and certainly didn't stop to look at files or records. He didn't seem to have any consideration as to the impact his words would have on me. He just said 'the family has moved away and we have no contact with them'. Then the line went dead.

"I felt so miserable after this experience, I wrote a three-page letter and I sent it to them to put on her file – just in case she ever got in touch. I never received any acknowledgement. Then she was eighteen and a woman called me from the Crusade of Rescue saying, 'I've got some information for you. Your daughter has been in touch, she'd like to meet you.' My initial reaction was she's alive! I think I said that out loud. Of course, I wanted to see her, so we started the process with an exchange of letters, followed by phone calls and finally an arrangement to meet. We met on the 14 of November 1992. It was extraordinary. I could feel something shifting in my physiology. It was like a readjustment on a cellular level. It was profound. She has never told me what the impact was on her, but it was powerful for me.

"It wasn't an easy reunion for a number of reasons. My daughter had grown up knowing she was adopted and had been told my name. She'd tried to find me when she was fifteen, which I thought was a very interesting synchronicity. She'd visited the Crusade of Rescue offices, and a social worker had located her file, then said, 'Sorry, you're not old enough'. They weren't legally allowed to give her information until she was eighteen."

I asked Diana what she felt about an adoption apology. She replied, "Because of my experience, there was so much damage and so much guilt and shame, and I was made to feel responsible for what happened. We have all been through such a terrible trauma without help or support.

"We need someone to stand up and say we're sorry for what happened to you, and we're willing to help you with trauma-informed support and free access to records, and all the things that we asked for when we approached the Parliamentary Inquiry. That would create a huge paradigm shift. Otherwise, if they don't provide support measures, it's just words … They need to apologise to shift the blame to the State, to the people who were responsible. That would take it from our shoulders and place it on their shoulders. Even if it doesn't free us entirely, it would at least lift the burden. It would vindicate everybody that has been carrying this for almost their entire lives, so that we can move through the world, knowing that we were victims of an injustice, not the perpetrators."

Diana tells me that she didn't have any more children and that she'd had a miscarriage. She said after her experience she was, "physically, emotionally, and psychologically damaged," and that as a result, she spent a few years with a partner who was "abusive". She has since settled into a happy relationship with her husband.

Diana now questions the contemporary adoption system, and wonders whether it is used as a way of saving money in the fostering system. These are questions that must be addressed in any apology. Lessons must be learnt. The proposed Hillsborough Law seeks to criminalise lying to the British public; the Government plans to introduce a duty of candour, ending the depressingly familiar pattern of cover-ups and concealments. But in addition, the UK Government needs to commit to research to fully expose the long-term impacts of historic forced adoption.

Anne

"I suspect the Government will hang it out until we are all dead."

Anne describes herself as coming from a sheltered, middle-class background, but she's forthright, clear and indignant about what happened to her years ago. She explains that at eighteen she became pregnant. Subsequently, on 28 January 1967, she was sent to a church army home in Bedford where she had her baby and then had her newborn taken. "He was *taken from me* for adoption in March."

Anne details how she was forced to work, and how in hospital, she was given no information or pain relief, and despite asking if she could keep her baby, she was told no. After losing her child, her mental health was severely impacted. "In those days nobody talked about postnatal mental health," she says.

In sharing her story, Anne was concerned that perhaps younger women wouldn't be sympathetic to the experiences of older generations, that perhaps they wouldn't understand the circumstances that prevailed at the time. For instance, in the fifties, she explains, "There was only a rumour that you could get the contraceptive pill and, even then, it was strictly reserved for married women. Abortion wasn't legal at the time." It's perhaps even more difficult for young women today to understand the material reality of older women's existence in a culture that didn't reference 'women's rights' and didn't recognise trauma.

Anne continues, "I was eighteen and working in a café. My parents were extremely strict, and we didn't have any discussions at the time, and I certainly didn't talk about going out with boys. It was all swept under the carpet. I met a man slightly older than me, and I just worshipped him. He was the type of boyfriend any mother would have thoroughly disapproved of, but I couldn't see that at the time. I was surprised when I found out I was pregnant, and I did whatever I could to try to prevent the pregnancy continuing.

"This included taking tablets that my friend obtained for me – she told me she got them from a nurse. In any case, they didn't work. Then I even tried to throw myself down the stairs, to no avail. I didn't dare tell my parents, and my secret only came out when I was seven months pregnant. I had managed to keep it hidden and had somehow convinced myself it wasn't happening. But one of my mother's friends had been to the café and noticed that I was pregnant and had gone back and told my mum that she thought 'it was a shame I was in the family way'. After that, there was a terrible row at home and my father even hit me. My father asked to meet my boyfriend and told him that he had to consider marriage. My boyfriend left me at that stage.

"Around that time, I finally went to the GP, and she also gave me a proper dressing-down for not attending for maternity care earlier. From that moment onwards, I stopped going to work and my parents forbade me from even answering the door. I was effectively hidden at home. To say they were ashamed of me would be a massive understatement. They called me a slag and all that type of thing – it was absolutely horrible.

"Shortly after, the GP put me in contact with a moral welfare officer. They arranged for me to go into a mother and baby home. It was a big, old Victorian place. Matron ruled the roost and reported my activities back to my parents.

"It was the usual story: you went into the home six weeks before the baby was due, then stayed there with the baby for a further six weeks, and you were required to work, to earn your keep while you were there.

"Actually, it was quite a lot of fun because the other mothers – about five or six of them who were expecting, and another six or so who had already delivered their babies and had them with them before surrendering them for adoption – they were all very supportive.

"I know that my parents were making a financial payment for me to stay in the home because later when I returned home, there was a row about how much I had cost them. Also, we had some money of our own – I think it may have been a maternity grant or allowance. Maybe I received it because I was working? But I know a few of us walked to the Post Office to get it, and afterwards, I had to hand some of it across to the matron of the mother and baby home."

I wondered what restrictions were placed on Anne while she was in the home. She said she was free to come and go, provided she let them know where she was going and went with another mother.

Anne said, "After we had our babies, we were allowed to take them out in prams for a walk. Having the baby wasn't very nice. I can remember that I was sweeping stairs when my waters broke and an ambulance was called, and I was taken into a nearby hospital alone. They were quite nasty to me, and I was never sure if it was because I was unmarried or just because that was the way they were.

"I was put in a small room with a single bed with no windows. I was given an enema and I was shaved, and was then just left there. There was no pain relief. My baby was born in the early hours of the morning. I was starting to push, and a nurse came in and told me to be quiet because I was disturbing the other patients. She then walked me to a cold, clinical delivery room for the birth. I had an easy birth, but they said horrible things to me like, 'You should regret what you've done.

You should never forget it.' They didn't really need to say those things to me because I wasn't going to forget – was I?

"I was put on a post-delivery ward for a week after and that was quite hard because every visiting time, men – husbands – would come to visit their babies, and it was so obvious why I was there.

"I did absolutely fall in love with my baby. I did ask if there was any way I could get help. I was told no, there was only help for widows. I went back to the home and looked after my baby for another six weeks. The home had a very strict regime: bottle-feeds every four hours. We weren't allowed to spend time with the babies, nor encouraged to play with them – but we did. Night-time was better because we had them next to us and we could do as we liked, and I would cuddle and whisper to my baby 'I love you' and to 'come and find me, come and find me. Don't forget me.'"

I was curious to know whether or not Anne had been encouraged to breastfeed, and she told me sadly that while she was in hospital, her chest was bound with bandages, and she was given an injection to dry up the milk, so she never had the option or opportunity.

"It was hard. It was traumatic and after six weeks, which of course I knew was coming, the moral welfare officer came to see me and said they had found a lovely couple – and she said, 'They are the same sort of class as you'! She told me a little bit about them, that they already had a natural-born daughter, but that they couldn't have any more and they needed to adopt.

"I asked her was there any chance I could keep him? Was there any possibility at all of help to find us both somewhere to live? This was just dismissed. My mum and dad had already told me that there was no way I could come home.

"On the final day, the moral welfare officer told me to get him ready and she came with the carrycot, and she took him away. I could see her car driving away down the road and that was it. That same afternoon, my mum came to pick me up and nothing was ever said about my stay at the home or my baby ever again. Nothing. I returned to work a few days later, and even when I was back at work, no one at any point, asked me how I was. I was told if anybody asked me why I'd been away, I was to say I'd had a kidney infection! Although I'm sure some people must have known why I'd been absent for three months. But nobody ever actually asked me."

It's almost impossible to conceive that somebody could have a baby and no one would acknowledge that fact. However, that baby was lost and then people said absolutely nothing. Under the weight of the shame, questions or enquiries and all concern were obliterated.

Anne asked, "I wondered how my mother could dismiss her first grandchild. I had a very hard time mentally after that. I had one photograph of my son, which I had requested from the social worker when he was taken away. It was given to me when I signed the final adoption papers.

"I think they genuinely believed that this process was the best thing, that you would get over it, forget about it, move on and meet somebody better to have another baby with, to become a mum – with a dad and a stable home. We wanted to believe them when they told us that.

"Looking back, I knew that I could have easily looked after my baby. At nineteen, I wasn't exactly a child; I would have coped. Funnily enough, I did meet a man who I married a few months afterwards. He was the one that started to make me laugh again. We didn't talk about depression in those days, but I think I had a very severe depression. We went on to have children together also.

"I think I've had a reasonable life since then. But nonetheless, I carried this secret with me my whole life, only telling my children *many* years later when my adopted son eventually came to find me a decade ago.

"I received a letter out of the blue from my adopted son's wife, who said she'd been doing some research to track down his birth mother, and that he desperately wanted to find out about me. I wrote back to say I was delighted. Of course, then I had to tell my children, but they were both sympathetic and empathetic – they were wonderful. We still meet up to this day.

"But there is a big hole in my life. All those years I was keeping this a secret, because of course once I'd met up with him, I was able to tell people – and that was such a big burden lifted from me. I know it sounds ridiculous, but before that, I always felt that somebody would find out."

"That's the legacy of manufactured shame," I pointed out.

Anne agrees. "Of course, the other sad thing about this is, although my family has accepted my adopted son, there can't be the relationships that there would have been had this not happened. They will never have that sort of ease with each other, nor will they ever share those decades and experiences together. It's fractured. My adopted son is like a distant friend to my other son."

Anne is correct, there is always a dissonance in families where this sort of fracture has occurred. Things can never be how they might have been. There are all those events where a person was absent, and now often events where people don't really quite fit.

Would an apology help? Anne says she's not sure. "Of course, there are women who desperately want that apology and I support them and I understand it. But I don't feel for me personally that an apology is going to put anything right. It's not going to make up for all those lost years and the heartbreak. I think it's too late. Overall, it's worked out okay for me. But I know that's not the case for other women. That's why I got involved with the MAA.

"It was very difficult when my adopted son got in touch with me – not just emotionally but also physically. I had significant issues because everything suddenly came back to me. I had to tell my children. I had to tell my family. I think I had a breakdown of some type. I also had Takotsubo cardiomyopathy, which is why in couples when one dies, sometimes the other follows shortly afterwards.

"My son, as it turned out, didn't have a particularly good adoption. The father in his adoptive family walked out whilst he was still young. He didn't have a great time, and it was so unnecessary, as with some support and some understanding, I could have done a better job. Instead, I was treated like an outsider and as if I'd done something terribly wrong.

"I hope that the Government will issue the apology because I know there's a lot of women who it will help and that's why I'm giving this interview because I'd like to support them. Because for some, lives have been ruined."

Jan

"The amount outstanding for David is £2.6.8d ..."

So reads the receipt that Jan passes across the café table to me. It's a bill for the foster care she was forced to pay, shortly before her baby son was placed for adoption.

In 1962, Jan realised she was pregnant. She had met a boy and had a very short relationship, which in contemporary times wouldn't be considered problematic. She didn't even consider the possibility of marriage.

She explains that her parents were more concerned about what the neighbours would think than about her well-being. As Christmas and CSE exams approached, without any choice, Jan was forced into St Faith's home for unmarried mothers in Bearsted, Kent run by the Church of England. She tells me, back then she was a very quiet and compliant girl. It is true that teenage girls in the 1950s–1970s are very different from their more confident and much better-informed counterparts today.

In common with other women I interviewed, after Jan was forced to surrender her baby, she left the family home and desperately endeavoured to replace the baby she'd lost. She explains this led her to make bad choices. Her relationship with her parents splintered, and in the end, she became a single parent, "the very thing they had attempted to shield me from," she says sorrowfully.

She remembers her experiences as if they were yesterday and tells me, "He's sixty this year and I don't know if he's dead or alive." Jan was fifteen when she became pregnant, and sixteen when she went into St Faith's mother and baby home. She's now seventy-eight and the memories of what happened to her all those decades ago are crisp.

"There were several sisters at St Faith's including Sister Holbrook who was an older nun and incredibly kind, and she delivered David in the delivery room in the home. She even sent me a congratulations card afterwards. However, in general, the home was cold. I couldn't go and have a cuddle with somebody like another fifteen-year-old living at home might be able to. Also, whilst in the home, I had to do work including scrubbing the floors.

"I hid my pregnancy. I simply couldn't admit to it until I was about seven months and, as a consequence, I went into the home a little later than the other girls did. I think there was a resentment towards me from the girls who had been there for longer as I was virtually at the end of my pregnancy. They had a system in St Faith's whereby you went into a room for a while and then moved into another room closer to the delivery suite as you neared your due date. The home was very large and imposing. There were about fifteen other women waiting to give birth, and those that already had their babies. We were all given duties like working in the laundry, which was in an outhouse with great big boiling pots of water and had to scrub the floors and do the washing. It wasn't easy.

"Every Sunday we would go in a crocodile down to the church so that the decent people in the church would get to look at us, *the fallen* …

"There were three or four of us in a room. All the facilities were shared. There was a set bath night. There was no privacy. You didn't even have a drawer where you could lock any possessions away. The antenatal care was given by the nuns, some of whom had midwifery qualifications."

Jan passes across the table a collection of cards, mainly Christmas cards that she received when she was in the home. She singles out the card from her brother. It says:

To my sister from your brother. XXX

I hope you are getting better. We all hope to have you back soon. I hope you have a very Merry Christmas and a happy New Year. With love as from above.

I noticed there are no kisses on Jan's card from her mother, which I imagine is a sign of those times when family affection was more limited, more restrained. It says: 'May this day of the Christ child's birth bring you every hoped-for happiness.' Jan goes on to tell me that her brother, seven years younger, had been told she had had a nervous breakdown and therefore had to be taken away.

It still makes her cross.

There was another card from her grandparents, which was much more consoling. It said: 'God bless and best wishes for the future'. This card is completely different in tone and lacks the judgment of the mother's card. I was moved that Jan had brought these along to our meeting. There was also a letter from Sister Holbrook, which said, 'I expect it feels strange to study and concentrate.' She referred to the other girls that were 'waiting to go', meaning waiting to finish their stint in the home with the baby.

"At this stage," Jan explains, "I was sixteen and about to do my examinations. I'm sure my mother did do everything with the best of intentions, but always it was 'What will the neighbours think?'

"St Faith's had a tough regime. The system was you looked after your baby for six weeks, and what do you do during that time, of course, you bond with your baby. You're encouraged to breastfeed but that's about building a stronger bond. We were told it was for our health, but really it was for the baby. Like any sixteen-year-old, I was vulnerable and naïve. I believed whatever I was told."

Jan was very concerned about breastfeeding because according to her own recollections, it did form that bond, and that was a problem for her with the adoption imminent.

Thinking about what other women had told me about their experiences of the problems associated with bonding prior to adoption, and the way in which cruelty in the homes was 'normal', I asked Jan if she thought it was possible that the creation of the bond was encouraged, so that the final surrender of the baby would be that much more difficult and punishing – so that the mother wouldn't forget what she'd done. Jan agreed with me that was very much the way it was.

Jan continues explaining what happened to her. "I had to take him to Gosport. My mother and I went with the social workers in her car; it was a very difficult journey because it had been a very hard winter. We drove down the road with snow banked on either side. When we arrived at the Adoption Agency, somebody said, 'I'll take baby,' and she took him from me. She said, 'We have a family, they're coming to get him tomorrow.' I was asked if I wanted a photograph of David and I said yes, but my mother interjected and said 'No, it will be too painful.' Of course, she meant it was too painful for her because it was her sin as well – you see.

"Then the nursing sister said to me, you can go and say goodbye. He was in a room on his own, lying in a great big cot. It struck me that he was so alone." The pain of this memory is evident on Jan's face.

Jan continues, "After, I received a letter from the social worker, asking for a further sum of money to cover David's costs."

Jan looks at this letter and then looks at me, before saying, "It beggars belief, doesn't it?" I can only agree with her. There she is, a sixteen-year-old; she's just taken her mock-CSEs, with her baby taken from her, and she's been left with the shame and a bill. It's a poignant moment. The last financial transaction – a final payment for a baby taken away and lost forever.

"We never talked about it at home." Jan is emotional as she recalls what happened after David was taken. "It was a case of now that's done, move on. Was it for the best? Was it for my best? Was it for his best? I was made to feel so ashamed. The 29 of December is a terrible day for me, as I kept it all inside until very recently; until I heard about MAA. They popped up on Facebook three or four years ago."

We discussed whether Facebook could have 'listened in' to Jan's concerns or, whether she triggered an algorithm that then served her the exact content that she was looking for. We both agreed that many women, many of the half a million who had babies taken from them, are perhaps actually using Facebook and other platforms to try to find information and given her age and demographic, and search history, maybe the algorithm served her what she needed at that time. We can't know, but Jan considers it incredibly fortuitous and speaks to a societal change where such important matters, once considered deeply private and deemed scandalous, are now much more in the public consciousness.

"It took a lot for me to contact MAA. I had already told my daughter and son that I'd had an illegitimate child years ago, but I didn't go into any great detail. They were both devastated and angry about how I've been treated. In particular, how my mum, dad – their grandparents – have treated me, how they'd locked me away and made me stay hidden. My son said he was very disappointed in his grandparents."

Jan says she still feels the shame. "I can't easily talk about it all. In fact, I asked my husband if he was going to come along with me today to meet you. He said, 'No,' very kindly. 'I think this is something you should do on your own.' He gave me a cuddle before I came out."

I asked about the birth. Jan told me it was a straightforward delivery. "In fact, it was like shelling a pea! My son is sixty this year, and I don't know if he's dead or alive. I think I'd like to find him, but it's too late for him. And it's hard for my two as well, although they both said they would accept him."

I asked Jan if there was anyone she knew that she could talk through her decision to try to trace her baby with, considering all the ramifications and complications involved. She didn't know who she could turn to. I suggested another woman from the MAA website, but she replied, "All of those women have also got all of their own pain and difficulties to deal with." I suggested that she would need not only an intermediary to help find her son, but at this stage may also need some therapy-based approach and support.

Jan agrees. "My first marriage broke down because of carrying my secret. My grandfather was very concerned that I should maintain the secret and was upset when he realised I had told my first husband. He said he didn't need to know."

After the adoption, Jan said she left St Faith's looking for love, trying subconsciously to replace the huge loss she had experienced. She very quickly married a man she already knew and admits, "We suffered each other for eleven years." This is a common thread among women I interviewed and a common outcome of forced adoption – the headlong rush into another relationship. It's very appealing to attempt to hide under this cloak of respectability. It balances the judgments that you've been under. In Jan's case, she enhanced her respectability in her family's eyes by marrying and producing grandchildren.

"We were seen as damaged goods. He is willing to marry me, so I thought I must, because I'll never find another man who will want me."

But she didn't get that quite right in the eyes of her ever-judgmental mother who accused Jan of behaving like a 'wog' when she had very little gap between children. This racist accusation hurt Jan very much.

At nineteen years old, when Jan was working, the trust between her and her parents was very damaged. She was expected to be home by 10.30 p.m., and on occasion, her dad would collect her from wherever she was. She had no possibility of forgetting her misdemeanour and, "In a way," she reflected, "my nose was rubbed in it."

Other women were treated in very much the same, heavy-handed, controlling way, but Jan's situation was different, her forced adoption was still very much a secret, with most of her friends believing that she had been away due to a nervous breakdown, which was the story the family promulgated.

"I've had a good career, starting as a secretary working in the House of Commons. I ended up managing a big department." Since retiring, Jan has been active in other significant roles. "I had to prove myself, didn't I? To myself, really. I also fostered two boys – difficult adolescents – they had to be difficult teenage boys, of course; I was paying back. I thought that maybe by helping foster children, I was in some way helping my own son."

After several years of marriage, her relationship with her husband broke down and he left her. It was a struggle financially and emotionally for Jan to manage. Jan is rueful. "It was fine for me to be a single mother having been married – but it wasn't fine for me to be a single mother and be unmarried. How judgmental society is. It was a very tough time, and it was then that I told them about David. I was very close to my children and them to me. We had a strong bond."

A chance meeting on the telephone forty-two years prior led Jan to meet the man who would become the love of her life, the person with whom she would build a secure future for herself. Proving that romance isn't dead, a wrong number led to a drink and, five months later, Jan married for the second and final time. The warmth of her story illustrated the power of love and how, even after such trauma, we are all capable of forging new, optimistic relationships. But it also made me wonder how many women – and I include myself – spent fruitless, dead years, sometimes with abusive partners, as a means of punishing ourselves, before we finally escaped the shackles of shame.

"He accepted me with all my history and drama," Jan says. In contrast to some of the women I interviewed who weren't allowed to mention their past.

"He saw through my mum; he was a great father and an absolute rock. I still think back sixty years ago. It's still so vivid in my mind: I can see the rooms, I can see the bed I laid in, I can see the delivery room, I can see the lying-in room. I can still see the journey down to Gosport and remember the imposing door and going through the doorway into this cold, cold room, and I can remember leaving my baby in this great big cot all by himself."

We discussed what needs to be done now. Jan says, "I can't see that there's going to be an end-point, not until the last person who was forced to give up her baby for adoption has died, or until the doctors involved have died, but even then, there is still the impact on the family, isn't there?"

I asked Jan what an apology would mean to her. She pondered this before saying, "I thought about this a lot. I suppose it's recognition that I don't need to be ashamed, that I didn't do anything shameful. I feel sorry. It's a very easy word to say without any substance behind it. So, a 'sorry' would need to have actions to back it up. To make sure the other children and families wouldn't ever have to go through the same. And that these things were followed up on. You hear it so often don't you? That we've learnt lessons. Really? Like the Post Office scandal? The impacts occur way down the line. For instance, I always avoided the area where my baby boy was taken from me."

After our interview, Jan agreed to be interviewed by a local radio station. She wants to do what she can to break the silence and to end the shame.

Pat

*"It was always the girl's fault ... The trauma travels
with you throughout your life.
It doesn't work its way away from you."*

Pat tells me, "I went into a mother and baby home on my sixteenth birthday in 1968. It wasn't exactly a nice celebration.

"I was living at home with my parents, and I'd left school at fifteen. I began working in a café, and it was there that I met a man and started going out with him. I realised I was pregnant, and I tried to keep it secret. I don't know what I thought was going to happen by keeping it hidden, I just didn't want my mum and dad to know because I knew what would happen. But eventually a woman at work took me to one side and asked, 'When's your baby due? We all know you're quite far gone.' I responded that I didn't have a clue and she offered to come home with me to talk to my mum and dad that night. Fortunately, my dad was away on a course at that time.

"My brother, who was slightly older and in the army, and did know I was pregnant, was supportive. But my mum said, 'That's it. You've got to go. Your dad is due home this weekend. You can't be here, he'll kill you.' I got ushered into a mother and baby home very quickly. Within a few days of being there, I was told I would never be allowed to go home again, which was awful, but I was still in a sense of denial, thinking this wasn't really happening to me."

I asked Pat how she knew her mum and dad would be very angry.

"My dad was extremely strict," she said. "I knew as soon as he found out that I would have to be gone. It was just instinct. He didn't like my boyfriend and, in any case, I was very unhappy at home and had run away two or three times before. I don't feel that my parents really wanted my brother or me.

"My mum had been to see the vicar at the local church, and he made the arrangements. He knew about my dad's temper and understood I would have to be out of the house before Dad got back. I went into a Salvation Army home in the south-west. Before I went in, I spent a few days living at home and Mum did everything she could do to keep me away from the neighbours."

Pat can't remember how she travelled to the home. Gaps in memory are perhaps inevitable with the passage of decades, but also indicative of the trauma suffered, which was common among the women I interviewed.

Pat continues, "When my boyfriend knew I was pregnant, he disappeared. Once I went into the mother and baby home, I never saw him again. He did say he would come and see me, but I believed he moved away out of the area for a job in another town. Eventually, I did manage to tell him where I was, and he agreed that we should get married, and I obtained the forms from the registry office, my dad signed them, but I never saw him again – even when the baby was born.

"I felt bitterly, bitterly disappointed and very let down because I had nowhere to go. The happily-ever-after dream that I'd had was for nothing. I knew I was in a terrible situation. I had nothing. I was stuck in a mother and baby home with girls in the same position and some who had already delivered their babies. Big friendships weren't formed in the home; everybody there seemed shell-shocked. We were all so young. I kept my head down. We all did.

"I had been very rebellious at school, but *this* knocked all the fight right out of me. I did try to keep my baby; I fought very hard to keep him. I believed I could get a job and somewhere to live. They knew exactly what they were going to do to get my baby off me, and I began to realise I had no chance."

We talked about going into labour. Pat explains, "We had to work in the home scrubbing and cleaning right up to the day we went into hospital. I know it sounds mad, I was so naïve, I didn't even realise where babies came from. We never had any antenatal care; the only thing we had was a test to see if we had any sexually transmitted disease. The night before I gave birth, one of the girls was talking about stitches, and I asked, 'Where do the stitches go?' and she replied, 'Well, anywhere you tear.' They thought that was hysterically funny. I got taken into hospital later that night; the labour was awful, there was no pain relief. They put me in stirrups because I was fighting against giving birth because I knew once I gave birth, they would take my baby off me. It was a battle. The birth was awful. They were shouting at me to keep quiet. They cut me and stitched me without any anaesthetic."

The standard of support, both clinical and emotional, in antenatal care and during labour has been reported to me as being appalling. Almost every woman I interviewed detailed the same disgraceful and shocking treatment.

Pat continues, "They called you 'Mrs', pretending that you were married, although everybody on the ward knew you weren't married. They didn't give me any help. For instance, I was struggling to breastfeed him. They didn't assist me, and they then said I wasn't being a very good mother and that he would have to go on the bottle. Now, I know this was all part of the plan for me not to get too attached. He was 6lbs 12oz; he wasn't tiny, but he was very long, and they said he was a 'puny thing' and they didn't mean it in a nice or jocular way. When I read that in the file I obtained many years later, I was so upset they recorded that he was puny.

"Then they started to take care of him and to take him away from me. That was all part of not letting me get too attached. To my mind, I thought I was still keeping him. I was determined that I would find a way.

I was in hospital for ten days and it wasn't very pleasant. I did bond with him though – as much as they would let me. I was still thinking that my boyfriend would turn up and make things right.

"After his birth, I returned to the mother and baby home and that's when they started piling on the pressure. My baby cried a lot – I don't know why that was – he wasn't settling. They told me I wasn't doing 'a very good job' and that I was a 'bad mother', and that there were other people 'waiting to have a child like him.' They just kept piling the pressure on.

"Then they said, 'You have to leave the mother and baby home tomorrow and you're not taking him.' The police became involved at this stage. They came and said, 'You have got to let him go. We're taking him whatever you say.'"

I explained to Pat that I could barely believe the brutality of this approach. She continued, almost in a whisper at this stage of the interview.

"After my son was born, he went to a foster mother for a couple of weeks or a month, whilst they sorted out adoptive parents. I had to pay the fee to the foster mother every week, and I had to provide a layette when I eventually, reluctantly, handed him over. I told them if his new parents changed their minds, could he please be returned to me."

She also recalls receiving some sort of benefit payment that went to the home for her upkeep.

Pat tells me that she was aware that a fee was paid for her baby when he was adopted, as it was in her files. She's not completely clear who received the fee for her baby ... Later in life, she came to believe her father did receive a payment in connection with her son's adoption. It's upsetting and distressing to Pat that she now believes her father gained a financial benefit for the child that was taken from her.

Pat returns to the topic of her father, who she explained had taken her to court "for being beyond parental control. I had run away with another girl whose parents were lovely and they turned her around because they did care about her. They didn't turn their back on her – they nurtured and loved her – and were not saying, as my dad was, 'I want you gone.' I think he was happy when I became pregnant because he could now finally get rid of me. I wasn't the dainty blonde, petite child that he wanted. I wasn't wanted; my dad had his favourite."

I reflected with Pat, on the fact that there is a need to be honest about the backgrounds women like us, who found ourselves in this curious 'care system' come from. The dominant assumption is that all parents, and mothers particularly, are loving and caring, but that's clearly not always the case. Pat agrees. She adds, "My mother was very weak and dominated by my father. That did right itself in the end, but it took many years. For instance, my dad banned my mum from coming to see me in the home, but my mum defied him and came to visit me along with my grandmother and my brother. So, I did have some support.

"Somehow, they found me a place to stay in a sort of halfway house with a woman – she may even have been a foster mother; she looked after me and one other girl. I stayed for three months, and she did our washing and cooked for us. But I was so upset. I couldn't talk to her. I stayed in my room most of the time and tried, somehow, to come to terms with what happened, thinking was there something I could do to get my baby back. But I didn't have a chance. They had him at that stage.

"During this time, I was still seeing my mum and she engineered an opportunity for me to bump into my dad in a shopping centre. She managed to arrange it so that we would all meet up and that was my preplanned opportunity to apologise to my dad and to say sorry for my behaviour. After, I would be able to return home. I needed to resume my life and to find another job. It was never ever mentioned by my mum and dad again."

I couldn't help but comment to Pat how astounding I found it that such circumstances can happen; something as important and life-changing as having a baby, and then the mother's parents not mentioning it ever again. This was the theme that played out in many of my discussions. Somehow, the parents of the women I interviewed seemed to me to be part of such a different generation with alien attitudes, as if they were from a different planet. They seemed to be able to witness their daughter's struggles, to see them so challenged, to know the physicality of what they were going through, and the pain of parting with a baby, but then never said anything about it ever again! Perhaps this is, in part, the legacy of two brutal world wars, when so many families experienced profound loss and tragedy? In a contemporary context, it seems so far-fetched as to be bewildering. I cannot imagine how this could happen today. It is another reason why unravelling the full context of the forced adoption era is so important. The lessons that we can glean through the shared experiences of these women are of vital importance in this information gathering. These are mistakes that should never be repeated.

Pat draws a deep breath. "You were told you can't say anything to anybody. You're not allowed to talk to anybody; you must just get on with it. You were expected to forget about it after a couple of weeks, but of course that never happened."

Pat confirmed that once they took her baby, they took everything, even the one photograph that she had on the birth certificate, explaining to her that she would never need them again. However, Pat says, "By then, I was completely ground down. Afterwards, I got married quickly to a man who was a few years older than me, and he wasn't very happy at home either. We convinced ourselves we were madly in love. I told him about my son, and he just said he didn't want to know and not to mention him ever again. But I hadn't signed the final adoption papers by then and, if he had been different, more open and supportive, then this situation could have been so different. We got divorced ten years later.

"When I met my second husband, I told him about my baby because I was determined not to have the secret hanging over my head. He was fine about it.

"In 1998 I decided to tell my children about the child I'd had adopted. They were absolutely fine about it and my son said, 'I always knew there was something wrong, mum.' I had some counselling at that time also, and they informed me that I could get another birth certificate. And I applied online for that, and it was lovely to see it; it was the only proof I had that I'd actually had a baby. I didn't do anything else because I was worried about causing problems in his life, assuming he was happy and settled. Also, I was concerned he might not want to know and I wasn't sure I could take that rejection.

"Eventually, with encouragement, I plucked up the courage and went through an intermediary in 2018. It took a while and, of course, it isn't a free service. Contact was established with my son who said he hadn't given finding me too much thought. He'd had a very happy childhood and his mum and dad were lovely, and his adopted mum had only ever said very kind things about me, explaining to him that I was very young and that I wasn't able to look after him. Therefore, he hadn't really felt the need to find out who I was.

"It took a year of occasional phone calls and stilted conversations to get close, but then it became easier. I don't see him all that often. I knew I had to take it slowly."

Timing is everything with attempts to reunite mother and child. Whilst women handed over a baby, in the passage of time that baby has become an adult. And adults, as we all know, very often have a lot to deal with, including eventually the bereavement of their adoptive parents who tended to be older than their birth mother. I noticed in the course of my research a seemingly strange pattern of the birth mother making contact with her long-lost child at the same time their adoptive parents were dying.

This, I presume, is because the birth mothers were young, and their babies were adopted by parents perhaps ten, twenty or more years older than themselves. There is little doubt that this represents a significant challenge to the child, now adult adoptee, but it's also something that the birth mother is often advised to be cognisant of, and to be respectful and patient, not at all easy when many women have waited what seems like the best part of a lifetime for this opportunity.

Pat picks up their story. "There's a lot I haven't been able to say to him, but I have been able to explain that I did fight for him. Which he hadn't realised. I haven't told him about the trauma of what happened.

"My son obtained all his adoption notes and offered to let me look at them, and it was interesting. They just sent his mum and dad a letter, which said that they had a baby and if they would like to travel down to the south-west to see the baby, they could decide whether to take him there and then. If they liked him, they could take him, but if not, not to worry, because there would be another baby along soon.

"That wasn't *quite* what we were told in the homes. We were told that great efforts were taken to match babies. Not that parents could turn up at any point and pick one …"

Pat expressed her gratitude that her son, "had enjoyed a good life and had those parents, because he could have had parents that perhaps wouldn't have been so good for him."

I asked Pat in relation to the call for a formal adoption apology if all these lived experiences – her experiences – were public, then others like her son would know that she was as much a victim as anybody.

She agrees, "Because it's all hidden, this isn't known. My son understands now that I didn't have a choice, but I didn't know that before I had contact with him, and I think his birth mother did instil that in him. People assumed we would just get over it. But you never do – do you? It leaves you feeling very numb. You do think about it every day, you think there's going to be a knock at the door, but when it doesn't come, you think what if? If we got an apology, it would reinforce to other people that we really didn't have a choice, how bad it was, and how inhumanly we were treated.

"To this day, I never tell very many people about what happened to me. So, very few people know. I still worry about what they will think of me … It was always the girl's fault … The trauma travels with you throughout your life. It doesn't work its way away from you."

Pat talks about what she read about herself in the file, and how it took her a long time to read it because she couldn't bear how she'd been characterised as overdeveloped and so on. She worried if her son had seen these details that he would form a low opinion of her. She also comments on the inaccuracies of the report.

"They got the number of siblings wrong; the county was wrong. They said I called my boyfriend 'a rolling stone', which I didn't, and that I was concerned about his drinking, that he was beating me up, which he wasn't. It all paints a very deliberate picture. It really upset me. I couldn't read it again for many years. I don't think that they ever thought we would see these files, and there's never been any accountability for what was erroneously written in them.

"Back then we had nowhere to go and couldn't obtain any help. We were told we couldn't get benefits, but I found out many years later that something was available, even in 1968, that could have been a help to keep him.

"Another surprise was that I only found out after my mother died that she would not have minded me keeping my baby. And that would've worked out quite well because she already had little ones. But that wasn't to be."

I thanked Pat for sharing her heart-wrenching story. Two thoughts remained with me: firstly, the very idea that the police could be involved in forcing a sixteen-year-old to put up her son for adoption. I can so easily place myself in her shoes: I can feel the powerlessness and the grip of fear. Also, the sadness that Pat has lived with for the greater part of her life, intuiting that her father derived financial benefit from her great misfortune and the potential sale of her son.

Anita

"They had a very strict timetable about when they wanted the babies to be born, because of the set up in the home – to keep the rooms turning."

Anita was the first person I interviewed for this book. I was nervous about prying into her personal life, but over a couple of coffees, overlooking the sea on a blustery day, she put me at ease. I'm very grateful to Anita – she set this ball rolling. This is her story.

"In 1966 I was eighteen when I got pregnant. At the time I was working in my first job as a civil servant as a mathematical clerical assistant. I worked in the same building as my dad, and obviously, I didn't want him to know, so I started to make plans to run away. The people I was working with in my department found out about my pregnancy and they went to the management, and they then called me in, and there I was, in the same room as my dad! They asked me what I was going to do and then moved me to a different office in another part of London. After that, they found me a place in a hostel for unmarried mothers. I paid my way whilst I was there and six weeks before my baby was due, I went into an actual mother and baby home.

"While I was in the first stage of my pregnancy, I did try for an abortion. A friend suggested I visit a doctor who could give me abortion pills because other girls she knew had used him. Another friend of mine, a man who had nothing to do with the pregnancy, took me to a doctor in Russell Square, London. I had a brief consultation and he offered me pills, at a cost of thirty pounds. He said if they don't work to come back, but as I was leaving, he grabbed the top of my thighs and rubbed them in a sexual way. It was horrible and I couldn't say anything because it was an illegal meeting. I don't think I could've afforded a hundred pounds for an abortion."

"One hundred pounds is now worth around two and a half thousand, which was a huge sum to find," I say to Anita. She nods in agreement.

"My friend had been pregnant," Anita continued, "and she secured an illegal abortion. It was performed in my flat, so I was there. This lady came and boiled up two bars of carbolic soap and after allowing it to cool, she then used it like an enema – inserted into her vagina. She nearly died; it was that lethal. So, when legal abortion came in, it was great for people – not that anybody ever wants to have an abortion.

"The hostel I was staying in was a big old house on Christchurch Road in Streatham and it was run by the Methodist Church. I paid for it out of my income. I can't remember how much the fees were, but it was a lot for my tiny civil service salary.

"My mum and dad were okay, but they didn't want me back at home until I decided what I was going to do. They didn't want me to have my son adopted. They wanted me to move with them to a different area. I was on six weeks' leave and then I could take six weeks off after the birth of my baby. I suppose in a way the civil service were quite enlightened back then. The civil service welfare officer dealt with me and transferred me to an office closer to the hostel. The welfare officer, a woman, was quite matter-of-fact and kind, and was concerned about any embarrassment to my father who was quite prominent in his role in the civil service. I think they were worried that I might do something stupid.

"The mother and baby home was very unpleasant with horrible little rooms, and it was deeply religious. There were probably twenty to thirty women from all walks of life, including a fourteen-year-old girl, and a black nurse who had got pregnant by a white doctor who couldn't tell her family. Some of the girls probably weren't all they might be. I thought one or two might be prostitutes. One of the girls in there used to steal our stuff, but that's desperation, isn't it? One girl used to grunt all the time; I think there was something wrong with her. The matron was reasonably nice; she was a normal woman, but the housekeeper used to refer to us as 'the fallen women.' She used to say to us, 'If it wasn't for people like us, you would all be in terrible straits.'"

Anita explained the day-to-day routine in the home. "It was a very rigid regimen. We were all locked up. I think we were allowed out one evening a week until eight. We didn't have a key – nothing like that. On Sundays we were expected to go to church. We would all walk up to the Methodist Church together along Streatham High Road, all pregnant, all looked at, all laughed at. We all had duties in the home – which was fair enough. All the cutlery had to be polished, and once a week one of us would have to climb up the stepladder in the larder, and it seems ridiculous now, but they would have to take out all of the jars of jam, then they would have to empty them. Then they would have to wash and dry the jars and put the jam back in! Really, they were hoping that when we went up the stepladder, it would bring on labour. They had a very strict timetable about when they wanted the babies to be born, because of the set-up in the home – to keep the rooms turning.

"Just before I was due to have my son, I fell over on the polished floor. My leg went black, and they called the doctor. He examined me and advised me to stay in bed for at least a week, but the next day I was told to get up and carry on. I didn't have any say in the matter; I felt astounded by this.

"Then you went into St George's Hospital in Tooting to have your baby. After you came out, you were supposed to be moved on in the next six weeks – that included having your baby adopted. We kept the babies with us in the home and even the mothers who were going to have their babies adopted would keep them with them. The home had a nursery and all of us mothers, irrespective of age, had to take a turn sitting with the babies while they were sleeping. Their mothers would produce a glucose drink and we would sometimes have to give this to the babies. Then at three in the morning, the mothers would come down and take over. Sometimes you had half a dozen babies that you were giving glucose water to."

I asked Anita if she'd had any previous experience with babies before going into the home. "No, but in St George's Hospital, they gave workshops not just for single parents, but for anybody, and they would run through the different things that you needed to do for the baby. That wouldn't happen now, would it? I pretty much made my mind up straight away – no way was I parting with him. And I remember going into labour. I was the only one in labour that night and it was lovely to see him finally with his big blue eyes. A lot of the girls though didn't have any family and I did sit with one of the other girls when she was in labour. My labour was calm, but she was very frightened."

I wondered did Anita bond with her baby quickly.

"Yes, straight away. They're your flesh and blood, aren't they? My mum and dad were quite happy. They sold their house, and they moved us to a slightly different area where nobody knew the background. When I was in the mother and baby home, the social services got involved, and I still remember the lady I was dealing with was called Miss Devon. She got my son's father to come there, and apparently, he'd asked if he could take the baby! They said absolutely not. She told me that afterwards. I'm still in contact with the baby's father now.

"I didn't have any power, but the worst thing – well, there were lots of worst things – but the worst thing was little Rosie, whose baby was mixed race, they couldn't get her adopted for three months. Nobody would take her. She was a very beautiful little girl, and when she finally was placed her poor mother wailed all night. Very sad. I don't think things are like that now. I think people are willing to take children of a different colour from themselves now." This is echoed by Phil Frampton, author and lecturer, born in a Cornish mother and baby home, who details the prejudice and racism he faced in his book, *The Golly in The Cupboard*. He explains that dual heritage babies were more difficult to place with adoptive parents at that time.

Anita resumes. "I had to go to court to get a maintenance order from my baby's father for £1.50 per week, which he often didn't pay. I used to phone Croydon Court. He was called the 'putative father', because he was the *supposed* father, but you can do things now to prove who the father is, can't you? The warrant officer from the court would go round to see him about every three months to get the money off him. He was about the same age as me. It was a casual relationship. There was no pill and no access to safe and legal abortion. I suppose that is why there were loads of us in St George's.

"It wasn't easy being a young single parent. I was a civil servant, still working, but it wasn't enough money, especially with the childminding fees. On one occasion, I went for a job when my baby was four months old. I handed in my CV, but I could hear them all giggling about me, saying, 'Oh, Miss Smith with a baby!' They came out and asked me, 'Is this child still with you?' and I replied, 'Yes, that's why I put it on the form,' and she said, 'Well, the person you want to see isn't here today, good day.' So, that was my interview finished." Anita looked humiliated as she told me that. That incident had left a mark on her all these years later.

She continues to tell me about her life as a young mother. "Eventually, I got married and it was a very short-lived relationship. It lasted five minutes." But she remarried and says, "My new husband was very good to my son, whose own father wasn't around, and then as he got older, my new husband went to see my baby's father and told him he should get involved.

"After I had my son, all my friends were unmarried mothers. There were a fair number that I mixed with, but not from the home, just people that I met locally. I'm sorry now that I didn't keep in touch with any of them. If my parents hadn't have helped and supported me, I would not have been able to keep my son. I'm thankful to them. My dad said, 'It's good to bring a child into the world, but it's just a bit inconvenient if you're not married.' He was very bright; they were both very good to me. They shared the car with me. We all went to work, and I found a childminder.

"I didn't feel any pressure in the home to have an adoption, but I know the others did feel pressure because they were told of families waiting for babies. My situation was different because I had parents that I could rely on; they were happy to have me back with the baby. Some of the girls had been kicked out by their parents. After I had the baby, I took him to my workplace to show him to everybody, and they couldn't believe that I had kept the baby. I did wear a wedding ring when I was pregnant but not afterwards.

"I had to work night and day. I worked with the civil service but also worked in a nightclub, wearing a skimpy outfit, to keep things going. I worked hard – it wasn't easy."

Anita brings me up to date. "My son doesn't now speak to me. I think he was jealous. When my mum died, my son got very angry about the inheritance. He's recently married again, but I didn't get invited to the wedding, but his dad did get invited. There is so much that went on. I had to harden my heart.

"When my daughter was coming along, I said to my mum, I'm not sure I can feel the same because I loved my son so much. I couldn't believe I could love another baby as much, but you can, can't you?

"I didn't realise for many years that my son had found the lack of a father in his early life so difficult and such a significant issue. Later, I told his father that he had been a very bad father to our son, and he agreed."

Anita went on to share with me how she felt that, "Men, fathers of children, could always walk away. I think men do need to step up to the plate."

Anita wonders how the impact of those early days of pregnancy, the uncertainty of being in a mother and baby home, and the condemnation of society at large for displaying flagrant 'moral incontinence' may have influenced her relationship now with her son.

It's an interesting point. Other women interviewed, including myself, share similar concerns as our relationships with children we love and fought to keep flounder. No mother wants to do harm to her child. What is the impact of the weight of illegitimacy and the legacy of 'bastardy'? I hope this book promotes a discourse in this area, for mothers who felt they weren't good enough (or married, or old enough), who carried that with them their whole lives and perhaps transmitted a sense of incompleteness and 'not-good-enough-ness' to their child, who in turn reacts, and fulfills that prophecy, like a dystopian Hans Christian Andersen tale.

Dawn

"I don't want anything from the Government.
I don't want any money. I just want the Government
to admit that what happened to us – what
actually happened – was forced adoption."

Because Dawn now lives in America, it was many months before we were able to meet face-to-face, which we did when she came to visit family in the UK. It was a pleasure to finally get together and hear her experience first-hand.

Dawn's story is unique. She became pregnant in the early 1960s, went into a mother and baby home, and had a healthy baby boy, who like many others was taken for adoption. In common with all those I've interviewed, Dawn reiterated, "There were no other options – only adoption." She looks deep into my eyes, her face a picture of trepidation, as if I might not understand the pressure she experienced.

At eighteen years old, Dawn had fallen in love with her boyfriend and believed he was in love with her. He repeatedly reassured her of this, saying that everything would be all right, that he loved her and would marry her. The reality for Dawn, as with others, was that she was soon discarded, and by somebody who was about to become very famous indeed. So famous that on the day I met her she laughed about her situation saying, "Even sixty years later there's no escape. You could be on a remote beach, and someone will turn up wearing a T-shirt with them splashed across it!" Dawn and her husband are constantly reminded of the father of the baby that was taken for adoption.

Dawn's family were strict Catholics, so the news of her pregnancy was a significant shock. Factor in Dawn's 'uneasy' relationship with her mother who scolded her, saying Dawn was her biggest mistake in life. Dawn's mum and dad were utterly horrified that she was pregnant, and she was left in no doubt about what they now thought of her – she was a tramp that had ruined them and herself.

In common with other young people in 1962, as soon as Dawn finished school, she was expected to get a job, and although she wanted to become a nurse and midwife, her mother had different plans, and she steered Dawn into hairdressing. Dawn started an apprenticeship at Claridge's. She lasted a week. Her mother then enrolled her into an upmarket hairdressers on London's Park Lane. She lasted a month. Her next port of call was with an up-and-coming stylist located in Mayfair, and she soon began working for Vidal Sassoon – a modern salon more palatable to her. Settled at work with money in her purse, she and her friend used to go to hear the newest bands play. "We would go to the Marquee and the Flamingo Club on Wardour Street." Dawn was having a ball; she met The Rolling Stones, Eric Clapton, and others who would go on to establish star status.

Dawn explains that because of regular contact with all the 'stars' that used Vidal Sassoon and living near to The Rolling Stones' manager, she wasn't fazed or dazzled by stardom.

Dawn met The Rolling Stones at the very beginning of their career when they practiced in The Red Lion pub in Sutton near to where she lived, and she tells me in those days, "They were quite unpolished." After a period of time, she happened to see them while she was on holiday in Great Yarmouth and, by this time, the Stones had perfected their act. Even so, Dawn was surprised to see girls screaming and swarming towards the stage when "the boys came on, the whole place erupted. Mick was a born showman: a bundle of energy, hypnotising the audience and gyrating diffused sex. The girls in the audience were hysterical, fighting and fainting." But Dawn had been a fan from the early days and saw the band as ordinary guys. They were very friendly towards her and her friend, giving them a lift from Great Yarmouth back to central London.

Dawn remains firm friends with Bill Wyman, recently enjoying a catch up over lunch together. It was touching to see the photos of them, still friends after more than sixty years.

It was 1964 at a party, when Dawn finally met Brian Jones properly. "He made a beeline towards me, asking me what my name was. Did I want a drink?" she says. "I manage to stumble out, 'I'm Dawn …'" and I get the impression it was at that precise moment she fell hook, line and sinker for Brian. She tells me when Brian asked for her phone number, she didn't hesitate. "Some days later, my mother shouted, 'Dawn, there is somebody called Brian on the phone for you.'" They went out for a drink together and evidently Brian had also fallen for Dawn. He told her that his life with The Rolling Stones, the fame, and the screeching fans had become mad and crazy, and that he hardly had any time to himself anymore, but then he said, "But you're alone with me now and it's so perfect." It wasn't just that Brian Jones said these words to Dawn, it was also the first time a man had ever been so romantic towards her.

Brian didn't leave Dawn in any doubt about his feelings and very quickly professed his love. They started to 'go out' together, and although Brian was constantly on tour, they managed snatches of time together. Dawn and Brian were besotted with each other, and Brian was accepted and welcomed by Dawn's family. At that point, Brian didn't yet have the Lothario reputation he later gained, and Dawn didn't realise that Brian was involved with other women. She believed his friend Linda was exactly that, nor did she know his drug use was a significant problem as he tried to maintain an impossible schedule.

By this time, The Rolling Stones had become a supergroup, perhaps the first to truly deserve that title. They were the undisputed 'bad boys' of rock and roll, surrounded by swarming fans, free-loving groupie-girls, and an adoring public who were everywhere. "The badder they behaved, the more popular they became," Dawn tells me.

In the mid-1960s, The Rolling Stones were on a rollercoaster, and Dawn was on the ride. She saw Brian whenever she could, and when they did see each other, they couldn't keep their hands off each other, their relationship was sexually charged. It was only a matter of time before Dawn became pregnant, and being a faithful Catholic girl, the reality was terrifying. She wondered how a good girl could find herself in such a situation? When she told Brian that she was pregnant, he promised he would, "make sure that everything was okay," and said he would "look after both of you." And, of course, he vowed that he "loved her …"

But if Dawn's love affair with Brian Jones had started like a modern fairy tale, it ended like an *Aesop's Fables'* nightmare. Dawn went to one of The Rolling Stones' gigs, expecting that as usual, she would be able to go backstage and see Brian, but when she got to the backstage door she was blocked and informed, "You can't go in. Linda is in there." Dawn explains, "I felt very perplexed. I didn't know what was going on. I looked at the guy blocking my way and he said again, 'I'm sorry I can't let you in because Linda is in there with Brian and their baby.'" Dawn tells me she didn't know whether she should cry or scream, adding, "That's when I knew I was on my own. Brian had been seeing Linda all along."

On her mother's instructions, Dawn found herself outside of a backstreet abortion clinic. "I stood outside the door in the pouring rain and thought I'm not doing that. Something inside me said no. My Aunt Eva helped me after that. I know if she'd been younger she'd have kept me. My only other option was to run away … anywhere would've been better than where I went …"

This is how Dawn found herself in Beechwood House, a mother and baby home in London. "The woman who ran the home, Matron, had no compassion. I had to clean floors, do the washing, cleaning, ironing, peel potatoes. When I was in labour, I had to clean the silver – twice."

Dawn explained she'd made a close friend in the home called Betty: "Her parents paid for her to attend the home, so she didn't have to work … her baby was taken away in the back of a car at the same time mine was."

Like other women in this book, Dawn received no antenatal care or pain relief during labour. She tells me, "I heard a girl screaming down the corridor and I listened terrified, knowing I would be next …" Like most of the mothers in the homes, none of the girls and women were prepared for birth. Pain and fear were part of the punishment. Dawn expands, "Even in the home, those who had given birth were kept separate from the pregnant girls. So, they couldn't talk to those who were still pregnant. They would have told us what to expect.

"We were told to give up our child and then to get on with our lives. That we could have another child later on … when we had a proper family. It's terrible. There were thousands and thousands of us …"

Dawn says this is one reason she'd like a formal apology from the Government, and also because, "Being adopted is like a death for them [the adopted person]. They go through absolute grief, then they get very angry about it and then they accept it. We, the mothers, also need the apology. So that it can be reaffirmed that we are not lying, what happened to us did happen. And what we have told our kids is true. They don't always believe us. They say you could have kept us. No, we couldn't. We were chained. An apology would unchain us."

Dawn later married, and she and her husband relocated to start a new life in America, a move that was very successful for them. But Dawn tells me as she sat on the plane, she felt certain the move meant her son would never to be able to find her. Dawn and her husband, Peter went on to have four children. In 1984 to her great joy, her first-born son, John did eventually track her down. He came across to America to see her. Dawn says, "He accused me of not caring for him: 'You gave me away.' I tried hard to explain, 'Well no, I didn't. I had no choice.'" I explained to him about what everyone told me, "If you really love your baby, you will give him to a good home, to real parents." What actual choice did Dawn have – what choice did any of the women really have?

This is another compelling reason Dawn believes an apology is overdue. It's extremely challenging for the current generation of women to understand, let alone believe, exactly how the practice of forced adoption happened. It's a sentiment both Dawn and I understand. Perhaps it is too difficult to understand a world where women seemingly had so few rights.

We discussed the young, unmarried mother as an historic archetype, presented to the public as 'the other', as women deemed *sluts* – someone with low morals and undeserving of decent treatment. We both know this wasn't the case – but that was the picture painted and seared into the public consciousness at that time.

Dawn describes the difficulties and complexity of reunion after her son found her. Firstly, explaining how she had to tell her own teenage children, who didn't know anything about Dawn's past. "I'd been a prude and super strict with them. In effect, I'd put myself on a pedestal, which I was about to fall off!" My son was very sweet he said, "Way to go, Mum!" because of whom I'd become pregnant by.

"My husband has been so supportive, but some marriages can't take that pressure plus the added pressure of the band still being everywhere, all the time. There's no escape we only have to put the radio on ..." Dawn says with an accepting shrug.

"It's difficult for John; my 'child' isn't my husband's, and although John is a sibling to my other children, they don't really know each other. It affects everyone ..."

After meeting John, Dawn was motivated to write her book, *'Not Fade Away'*, and she says, "I wrote my experience so the reader could understand what happened from my point of view. I think any Rolling Stones fan would like it, and I hope anyone reading it now would understand what we women forced into adoption went through. I'd like to think that people thinking of adopting a child now would also read it. I capture lots of different perspectives – like my mother's – I still wonder how she could give her grandchild away." In *Not Fade Away*, there's a line Dawn writes, which struck me as very powerful, "Adoption is a permanent solution to a temporary problem."

Dawn shares more photos with me, pointing out sweet-looking grandchildren and a gorgeous great-grandson – who is the spitting image of his grandfather. I can see how her early experiences never fade away. We both laugh aloud at the striking similarity.

Dawn and I have several surprising things in common: we have both very sadly lost a child, and they are buried in the same part of North Nottinghamshire. Briefly, Dawn and I touch on how weird it is to have a son and grandson that looks so like your first and long-lost love. How that can momentarily and disconcertingly tilt your world. I love the way these interviews have gifted me such a rich and deep bond with other women. There is such strength in knowing other women have survived – and thrived – despite life throwing the worst at them. I look at Dawn and I see a marvellous and inspirational woman.

Dawn continues, "I never wanted to be a victim. I knew two women who committed suicide because of forced adoption. One a year afterwards and one straightaway. Adopted kids are also more likely to commit suicide. In America, they are looking at this."

I think of MAA's requests for better research and of the many frank disclosures about suicide ideation I have heard. I also think about the passing of the years and how grief may become a less frequent visitor, but its poison is as potent as it ever was. That's how these women suffer. It's what I see, feel, and otherwise intuit during every interaction with the MAA women and adopted people I've encountered.

Dawn hasn't been alone; whilst in the US, she's networked with the American adoption movement and speaks highly of Anne Fessler. "Do you know her work?" Dawn asks me.

"Her book's in my bag!" I smile. "Her work is what inspired me to write this book." We laugh and drain our cups. Of all the outcomes I'd anticipated in writing this book, sisterhood and friendship weren't the two I'd expected.

Finally, I asked Dawn what she wanted now. "I want a plain, old-fashioned apology from the PM. I don't want any money. I just want the Government to admit what happened, happened. Then our children will know we are telling the truth."

Jan and Gaynor, mother and daughter

"Although I can't say I was forced into surrendering my baby, I really had no other option," Jan.

"They did spend most of their lives playing us off against each other," Gaynor.

Jan and Gaynor are a friendly, chatty mother and daughter who have been reunited post adoption. They are on the call together, and they agree to using their first names. Gaynor contacted me initially to talk about how she'd been adopted, and in our initial conversation, she suggested she would ask her mum, Jan to join us. It's evident from their communication that they have a loving, powerful and important relationship. Whilst interviewing them both, I was repeatedly struck by their similarities, the lilting tone of their voices, the turn of phrases they used, and the views and opinions that they shared. This caused me to ponder afresh the nature versus nurture question.

Jan starts the conversation. "I'm seventy-seven years old and when I was just sixteen, I went into St Saviour's mother and baby home in Northampton and I had Gaynor. It was a harrowing time. Although I can't say I was forced into surrendering my baby, I really had no other option. There was no way my parents would allow me to stay at home and have her, even though I was still seeing her dad. We did eventually marry, but it didn't last because we were so young. We went on to have two more children, siblings to Gaynor. He and I are still best friends although we are divorced.

"St Saviour's itself wasn't horrendous. There were fifteen girls from all different walks of life, all with different reasons for being in there, except they were all unmarried mothers. I was possibly one of the youngest and I was there from January to April. There was a little bit of bullying when I first got there, but I managed to cope with it. I had my baby in early March and then stayed for another six weeks. We were expected to look after the babies ourselves. We had to do the housework, the cooking and all of that. It was such a big shock to the system especially as I hadn't been away from home before. It was such an unpleasant time. I don't think I ever got over it. Well, you can't, can you, something like that?

"You get on with your life after – you have to. My mother had a hard life herself and my family was very poor. She lost her father, and she had a very strict outlook on life. Her attitude towards the adoption and me was, 'Oh, you'll come home. You'll start again, you'll get over it.' Of course, you never do.

"It put me off religion and church because it was rammed down our throats. We were looked on as these terrible sinners. The church was just over the road from the home and the vicar used to come to the home and check in on us. Also, we had to go to church every Sunday. The church would have an evening gathering mid-week where we could get together with other parishioners, but the lads in the choir would just treat it as a huge joke. It was quite condescending."

I asked Jan about what antenatal care and preparation for the birth she received. "We had a doctor come in every week. I had to have my baby manually turned every week for many weeks. It was most unpleasant. They don't do it anymore." Jan bursts out laughing and says, "She was the wrong way up – trust her to be awkward." Then they both laugh. There is a sense of love between these two that is as evident as it is joyful.

Jan continues, "She righted herself for the birth in any case. If the birth was expected to be straightforward, then you went into a delivery suite within the home. There was also the local hospital. Some girls were given a fake wedding ring and shipped off there. There was also an area in the home specifically for new mums. Then, after a few days, the mothers post-birth would go into a dormitory, and every woman would take a turn for a few nights in the nursery, looking after all the babies. We were put on a rota. You looked after ten or twelve babies at a time, so you didn't get a lot of sleep. And when we could, we slept on mattresses on the nursery floor. I had to help with washing, the sluicing, and the general cleaning of the place, and then we'd all sit round in a circle and bottle-feed our babies – because none of us were allowed to breastfeed because all our babies were going to be adopted. We were all given Epsom salts to stop the milk coming in.

"Whilst in the home before we had our babies, we were able to go out. I think I went to the pictures one afternoon and we had visitors including Gaynor's dad. My mum and dad also came to visit. We used to put babies in these prams and take them for a walk or put them in the garden so that they got fresh air. They were dressed in the clothes from the home: they were grim, all grey and over-washed, not what you'd choose to dress your baby in. But when you were leaving, you had to provide a set of clothes, a layette, for the baby. I remember my mum bringing Gaynor a little dress and cardigan, and I dressed her on the day. After, we went into matron's office, and she was put into a carrycot. My social worker took her away. All the girls would rally round on that day. And then mum came to fetch me later that day."

It was unusual that a girl in a mother and baby home would still be going out with her boyfriend – the father of the baby. I asked Jan about this. "He was supportive, even though he was only seventeen, an apprentice who had no money. But he would write and visit. When I left the home, we carried on courting. We became engaged and married when we were both nineteen. He would've married me before, but both our families said we were too young. We stayed married for almost thirty years, but then we divorced. I think we got married too young. We still get on, and Gaynor sees him."

Jan reflects on her experience. "It was a pretty bad time that you don't always want to think back on. I do find it difficult sometimes too, because as you get older you do think more about the past and I still find it distressing. I think the fact that I did have my boyfriend did make it slightly easier. Most girls suffered two losses: their baby and their boyfriend, whom very often they believed they were in love with. And I had a family to go back to. So, it was just a bit better – if you want to call it 'better' at all."

I wondered what Jan thought about an apology. "We are owed an apology for the whole situation – for being thought of as terrible women and girls. I know it was worse in Ireland, for instance, but we didn't have other options. It does take two to make a baby and the men were never frowned on – the women always were. The outlook at the time was wrong, and we didn't get the support, and it wasn't like we were terrible criminals. It was a big secret at the time, and even now I don't tell everybody – only close friends. After being in the home, I went back to work in the same job as a wages clerk, but I had to lie about where I had been. I told people that I'd been with my sister because she just had a baby. You couldn't say you had been in the mother and baby home … And that was hard, my sister having a baby – my mother's grandchild – which they celebrated, unlike my birth.

"It was all swept under the carpet. There are people who still think I only have two children. It was ten years before we felt settled enough to have another baby, although we tried for five years to conceive unsuccessfully. I had heard of situations where women didn't have more babies and couldn't have more babies after adoption.

"I did receive a letter from the adoption agency to tell me that Gaynor was settled and happy with her parents. When I showed that letter to Gaynor many years later, she disagreed with it. Also, they sent me a photograph. Then I had to sign the adoption papers and her father didn't want to. We had to go to Magistrates' in Peterborough; the social worker was an old spinster type, she really looked down her nose at us.

I asked Jan about costs. "My boyfriend paid some money towards the home and my mum paid the rest. I think I got some maternity money from the State and that went straight to the home. I would've had to pay for longer if Gaynor had gone to a foster mother, but she was chosen by adoptive parents very quickly."

I pointed out that from research it seemed girls were in favour, chosen more frequently by adoptive parents than boys at that time. Gaynor chipped in, "My adoptive parents wanted girls …"

I had detected that Gaynor's experience with her adoptive parents was something they both now questioned. Jan takes up the story. "Gaynor never really got on well with her adoptive parents. She and her adoptive mother never really bonded. Some people shouldn't have children. But it was the expected thing back then …"

Gaynor explained, "That was society then: you got married, then you were expected to have children and people kept asking you, 'Why haven't you got children?' The opposite of what happened to unmarried mothers. It was recommended practice by social workers at the time that children such as me should be brought up knowing that we are adopted. It was called *being chosen*. My sister was adopted about twenty months later from a different family, and she and I grew up always being told we were adopted, but we weren't allowed to ask any more questions; it was established as a taboo area. They didn't want any of their friends knowing they had adopted children, so they moved house quite soon after my baby sister was adopted so that the new neighbours didn't know my mother hadn't been pregnant. We moved to a village, and nobody really knew us and our adoption wasn't something we could talk about. If we did, we got severely told off, especially if we mentioned it at school. That was a big no-no. Because they wanted everybody to think that we were theirs.

"I always say my childhood wasn't too bad; they were ideal parents – on paper. They owned their own house. They moved to a bigger house. He worked hard and she didn't have to work. She was a stay-at-home mother all the time. It was a middle-class lifestyle with dancing lessons, swimming lessons, and Brownies. All the things we ever wanted to do – if I wanted to try horse riding, I could. We had summer holidays in Spain.

"The Church was also a massive part of our lives. My adoptive parents were helped to adopt by the Church. You were deemed a much better person if you went to church and if you had connections with the Church. The vicar was a key sponsor for them to be able to adopt my sister and me, and they carried on being 'church people' all their lives. We started going to Sunday school whilst we were little, and then we got involved in other activities, including the church choir and bell ringing. We were well into it – indoctrinated into the Church way of life.

"But then slowly, you start to grow up and form your own opinions. You learn to say no; you realise some things don't suit you. You start to understand that you're not actually like these people and that you're totally different in many ways. As soon as we started to get our own personalities, that's when life turned harder and more difficult.

"It was worse with puberty, but before that, there were occasions where my adoptive mother was a nightmare – and a nasty person. You don't think about it at the time, but she was a narcissist, and he was the sort of person that thought his opinion was the only opinion and nobody else's views mattered. He was always right! And they fell out with so many friends and family members over the years, those who didn't or couldn't tow their line.

"I tried my absolute best to conform. I did go to church three times on a Sunday. I met a boy from church, went steady with the boy from church, and we got engaged. We weren't allowed to live together. No sex before marriage and, of course, I came from a fallen mother! I had a very strict Victorian-type upbringing. My boyfriend was allowed to come to tea, and he came on holiday with us, but we weren't allowed to go anywhere on our own. So, in that way, I was forced into a marriage with someone who I shouldn't have married … That marriage didn't last."

Jan interjects, "You forgot to say you lived next door to them …"

"Yes," Gaynor says, "the house next door to them became available. And although we'd been saving enough for a deposit on another house that we'd found and liked somewhere else, and had even paid a deposit on it, *they insisted* that we moved next door to them. That was horrendous. When we first got married, my adoptive mother would say, 'Who was that at your door? What were you doing? Why weren't your curtains open?' It was never going to last, was it? After that, my relationship with them started to falter. We had a massive bust-up and didn't speak to them for a year, but then we'd end up being on speaking terms again – it was the same pattern for my sister.

"They didn't approve when my sister got married, so they didn't go to the wedding, and they forbid me from attending the wedding as well. I was 'in favour' at that time. That was the kind of rocky relationship that we had. They never seemed to be able to be friends with my sister and me at the same time. They did spend most of their lives, playing us off against each other. After my marriage broke up, which I can't say I regret because it gave me my son, I met the man I'm married to now. We've been together for thirty-five years. They didn't like him – he wasn't controllable.

"At the start, we tried to do the things that they wanted us to do. We let them have a lot to do with our son. Luckily, when they retired they moved to Scotland, which gave us that gap and very slowly, I managed to get away from them. I became estranged from them for the last twenty years of their life.

"When I found out that my adoptive mother had died – she was the last to go – it was a massive relief. Like a weight had been lifted off me. And that's when I wrote my memoir, *An Adoptee's Journey – Letters of My Life*.

I could say what I liked without anybody criticising me. It's the best thing I've ever done! I'm currently recording the audio version. It was very cathartic, writing it all down."

Like others, I had interviewed, and myself, there's a pent-up need to speak the truth about what happened, an ambition 'to set the record straight'.

Gaynor explains how the desire to chase her biological mother grew. "After I'd had my own children, I started to think about where I'd come from. For me, it was a case of looking at my baby in my arms and wondering how somebody could've given me away. I joined Norcap back in the day and they helped me to begin the research. This was pre-internet: you needed to physically visit the records office. You start by getting your file from the relevant council. I also had good support, and I was lucky in that my birth parents have a slightly unusual surname. I worked out where they were from and that they were still in the area. Then I used the old-fashioned telephone directory and I obtained a telephone number. I called and asked to speak to the man I presumed was my dad. A girl answered the phone and said he wasn't there, but she confirmed that he was her dad and that he would be back later. She was a bit diffident with me, but I couldn't tell her anything at that early stage. But I did ask her if her mum was called Jan and she said yes, so I simply said, 'Thank you, I will ring back later.' In the event, I was too frightened to make that call so I asked my husband to do it, and he asked for Jan and she came on the phone."

Jan continues, "I didn't know who this man was – and unfortunately, my husband had been in an accident the week before, and I thought the phone call was something to do with that. So, I was a bit stern with Gaynor's husband, and he asked, 'Does St Saviour's mean anything to you?' and I said, 'Yes,' and then he put Gaynor on the phone."

Gaynor adds, "Of course, Mum and Dad had always thought of me all those years as Cherieann, the name they gave me at birth, and they had to get used to someone coming along with a different name. I changed my name by deed poll to Gaynor Cherieann. They only lived an hour away from where I was brought up. We've only ever been an hour away from each other.

"Within days, they came to see me and, even though they were separating at that point, they came together. My youngest was about a year old and I went on to have another child. It was great that my mother was in my life by then. It was very hard initially to explain these new family members to our children because we were still in touch with the 'adoptive people'." (That's the phrase both Jan and Gaynor used to describe the adoptive parents.) "And I absolutely did not want them to know. So, at first, I had to tell my children to call them auntie and uncle. I just had to tell them that these were people that I'd known when I was a little girl until they got to an age where I could explain who they were and what they were to me. Because of the adoptive people, I couldn't be completely honest. At one stage, when I was still in contact with the adoptive people, I thought that I should be honest with them – I didn't want secrets and lies. So, I went to see them, with all my records, documents, photographs. First of all, they were shocked and initially seemed okay, alright. They seemed a bit put out, but they didn't show it. But it wasn't long before things started to go very wrong, and I knew that disclosing my contact with my natural mother was another nail in the coffin of our already fragile relationship."

Jan adds, "I'd actually hoped to meet her and to say thank you, but she wasn't that sort of woman and she didn't want to know. I never met her."

"Yes," Gaynor continues, "once she realised you'd met my children. She only liked the eldest child – she would say to him, 'Oh, you're special. It's a terrible thing that your mummy and daddy have split up.' She really put him under pressure. She tried to maintain a relationship with him and, in hindsight, I shouldn't have let them, but you look back and you think they did love him, and he did love them.

Talking of Jan, Gaynor adds, "We've had to get to know each other. We've got a brilliant relationship; we can say anything to each other."

"It wasn't easy," Jan adds. "I parted with a six-week-old baby, and then when we met up, it was thirty years later and she was a person."

"Not only was I an adult, I was a mother myself …" Gaynor agrees. "We took it fairly slowly."

Jan elaborates. "We've heard of situations since where they've rushed. Where they've had Christmas together and so on. Then it's all gone sour because you're two different people. But we are alike in a lot of ways. My youngest daughter came over from America and she couldn't get over how much Gaynor is like me. She says Gaynor walks like you, talks like you, she's really like you, Mum!"

Gaynor continues. "I have one (newly found) sister that I really get on with and one where there's no real relationship, and I accept that. It's fine. It's no good upsetting each other when you come back into another family. I was taken from the family that I should have, from the mum and dad I should've had, from the life I should've had. All my history was taken away. But I have no regrets because I wouldn't be the person that I am today. But still, I had – we had – no choice, that's why we want an apology because we weren't allowed choice." Jan echoes her daughter, "No, we had no choice."

Gaynor adds, "There were women who did freely adopt their babies. Good for them, they knew they couldn't cope, or they decided they weren't cut out to be a mother. That's fine. They decided adoption was what was right for them for whatever reason, but that wasn't us. But those that were young like Jan didn't have a choice, they had their babies taken from them. Jan was forced – absolutely forced – what real choice did she have? There was no money, no state benefit, where would she have lived? She didn't have a choice – other than being on the streets with me?

As our conversation drew to a close, Jan added a little more context. "I didn't know what I was doing. We didn't have sex education. I was shocked when I became pregnant."

I found it slightly sad and touching that Jan felt the need to explain how she became pregnant all those years ago. It's very much a reflection of the shame she was subjected to all those decades ago, which still resonates.

Lin and Mark, mother and son

*"He said, 'I think you're my mother,' and I
replied, 'I think you're my son.'"*

"In 1956 I was sent to Rosemundy House in Cornwall, a mother and baby home fifteen miles from home," Lin, now eighty-seven, explained before describing daily life. "To be quite honest, I didn't expect a holiday camp, but it was like a prison. They had old-fashioned boilers; I had to do all the washing, the sheets and blankets, the nappies – everything – no matter what state of pregnancy you were in, even if you were about to drop. You had to lift the heavy wet sheets out with wooden tongs. You had to do all of this, and it was hot and sweaty. The people who oversaw the home also brought their personal washing in.

"You'd get up and have breakfast, and you had to work around the house, scrubbing the slate floors. We were all assigned to different things each day. To put it quite plainly, it was bloody hard work!"

I asked Lin how the work was organised and who checked the work. I was told in one word who was responsible for this: Matron, and Lin didn't hold back in her description!

"Bitch! She was "hard-faced." Lin elaborated, "Her thing was that she didn't hold back in sharing what she thought about the women and girls in the home. She frequently called us 'slags' and would say, 'It's your own fault you're here and you've got what you asked for." Lin told me she had no pity for anybody.

"But there was one nice nurse." Lin explains that "The Home had quite a lot of people in it, and this included some children. There were a couple of twelve and thirteen-year-olds; we all had to look after each other because they were cruel. If you were on breakfast detail, you had to serve everyone else. You didn't get to have your breakfast; you could only have what was left over after you had cleared up for everybody. It was as simple as that."

Lin remembers the circumstances that caused her to enter Rosemundy. She describes it as a year she will never forget. "The year everything went wrong. I was going to get married to my fiancé, and after a lot of rows and pretend 'heart attacks' from my future mother-in-law, I walked away and left mother and her son to get on with their lives, to get on without me and the baby I was expecting. This meant I had to go to Rosemundy to have the baby, in the knowledge that it would have to be adopted when it was born. In those times, there wasn't the help for single parents that there is now, but I had no idea what was going to come … You were treated as if you had committed the worst sin in the world and you were going to pay for it. This was the place you learned what hard work was. Everyone was issued with a list of jobs to be completed for that day, and the only way to be excused from them was to go into labour!

"You did get the chance to go into the local village to either shop or just to stroll around. Some of the villagers couldn't accept that you were in the village; some were extremely rude and nasty. I thought to myself, there but for the grace of God go I."

This was a phrase Lin referred to several times during our interview. I think there was a sense in the 1950s (and later) before contraception was available, that for a large percentage of women, there was an aspect of Russian Roulette in their relationships with men as they became sexually active.

Lin continues, "The villagers would say things like, 'There's one of those things from Rosemundy House – one of those sluts'. In Cornwall, people speak their mind. We had to go to church every Sunday – a Church of England service. They would march us up the hill with tabards on over our coats and bumps; we were basically labelled. If we arrived early, we'd have to wait outside whilst all the 'goody-two-shoes' went in, and they would mutter at us as we filed past. When they were all in and sat down, then we were all paraded! We'd go right down the very front to go past them all again! They would look us over. After, we were made to leave the church first, again parading past them. Finally, we were allowed to go back down the hill to the house. You were in full view all the time for people to talk about you, to say what they liked, and you didn't dare say anything in response.

"It was like being branded. The vicar would also come to the home to give us a lecture about drinking and sex, but what did he do when he left there, he'd go up to the Railway Inn for a drink." Lin chuckled about this, and I couldn't resist asking her, how she knew what the vicar got up to. "I had relatives in the village." The presence of gossip in that village was palpable.

"The worst part for me was when Mark – he was called Simon then – was adopted. The prospective parents used to come to see the babies. Rosemundy was a big country house with lawns all the way around it. We had to get our babies ready and leave them outside in their prams. When the parents came, we were locked away in the dormitory upstairs; we could look out the windows, but if anybody looked up at you, you had to come away from the window straight away so that you couldn't see whose baby they were looking at. You always knew when it was viewing day; you were told to go upstairs and get on with all the tasks."

I asked Lin to tell me more about the viewing days. She recalled, "You weren't allowed out of the building at all. You were basically locked in on the first floor until the parents had gone. It would be two or three sets of parents that had been booked in for the day – like going to the car showroom and picking your car – the same sort of thing. And after they had gone, you didn't know if you were going to keep your baby – they might not have chosen yours. I was with my baby for three weeks after he was born and then I had a notification that he had been chosen. The worst thing was, I had to go by train from Cornwall to Bath on my own with my baby and also with his baby layette set, which I had to make. We all had to knit sets of clothes for the babies, and if you couldn't knit you had to learn very quickly … We had to make two sets of clothes, bonnets, a matinee jacket and leggings. Matron would provide the wool.

"When I got to Bath, I had to take a taxi to the 'adoption rooms'. When I arrived, I was instructed to go upstairs. It was just bare boards in a room with a desk and a chair. It was only one person at a time. Then a woman came out and called your name, and you gave your name, then the child's name. 'Come over here,' she would say, 'give me the baby.' It was like handing a parcel over at the Post Office. Following that, she took baby into an adjacent room. I knew there were people in the other room. She came out and asked for the layette and then instructed, 'Hurry up. Go and get your taxi.' The taxi had been instructed to keep the engine running and wait outside. She said I should get back on the train and return to the home, and to wait until my baby had been adopted. I cried all the way back."

Lin told me this in a very calm way, but I'd never heard of such diabolical mistreatment. She replied, "It was just how it was at the time and Cornish people are very straight-talking." She added, "Even now, the older Cornish people don't move with the times; they are old-fashioned. It's always been the same. If they see someone's with child, they'll say, 'I wonder whose it is?'"

Lin has obviously thought long and hard about her experiences and I asked her why she thought they treated her that way, she replied, "Because you were a slut and you had to be *shown*, made to realise what you had done, and what your responsibility was. You had to have your nose rubbed in it all the time."

Lin went on to talk about the delivery. "They had a delivery suite in the Rosemundy home. I had a forceps delivery; a doctor came from Truro to deliver her. The delivery suite in the home was for pop-outs." She laughed.

I asked about antenatal information. "I gleaned what I could from the other girls. I couldn't breastfeed. I wasn't a good little cow, so I had to bottle-feed and that was another disaster because you were expected to breastfeed that child so that you didn't forget what had happened. But if you can't, you can't. They put everything down to you being a loose woman. If they saw you doing something and they didn't think you were doing it right, they would say, 'Come on, you slut, get on with it!' And if ever you answered back, you would get double duties – so no one did. The average age of the women was thirteen to about twenty-six. Nearly all babies were given up for adoption. There was one thirteen-year-old who cried so much that her mother did say, 'Okay, you can keep the baby. We'll have you back at home.'"

"Did you have contact with your family or friends?" I asked.

"We had visiting days, but they weren't allowed to take pictures of the baby."

Lin went on to say that she had written and published an article for a magazine in the north of England. I find it interesting that among the women I have interviewed around thirty percent of them have written books and articles. It seems to me as if there was an absolute imperative for these women to tell their personal histories. Much like I had done myself. I wondered what this was about. Was it about being told you're shameful, and wanting, as I did, to set the record straight? To say, 'Hold on, there are other reasons which contributed to my situation.' Or was it a desire to respond to those critics who called you a slag and a slut? Or was it, as I've come to understand, the fact that you are forever marked as a 'black sheep' and worse? This is a message down the decades to those babies that so many women lost, and still so many women haven't been able to connect with. Is it a message in a bottle, I wonder?

Lin continues, "I was lucky. My son was adopted by a head teacher, and they were good parents who also adopted a little girl. They saw him right. They educated him and he's a lovely lad. He's got his scruples and his manners, and I'm thankful he got somebody like that because you do see others where adoption isn't so successful. It's funny how our circumstances have crossed. For instance, I had a job, which meant I travelled, had to go down to Portsmouth, and when I was there, I noticed a row of houses up on a hill and a little boy kicking a ball. I'd watch him and it always came into my mind that my son would've been about that age. When we finally met up, fifty years after I gave him up, he then told me he knew exactly where I meant, and said he lived on that exact hill. I described it to him and he said – that was me! And there were several other places where I went on a regular basis, and it turns out he was near those areas too."

Lin had made several major moves during her life before eventually retiring to the south of England. I asked Lin how contact between her and Mark had come about. She explained she'd moved south, and it was her oldest daughter who contacted her to say there had been a phone call for her whilst she was out.

Lin takes up the story. "I was told someone has called for you asking for you in your maiden name and we don't know whether to pass on the number. So, I decided to ring them back. A woman answered. I said to her, 'You rang Buckinghamshire [where Lin had lived sometime before] for something. She said she'd called on behalf of her partner. My head went ding. I asked why. She replied because he wants to ask you some questions. I then gave her my number, saying he can ring me any time. At ten p.m. that night, he rang me back and I said, 'Is it concerning adoption?' He replied, 'Did your baby have to go to hospital?' I replied yes. He asked, 'Can you tell me what for?' I said a ruptured umbilical cord. He said, 'I think you're my mother,' and I replied, 'I think you're my son.' Then he informed me that he was coming to Cornwall in a week's time, 'Can I come and see you?'

"When the day came, my husband was leaning out of the window and shouted to me, 'I can see two men coming up the path. I think one of them is your son.' I said, 'Hang on a minute, what sort of yarn is that?' He said, 'One is carrying a bunch of flowers. The other one isn't.' I came around the corner and had a look and said, 'The one not carrying flowers is my son.' You see, I could see my gran in him. 'He's my son!' I said. 'Are you sure?' my husband asked. 'Absolutely!'

"We just stood there, looking at each other. We never said a word. We just threw our arms around each other and that was it. Later, I took him out to Rosemundy, which was then a hotel. I said, 'If you want to go in you can, but don't expect me to go in with you. He went in and collected brochures, and then we returned to my home."

During our conversation, Lin outlined to me how she always kept her son at the front of her mind; she'd heard Phil Frampton speaking on Radio Lancashire about being adopted from Rosemundy House. How he was now trying to contact people who had also been born in the home. This led her to start examining her own history and she was also interviewed on Radio Lancashire.

She explains, "I rang Radio Lancashire and did a broadcast with a politician about forced adoptions, and he more or less snapped, 'Well, what did you expect!' Exactly the same attitude as the people in Rosemundy. I replied, 'I didn't expect *that* sort of treatment from the Church, and nor from you.' I went on to say, 'I expect, mister, it's a case of there but for the grace of God go I. Perhaps you've been lucky in life?'"

We then discussed fees for the adoption. Mark had diligently looked for Lin, eventually turning up records that led him to visit Lin's mother's house, and of course not finding her. Lin says, "It was like a lottery; he tried every way to contact me, including through the adoption services.

He was hitting his head against a wall. It seemed as though we weren't allowed to do this, wasn't allowed to do that. In the end, he went to the local library in Portsmouth and got them to look up my married name and that's how he found my ex-husband, and that's how come he was able to contact my daughter.

"I explained to him that I had also spent many years trying to find him, but I wasn't allowed access to records, and he said that social services had been little help to him. If he hadn't have done it himself, he would never have found me."

This raises an important issue, which Lin points out. "Since the late 1970s, unmarried mothers have enjoyed access to support and rights; they don't face the same pressure to give up their babies. Even though it's still incredibly difficult for so many single parents, they can put a roof over their own heads, and they can access benefits – even if it is somewhat of a pittance compared to real need. The contemporary situation has perhaps created an impression that all those years ago mothers *really did choose to give away their babies*."

It would be easy to see how that belief could be formed if your point of reference is how single parents are treated in contemporary society. It takes both research and imagination to begin to understand the pressure that those mothers – at that time – were under.

I reflected on my own circumstances to better understand this. I was just fifteen in 1978 and very green; I would say I was a young fifteen-year-old. I was in a mother and baby home, completely absent of friends, relations, or teachers, and no idea at all of my rights, or where to even go for help and, of course, I had absolutely no grasp of the benefits system, or even the faintest conception of what housing was available through the council – let alone access to the judiciary. I was a schoolgirl and those sorts of things hadn't registered with me in 1978. I described myself as a 'Gonk' – I stand by that description.

This lack of rights, and the forceful, ever-pervasive cloak of shame, drove communities into a moral panic about unmarried mothers – concern about perceived promiscuity led to a feeding frenzy, not only to deny mothers and babies of their vital relationship but also providing an opportunity for monetisation of shame.

My sympathy is with Lin and the others like her who, for complex reasons, not least of all their lack of rights, and dearth of financial support, were driven to make such heart-breaking decisions, which weren't decisions at all, because there was no choice at all.

Lin points out, "This is off the back of two world wars when many working-class communities are struggling, and many families have lost fathers, grandfathers, brothers and sons. Little wonder women were driven to give away their most precious cargo."

"Nowadays, unmarried mothers have got everything, haven't they? They get benefits. Back then there was nothing. My mum was living on her own after my dad got killed in the war. There was no help. No benefits. If it hadn't been for a chance conversation with the local postman, I don't know what would've happened. He came round and said to my mum, 'I haven't seen Lin lately,' and my mother told him that I'd had to stop working and was going to have the baby adopted but didn't know where to go, and it was the postman that suggested Rosemundy."

As with others that I have spoken to, Lin has been reunited with her son and, as welcome as that was, she has also found a whole new family.

"I found out that I had three teenage grandchildren. They're all married with kids. I get photographs of them, but there's always something that gets in the way of me visiting them, like I broke my shoulder and I couldn't travel; it's just been bad luck. I've seen the youngest one more than I've seen the others, and she is the spitting image of my youngest daughter. And she's got the same interest, which is weird: she's a horse rider, she does dressage, and my youngest one teaches horse riding. Another thing, my son is car-mad and so am I. We are petrolheads! We both had classic cars – Triumphs. We have long conversations about what work he's done on his cars. I'm very interested in this." But the coincidences don't stop there. One of her grandchildren is very interested in needlework and Lin's mum was a seamstress.

I wanted to know how Lin felt about a formal apology. She was disparaging about the role of the Conservative government and their failure to acknowledge the instruction for an apology or to act on it, adding, "It would mean a lot. People say you're only doing it for the compensation, but I tell them I'm not interested in that. I tell them I was treated badly and I want somebody to recognise that this terrible practice went on. It isn't just about the Magdalene Laundries in Ireland. It went on everywhere. Australia and New Zealand have given an apology, why the hell can't we? It's like that politician said to me, 'Why should we apologise? It didn't happen in my time.' I explained to him as each set of politicians take over, they take over the past too. They take on the responsibilities for the former government. We don't care whether that apology comes from Labour, the Liberals or the Green Party, we just want the apology."

I wanted to know how Lin had got back on her feet, after such a terrible experience in Rosemundy. Firstly, there is the experience of finding out that you're pregnant and often the added dimension of a relationship ending. It must have been very difficult to think you could have married and pregnancy would not have been an issue, might even be welcomed. That's without considering the bond she might have formed with the prospective father. That would have been complex and difficult to deal with at nineteen. As we've heard, Lin's family were impoverished, and they had the additional worry of what to do and where Lin was going to have the baby adopted.

It's worth stating that there was an absence of easily or freely available contraception for unmarried women such as Lin; aside from going to a backstreet abortionist, women couldn't prevent themselves from becoming pregnant and couldn't terminate an unwanted pregnancy.

The Abortion Act which allowed safe and legal abortion didn't pass into law until 1967. In 1956, despite growing support to legalise abortion, illegal abortion killed or ruined the health of many women. They had none of the rights we take for granted today. There wasn't a benefit system you could lean into for financial or other support. The shame of having a child without a father, almost regardless of where you lived, let alone in the tightly knit Cornish community Lin was part of, where gossip was potent and ever prevalent – the idea of a young woman bringing up a baby without a father was unthinkable. The pressures would have been unbearable.

When Lin returned to her village, she knew she would be able to return to work at the garage across the road from where she lived. Her mother was informed, 'Lin's job is here when she comes back.' An act of kindness, no doubt. Lin worked there for a decade, delivering cars across the country. She says, "Going back to work after was awful. A couple of the boys in the garage started to dig me about it, asking me, 'What's it was like to have a baby, a girl of your age and you're not even married?' The boss told them to leave me alone and if they didn't they could see themselves out the front door and don't come back."

It was employment that Lin really enjoyed, providing her with skills and financial security. She comments, "It taught me to think like a man. Not have anybody push me down. People would say she's a strong character. I didn't mind that."

Our conversation turned again to the apology. "Even if we get an apology, it won't take it away. It'll always be in the back of my mind. It's like a computer you can't ever turn it off or wipe the record – even if you delete everything. It's still there. It eased when I met Mark. It halved. It took a weight off my shoulders. Being reunited was half the battle. It was such a Dickensian way of treating people, the way they treated me – and him. Even in Victorian times, if a woman fell pregnant, she was sent away not separated from her baby. Often it was 'adopted' into the family. Why can't the Government turn around and recognise how we were treated and say sorry? That's all I want."

Mark

"I always had this nagging feeling at the back of my mind, who am I? Where am I from?"

I was extremely pleased to be able to speak with Mark, following my interview with his mother, Lin. Mark takes up his side of their shared history.

"I was told I was adopted at the age of five or six, possibly earlier. I also have a younger adoptive sibling. When I was about ten, Mum said (and by my 'mum', I mean the woman who brought me up, and 'mother' is Lin) here are your adoption papers, which contained letters to and from the adoption agency, detailing who my birth mother was, the Bath adoption agency and the Rosemundy house details. I said, 'No, I don't want them. I'll probably mix them up with my Beano comics and you'll tidy up and throw them out.' I asked her to keep hold of them so that they wouldn't be lost and eventually I would look at them.

"I had a lovely childhood. We had a lovely place with lots of land. Dad was a headmaster. He got a promotion and we then moved. When I was thirteen, we moved back down south towards Plymouth. Everything was going fine. I wasn't brilliant at school, and I didn't really know what I wanted to do, but life was good. I suppose I got a little lost … I got married and had three children, but I always had this nagging feeling at the back of my mind, who am I? Where am I from? I knew I was from Cornwall, born in Rosemundy home. But that was all I knew.

"Eventually, about twenty years ago, I was going on holiday to Cornwall with friends and I happened to have an address in Falmouth. Towards the end of the holiday, I went and knocked on the door and asked, 'Did you know, Lin?' I used my mother's full name, which is very distinctive. I was told, 'No, mate, I've only been here for a couple of years. I suggest you knock next door but one and speak to the old girl who's lived here all her life.' So, I did. She said, 'Oh, yes, Linda and the girls.' So, then I knew I had half-sisters. The lady then told me that Linda used to sell wool in a particular place, which gave me my next lead. I had to wait a full twelve months before I could return, but then went back to the town the lady had mentioned and went looking for wool shops, hoping I would find my birth mother there. But I couldn't find that shop, and in any case, later, it turned out not to be a shop but a market stall!

"I didn't really make any progress tracking Lin down, so I had an idea to contact the local newspaper. Initially, they were keen to help me track down my birth mother but then had to turn down the idea because previously it had caused them trouble when somebody was traced who didn't want to be found. But the reporter I was speaking to there did make a really great suggestion to check out the local births, deaths and marriages in the library.

"I tried a different tack. I tried an adoption database, but this was also a big problem. You only get connected if both of you – child and birth parent – were on that database. And the birth parent had to know the child's new adoptive name. Otherwise, it doesn't work.

"Then I went to social services and they said, 'Oh, we don't know. It's a tricky situation.' They said we'll need to make sure she wants to be contacted and then you'll need counselling as well. I thought to myself, oh, my God, I'm not a twelve-year-old, I'm knocking fifty! I felt that they didn't want to know, and it was all too much trouble.

"With no other avenue open to me, I booked a slot in the nearest library and sat going through the microfiche to try to find my mother and I knew before I started it would be difficult. After a long search, I found her at an address, some eleven years prior. She had got married eleven years after I'd been born, and I knew roughly which area she lived in. I was on a high! I was on an absolute buzz, but the library was closing … I was leaving the library when I noticed some phone books for the area Lin had moved to. Now, knowing her new name since she's married and the area she had moved to, and thankfully it was quite a distinctive name, I was able to make a list of four likely people. I went to a phone box straight away and started to make those calls. First person, no answer. Second person was a young woman and so I ruled her out. Then I got a voice recording of an old man and I didn't think I could just leave a message with him. So, again, I ran out of leads to chase – or so I thought.

"At around this time, I met a new partner, who I am now married to. I explained to her how I had been searching for my birth mother for many years. She urged me to continue my search by pointing out I wasn't getting any younger, and certainly, my mother wouldn't be getting any younger, and she pointed out that she might actually be dead. That spurred me on. I explained to my partner about the numbers that I had tried, and that only one seemed to fit the bill – the old man.

"My partner made contact and this time she left a message, explaining she was seeking contact with a woman called Lin. The old man was Lin's previous husband. Since then, Lin had remarried and moved away. It was one of Lin's children that received the message and let her know someone was looking for her."

Lin now gave her permission for the mystery caller to be given her telephone number.

Mark continues, "I asked my partner if she could phone her and, to prevent another false hope, I gave her some questions that only my mother would know about. That would *prove* the connection. My partner said she would do it. She phoned the number and again left a message and the now updated name of the woman she was trying to find. Just thirty minutes later, she got a return call … 'Hello, I hear you're looking for me?' It was Lin, my birth mother – finally, we had contact."

Mark explains he now knows that his mother gave him up because she couldn't afford to keep him. There was, at that time, just his mother and her mother. The grandfather had been torpedoed in the Irish Sea as a merchant seaman. Lin had no options.

Mark goes on to say, "I have now become quite involved in the campaign for adoption apology, appearing with my mother on various TV and radio shows." He sounds very impacted – not just by 'being handed over like a parcel' as he describes the process when his adoptive parents chose him at Rosemundy House, but he also recognises the difficulties of other adopted children, and his and Lin's lengthy and difficult struggle to find each other. He tells me a story that he uncovered whilst he and Lin were undertaking media interviews.

"Two lads were taken to a farm to be adopted, and apparently something went wrong, causing the farmer to severely beat one of the lads. The next day, the poor boy was dead." It's not hard to understand why this story moves Mark – after all, that could have been him.

Mark also tells me how during filming, it was incredibly difficult for his mother to enter or even be near Rosemundy House, which would cause her to break down. "To me, it just sounded like a sweatshop. It's been pushed under the carpet." After this, Mark was motivated to contact moral welfare homes – another title for mother and baby homes – in his own area of Havant. He hit a brick wall as neither the council nor the local MP were particularly interested.

"Of course, if you're adopted, you don't know your medical history," Mark says. "My doctor asked me if there was any history of high blood pressure and I replied to him, 'I don't know because I am adopted.' And that's a good point really because many adopted people don't know – can't know that antecedence or whether they have a hereditary illness. Those details are never passed from the birth mothers' doctors to the adoption agencies.

"People ask me if there's a stigma to being adopted. I say no, I'm very grateful for my life actually because I don't know what my life would've been like otherwise. I've had a lovely childhood, a lovely life, and I'm a very lucky person with children and grandchildren of my own. Yeah, I'm a lucky person."

One thing I'm intrigued by was that both Lin and Mark shared an interest – bordering on obsession – in cars, particularly Triumphs, so much so that they often have long conversations about manifolds, brake pads etc. Mark explains how Lin owned six Triumphs at once. They are clearly likeminded.

I ask Mark about his notes and whether they contained any reference to fees. He says that nothing went to Lin, but he believes that a fee was paid to the adoption agency in Bath.

As our conversation begins to wrap up, Mark restates how poorly his mother, and women like her, had been treated. Lin had kept a postage-stamp-sized photograph of him in her purse, which she showed him when they met. It made him very emotional. He recounts their first meeting and his timid steps towards her front door.

"We just stood and looked at each other. I was totally welled up. I really was. And so was she. After that, I was invited in and her husband joked with her, 'Have you got any more skeletons in the cupboard?'" And this is where Mark points out something very serious that impacts a number of the women I've interviewed. Lin's previous husband had forbidden her to ever mention her past to their children – never to talk about Mark's existence.

Regarding the need for an adoption apology, Mark is clear, "I don't just blame the Government – I blame the Church as well because they were complicit in this. I really think that going for an adoption apology is flogging a dead horse with this government [Sunak's government in

2024]. Or with any government in Britain. You've got the Canadians, the Australians, the Danes, and the Irish all came out in the past five years and apologised. I don't think the British Government are going to come out and say we are sorry about this. You've got the likes of Ed Davey being interviewed the other day about the Post Office Horizon scandal. All he could say was that he deeply regretted it. He was pressed again to say sorry, and he just couldn't. Again, he said, I just deeply regret it. They just sidestep the question. I'm sorry I don't trust politicians one bit. You don't get a straight answer from them. I can't think of one politician who has put their hand up and said, 'Yes, we did that I'm sorry.' I don't think these women want money, they just want their suffering and their anguish recognised by the Government. To get that apology, and for the circumstances to be seen for what they are – a massive cover-up."

Last, but not least, Mark says, "Why can't the Government get their act together and issue this apology? Even Starmer won't apologise. Politicians dating back to the fifties have got a lot to answer for. They've all shoved it under the carpet. They really have." Mark's disgust is palpable. "Unfortunately, a moment of madness in your teens and you're labelled as a dirty person – branded for life. It shouldn't be the case."

Marie

"My daughter was whisked away ..."

Marie wrote the following email to me detailing what happened to her and her daughter, after reading my request for information on the MAA website. I'm grateful to Marie for her contribution, especially as it relates to events in 1982 when it was assumed these practices had abated, and because it shows how widespread the reach and scope of forced adoption had become.

How many other women suffered in this way? Had their babies taken from them unethically and possibly illegally? Circumstances such as these indicate that more research needs to be conducted.

Dear Karen,

I hear that you're wanting information about mother and baby homes, with reference to forced adoption practices. My situation was perhaps not the usual Mother and Baby home set-up, but if I explain a bit more, it's pretty close, and ultimately, I of course lost my firstborn child.

I was born in 1959 in Scotland, third child of four kids, born in very quick succession, four years later 1964 mum died. Dad didn't cope, and he was an alcoholic. We ended up in various children's homes, often in the middle of the night. And quite a long stint in foster care but somehow, we four stayed together, Dad miraculously kept his job and one day he picked us up from school, and drove us to Cornwall.

Multiple houses later we settled into our new home, I went to high school, and somehow survived a rather crazy childhood. My brother went to university at seventeen, my sister went to a technical college at sixteen, and I went to do a college course at fifteen, our youngest brother had to wait a short while but got into the armed services as soon as he could. I got the required O levels, did my nursing training, and followed that up with midwifery training.

Late 1982 I found myself pregnant, being a good catholic I went to confession and told the priest I was pregnant; I think he hardly knew what to say or do, so he told the catholic children's society and I had my first counselling from Marg and Maud when I was about six weeks pregnant.

I had secure accommodation in the nurse's home for as long as I was working, but to cover my shame I felt I needed to leave work as early as possible. So took all my annual leave for the year, just prior to my maternity leave.

I had known a family in Devon. Jane and Paul who were both in professional roles. They had two adopted children, one who had come from the catholic children's society, and two naturals. I approached them for help, it was a bit squashed, but I shared a tiny bedroom with the eldest girl and paid them the same rent I had paid when at college. Sat besides the telephone in the house was a small collection box, clearly for the catholic children's society, so anyone who made a call could 'Pay-it-Forward'.

Marg and Maud were delighted at this arrangement, knowing that this family would also be encouraging me to give the baby for adoption. I had visits from M&M every four weeks, plus letters, and phone calls, possibly to prevent termination of the pregnancy. Jane and Paul knew nothing about social benefits available to me, and with a rather busy household, didn't have time to even point me in the right direction. It wasn't a relaxing time, and yet I believe it was safe and they were generous to have me.

I spoke a little with their daughter who I shared the room with. M&M from the adoption agency never told me anything about benefits, or in fact any other options available to me, except relinquishing my daughter. From the first meeting, they worked on shaming me into silence. And spoke about wonderful adopters. One couple had an inheritable disease, and sadly infertility. It seemed a sad story. I wasn't told the disease was severe bi-polar disorder, and infertility was due to separate bedrooms.

I went into labour when I was out, and with them working, a friend took me to a smaller maternity unit, not the local one I had worked at. I gave birth, and two days later, my daughter and I were picked up by the family and taken back to my accommodation in Devon. I breastfed my daughter for seventeen days, she fed and slept well. My roommate never lost a moments sleep.

I walked to the hospital well baby clinic, with my baby in a borrowed stroller. I asked to see someone about my daughter being removed from me, but they couldn't find anyone suitably qualified. After a long wait, and another breastfeed, I walked home. M&M came to visit me to try to persuade me to stop breastfeeding, its fairly clear in the notes I obtained. I had no idea how I could even afford bottle-feeding. They also took my child benefit book off me and the coupons that gave me nine pounds per week as a single mum, at this stage I still had my daughter in my custody. They also took my daughter's full birth cert which was about five pounds, and of course it was irreplaceable.

M&M had been making arrangements with the family about picking up my daughter, so Jane took a day off work, which was rather unusual. My daughter was whisked away, and Jane took me on an extraordinarily long walk, the youngest son also was gifted a day off school to accompany us and lift spirits. We didn't talk about anything, and when I got back to their home, I bled and bled all night, embarrassed I didn't say anything. I moved out of this accommodation about twenty-four hours later. I was penniless, and stayed with a friend as I couldn't go back to work, as I was still on maternity leave, so I couldn't live in the nurse's home.

At my first meeting with M&M after I lost my daughter, I begged to have her returned, they announced that she had been baptised the previous weekend, and so now in God's eyes she belonged to them, their name is on the certificate. I have had an apology from Cannon Bede Davis from the Plymouth cathedral (now deceased) saying this should not have happened.

Thanks for the opportunity to have a say.

Marie

I have many questions about what happened to Marie and her baby in 1983. There is no doubt that this testimony represents not only a startling abuse of trust by 'friends' and the Church but also demonstrates a frightening degree of coercive control. I wonder also about the role the health services played, knowing a young mother seeking help was so abjectly failed. Was there no protocol in place that would have afforded her some support?

Rachel

"She could never be my mother because I had my mother, but there was just this bond. I was just part of her."

Rachel is fifty-six and married with two grown-up children. She tells me, "In 1967 Barbara, my mother, who was seventeen, found herself pregnant by her long-term boyfriend, and she immediately finished that relationship." Since then, Rachel says, "I've been in touch with my birth father and this came as a surprise to him. He was very teary, and he was still very fond of Barbara. At the time they were going out, he was about eighteen and they had been dating for a year and a half. Barbara was still at school and he was still doing his apprenticeship."

Rachel says, "I didn't contact him until after Barbara's death because she didn't want me to. When I did contact him, he said at the time with Barbara coming from a Catholic family, he would have also wanted to marry her, and that would've been very much expected by his family." Rachel laughs and says, "I don't think my mother wanted to get married to him." At the time, she lived in Hampshire, with her mother and father, Mr and Mrs Smith, and her mum worked as a practice nurse in a nearby surgery.

"When her mum, Mrs Smith, eventually found out that Barbara was pregnant, it transpired that her own mum was also illegitimate and had been kept by her mother and her grandmother who lived with them. Mr Smith, who would've been my grandfather, was himself adopted at the age of twelve. My great-grandmother was very keen that history wouldn't repeat itself with me.

"Both my grandparents understood in their own way in their own time, what it meant to be an illegitimate child and to be an adopted child. Mrs Smith was very much in the driving seat and understood the stigma that surrounded illegitimacy. She said, 'This can't happen. Society won't allow it.' So, therefore, Barbara became a prisoner in her own home. She left school in the July and just didn't go back until November. Her dad took her out once a week for a walk, driving to a beach many miles away. Nobody knew that she was pregnant, apart from those she lived with and her best friend Rachel, whom I was named after and with whom I'm still in contact. We are both devastated that we lost Barbara in 2022. I'd known her for sixteen years before we lost her.

"It was the doctor's surgery that Mrs Smith worked for that helped her to find a home for unmarried mothers. They couldn't really afford to send her, so she actually went in the day she went into labour. She had a horrendous labour – I was a forceps birth. We were in the home together for three days. She wasn't encouraged to see me.

"After three days, I went off to live with a foster mother until I was adopted at eight weeks. Barbara went straight back to school – with stitches – as if nothing had happened. She just turned eighteen. It breaks my heart, thinking of it."

Rachel tells me that prior to our conversation, she discussed whether to go ahead with our interview with Barbara's husband; she was in touch with him and also her half-brothers. She clarified that he is "very happy for this story to be told because she would've been absolutely on board with this. It was an absolutely awful time for her."

Rachel continues, "The main thing for Barbara was that she gave me away as a tiny baby and we were eventually reunited when I was thirty-eight years old, but I know she really loved me. She said I was a gift to my adoptive parents. I instigated contact with her via the local council when I was eighteen. I made contact with Mr and Mrs Smith, and Mrs Smith did her very best not to meet me. She didn't want Barbara and I to be reunited and that really hurt Barbara. Mrs Smith did pass along the message, telling her daughter that her child had been in touch. I was in touch with Mrs Smith for a long time, trying to get through to my mother. I think it really hurt Barbara that her mother had been in touch with me for such a long time when we hadn't yet established that contact. That didn't happen until after Mrs Smith died, then Barbara went through her paperwork and found my contact details. Why she didn't want to ask her mum for my address, I don't know. It took twenty years from my initially looking for her to actually meeting her. But we were in contact for five years before we met. It turns out, we are both cut from the same cloth, and we're both extremely hesitant and careful, both not wanting to upset the other in any way."

Rachel continues, "Mr and Mrs Smith were the gatekeepers. They met me in the interim period; they sized me up, writing letters to meet, occasionally phoning, but they never really wanted me to meet with my mother. When she and I eventually met up, my mother was deeply hurt by this behaviour – and she never got over it.

"When I was thirty, I had my first child. We went on holiday with my husband to France and we sent Mrs Smith a postcard. Mr Smith had died. Mrs Smith was in hospital, and Barbara happened to pick up the postcard … She took the card to the hospital and asked her mother about it, saying, 'You've had a postcard from somebody called Rachel? Who is that then?' Mrs Smith threw the postcard across the ward and said, 'That's your daughter.' Barbara was very upset by this. Barbara, it transpired, had written letter after letter to her daughter, but for whatever reason hadn't been able to post them. She was guilt-stricken.

"Barbara and I have talked endlessly about why her mother and her father acted in the way that they did. In fact, Barbara's husband, who she met when she was in her early twenties, while she was doing her nurse training in central London, who I spoke to this morning, said he knew about me from the moment he asked Barbara if she would marry him. She told him she would love to, but there was something she must tell him first. He said, 'That's absolutely fine, let's go and get her back.' He just thought they could go and pick me up! Barbara had to explain that I had been adopted. But he knew that the Smiths were aware of my existence, but they never broached the subject with him, and out of respect for Barbara, he didn't want to raise it with them either.

"So, I was this massive secret. And it was only after the death of Mrs Smith that this shifted. Her ashes were about to be scattered in the Lake District and I was invited to join the family, and my uncle was there. He said, 'So, you're the big secret.' He had also been sworn to secrecy.

"Also, I found out that my mum had asked for a photograph of me and that photograph had been taken and sent to the Smiths, but they never handed it over to Barbara. On my second birthday, Barbara mentioned that it was two years since she'd had me, and she was left under no illusion that she should never mention me again. Never to talk about it again.

"The Smiths were loving parents, but this treatment of both Barbara and myself was very harsh and I wondered why this was. Is this what they were told to do and, if so, who told them? Whenever Barbara and I talked about it, tears would well in her eyes.

"Eventually, Barbara and her husband came to visit me and my husband in my home when my half-brothers got involved and encouraged her saying, 'You've got to do something.' From the moment she came here that first day – that was it. She was my best friend. She could never be my mother because I had my mother, but there was just this bond. I was just part of her. She was the first person I've ever met that was related to me – apart from my own two children, but that was different.

"I came from her, and I am a blueprint of her. We didn't have to spend a lot of time asking each other how we felt because we already could 'catch' each other. We understood each other. We were absolutely in tune. We'd finish each other sentences. It was just bizarre.

"This trait also runs through to my eldest son. When the three of us have a photograph taken together, we are obviously the same genetics. My younger son is more like his dad. And in fact, when I had my first child, I had to have counselling, because it just blew my mind to meet somebody that I was related to.

"My mum and dad did accept me tracing my biological mother, but my mother was dreadfully hurt and upset by it also. She says now, 'I was just jealous. I didn't feel good enough.' But I felt I was swimming in an ocean without anything to be tied to. My parents went on to adopt another boy who isn't related to me, so we are separate biological children. And then they managed to have one of their own."

I asked Rachel what it was like growing up as an adopted child. She explained, "It felt very different, not the same as anybody else. Particularly around puberty, and as a little girl, I told all my friends at school that I was adopted. I was very open about it and there was a time when my friends would say, 'You could be a princess', 'you know your real mummy could be …', so I began to see that my family wasn't necessarily the same as other families."

I was surprised that there was no specific help from the agency, the council or social services when eighteen-year-old Rachel applied for her files.

She elaborates, "At the initial contact with the council, I was invited in and my mother was encouraged to attend a meeting. At the meeting, my mother was excluded, which left her feeling very upset, whilst I was invited to discuss my feelings in private. Those meetings didn't continue. I wasn't offered any ongoing support. Later on, I applied for files so that I could share them with my mother to try and help her heal. I had to have a meeting with a social worker to talk about my file and I wanted to take Barbara with me, but they said, 'Absolutely not, that wasn't possible at all.' So that was the only point, in my forties, when anybody recognised I might need some help dealing with this."

I asked what was the value of an adoption apology? Rachel had asked Barbara's husband about this. Interestingly, he knew nothing about the Parliamentary Inquiry, which she found surprising because she had sent links to the story of the adoption apology in the past few years, including a link to the consultation event. It seems that Barbara, for whatever reason, hadn't shared this news of an investigation and a potential apology with her husband. Rachel doesn't know if her mother participated.

Like many other mothers who lost their children through forced adoption, she went into the caring profession. Rachel thinks her mother did have some closure. "Eventually, she was able to say she had three children, not two." Since Barbara's death, Rachel is extremely sad that she's lost the only other person on the planet that could 'get her'. She adds, "She was the closest friend I had. So, for me being adopted, I feel that there was a stigma about it. And I've had a good childhood. Barbara did say, 'Nobody ever told me there were benefits. Nobody ever told me there was help. It's not like it is now. No, there was no help for the family, or if there was, it wasn't talked about.' Knowing Barbara, as I grew to know her, there was no way that she would've been able to ask for this information.

"There was one strange coincidence, which was when I was adopted, I went back into the area that my original family was from, and it was Mrs Smith, my own grandmother, who delivered my childhood immunisations, by chance, before I left to be with my new parents. Barbara had left her baby in a Southampton hospital, and I was just around the corner in Hampshire for the next six weeks. When Barbara realised, she was really upset. We could've been on the same beach, at the same time, when I was younger – and that haunts me too. As a child, I always wondered if she was going to turn up, if she would come and find me, or if I had walked past her in the street and, now all these years later, it seems that there is a likelihood that I might have done!

"Barbara and I went on a pilgrimage, and she showed me where I was born – she wanted me to know everything – she was wonderful like that. She had to stand there, bless her with all those memories flooding back.

"So, would I like an apology for Barbara? Yes, I would! I know it's too late – she suffered. And she wasn't alone. There are thousands of girls who were treated like this. There's got to be an apology. Unfortunately, we're not going to get one from this government, but when this government go, the Labour Party need to take up the baton for it, don't they?"

Rachel and her mother thought about working together on some sort of record or guide. She says, "I don't know if I can do it on my own. This is why I really wanted to talk to you and get the story out there. My half-brothers, who found out about me in their early twenties, could not believe that Barbara had been forced to go through this.

"This current generation doesn't understand – life is so different now. They have more determination over their life and choices, whether they have a baby, whether they are gay, whether they're transgender, whatever the issue is, there is generally support out there. Even from the Government. It might take a while but there is support there. I don't think people have any idea how awful it was, certainly not my brothers. They had no idea and, after that, their relationship with Mr and Mrs Smith became very strained. They couldn't believe they'd forced their mum into giving away a baby."

Jane

"Even rape was hushed up ... young women were left in no doubt that they were to blame ..."

Jane explained to me that she was born in 1959 and adopted in 1960. She outlines her story calmly. "My birth mum was raped, and I'm the result of that. So, there was a lot of pressure on her to give me up, and because her mother's partner had just left the family. So, you know, it was an unstable family unit really. My mother didn't talk much about what happened, and she's not alive anymore. I want her name – Jilly Pulford – included in any apology, even though she's not alive anymore. I think it's important. I don't want her to be anonymous anymore. But I remember growing up and it was all 'Your mother got into trouble.'

"I didn't discover I was adopted until I was called a 'bastard' at school. You know how kids overhear their parents and then repeat it ... You learn your mum and dad aren't your *real* mum and dad, and I had all of that to deal with when I was about ten. It was devastating because I had no idea. My parents later said they were always going to tell me, but I guess they found it hard to know when the right time was to do something like that. I didn't know what it meant. I remember being given a booklet and sitting down to read it alone in the front room. It was about children that were *special* and that's why they were adopted. I thought to myself I don't understand any of this. It was extremely hard to speak to my parents about it. They didn't really know what to do. They didn't know how to handle it. I think my adoptive mum had had her own baby which died and, after that, she adopted.

"My parents were a little bit older, and they found it challenging to talk about these things. Of course, I was always pushing them for more information. I knew that they knew things that I didn't, and I disliked the idea that they had secrets that they weren't telling me, even if that was for good reason. They were wonderful parents. I had a good adoption. I just never felt that I belonged. I think it probably made me too sensitive. Once I understood I was adopted, I simply didn't trust anything after that point, including them, and I also didn't trust *anything* would last for me. It was about insecurity, but I didn't understand that. I didn't know what I was. I didn't know who I was. I didn't know where I belonged, and I didn't know why I was there. I just felt completely displaced.

"In later life, when people said things like, 'Just be yourself', I thought I've never known who I am. Until I met my birth mother in the 1990s, and that was great, but there was a problem with my adoptive mum. She found it difficult, but I also found it difficult with all the secrets, and people knowing stuff about me, but me not knowing. I didn't know where I came from. I didn't know what my ethnic make-up was or anything. I felt like I didn't belong. I found it hard to fit in because I found it hard to be honest about who I was – because I didn't know who I was."

The sense of displacement was palpable and had clearly dominated Jane's life. I asked Jane to describe more about that feeling.

"When I was young and growing up in a small town, it was the same old story really. I couldn't wait to leave home, and once I got to London in the eighties, then I felt I could be anonymous. Some people didn't like that, but that was exactly what I liked. I'd grown up not knowing how to be with people or feeling that they knew something about me – like they in fact had done in my hometown. The people that I now met in London, I could tell them about myself and tell them what I knew, feeling comfort that they weren't judging me. That's always been through drama – at last, I found my tribe! That's always where I felt most at home when I'm involved in a play, where I'm with a creative group of people and we are working towards the same thing, and it's non-judgmental."

I wanted to know more about how Jane came to meet her birth mother.

"I was rehearsing a play, and there was a woman in the cast who was also adopted, and she put me in touch with Norcap." (Norcap then ran a variety of adoption services for adults including searching and tracing, intermediary services, birth record counselling and the Contact Resister; these are now provided by Family Action.)

"I was assigned a social worker and received a lot of information. At last, I knew my mum was still alive, but also I found out that my dad had been dead a long time. Suddenly, I knew her name and some, but not all, of the circumstances, including that my dad was married to another woman. I didn't know what to do with the information, so I sat on it for quite some time. I got back in touch with Norcap and they guided me through.

"It was good that I had a counsellor assisting and supporting me, because I thought, what if I ring my birth mum up and she doesn't want anything to do with me? I would experience that as even more rejection. I didn't know how to tell my adoptive mum either. It was really difficult. In the end, I thought I really need to do this for myself. If it hurts people, well, I've been hurting for a long time too. And I'm sorry if it hurts someone, but it's my mum I need to know so …

"I didn't tell my adoptive mum at first because I simply didn't know how to tell her, instead I confided in a trusted family friend who was like an aunt, and because she was my health visitor when I was born. Unfortunately, she broke my confidence because she told my mum. I was always going to tell Mum, but frankly, I didn't know how to do it. That was hard. It was hard to have that conversation with Mum because she's my mum and Jilly is something else – she gave birth to me and her circumstances were difficult, so she had to have me adopted. It was hard to explain to my mum that it didn't mean that *our* relationship was different. She was still my mum. Mum came to terms with it after a while and we chatted about it from time to time. I said to her you can ask me anything, but I won't bring it up. I knew she did find it so hard."

Jane explained that her brother, who was also adopted, created a lot of tension in the family, and between Jane and her mum. "He'd stir things up, it really didn't help. Because of course, he was an adoptee and he, too, was fragile and insecure."

Jane continued, "I don't regret doing it, but I've often thought I should have done it a different way. You always bear the guilt when you are the adopted one. I wonder what have I done wrong. And I self-remonstrate that this is just circumstances. I'm just trying to make the best of this, and I've got a right to know who I am and where I come from. However, there are so many barriers in the way; it's like you don't have a right to know about yourself!"

I asked Jane how she forged in her mind the idea that she had the right to know about herself, even though the idea of individuals having rights wasn't as prevalent through the eighties and nineties as it is now.

She explained, "I just thought to myself, what am I waiting for? I could be passing this person, my biological mum, on the street. I could have other family – siblings. I think living in London made a huge difference. The anonymity of it; also going through Norcap and being supported. They were there to pick up the pieces if I was rejected again. There wasn't a single lightbulb moment, but it had been festering for so long. I would've exploded with it all if I hadn't done something. I thought I've got to know. I'm going to do something about it … And whatever happens, happens. I was at that point – I've got to do that now and that's it, and I'm sorry if I hurt people but I've been hurt for too long myself. People knew things about me that I also have a right to know. Why are they keeping it from me …"

I asked Jane about meeting her birth mum, Jilly, and she explained the process. "It was around 1995. First, there was a telephone conversation with the social worker at Norcap. Then they phoned Jilly, phoning me back very quickly to inform me, 'She's waiting for your call.' I thought to myself, oh my God, what do I do now? Well, I thought, this is it! I phoned her and the first thing she said to me was, 'Are you happy?'"

Jane became emotional at this stage and continued, "I thought, this is so cruel, what happened to Jilly. She didn't know whether I was dead or alive. That really hit me. The first question was followed by, 'Did you have a good adoption?' I can't remember the rest of that conversation, which is really quite bizarre. It was such an important thing in my life. Then she came up to London with her sister and we met at Victoria coach station. I felt *something* and I just turned around and looked at this person and I *knew* it was her. We then spent the day together, talking about things. She told me the day I was adopted was the worst day of her life. She tried to keep me, but it wasn't possible. It was just too hard and obviously, I never blamed her for any of it because I understood the circumstances. And then, after that, her family was really welcoming and I was sort of leading another life, a double life at that stage. I couldn't tell my mum any of this; it was very strange that I was with these people that I was related to – blood relatives, who I'd never known – and then I had my mum who was always my mum. It was very difficult. It was another bit of deception in a way … It was deception. I did feel guilty about it, but I did have to embrace it. We went on like this for maybe a couple of years until the auntie breached my confidential disclosure. In one way, I was relieved that Mum knew but not the way it came about, and then my brother doing all the stirring up – that didn't help our relationship at all.

"He did the same thing when he found his family. He didn't seem bothered about knowing his family. Maybe that was the difference between us. He'd say things to Mum like 'She's got her other family now, but you've got me.'

"I have other half-sisters and brothers, but I kept this very close and I thought it was a shame that we couldn't all be friends, but there's so much going on emotionally. It's such a highly charged dynamic.

"I know that some of the carers in the mother and baby homes were intentionally cruel, but Jilly never told me anything like that. Except I did get to find out that she was in labour with me for twenty-seven and a half hours. I only discovered that a few years ago because I was power of attorney for her and I saw all her medical records. She had dementia and even when I went to see her in the care home, she suddenly grabbed hold of me and said, 'I tried to keep you, I wanted to keep you. I tried to get you back,' and I wasn't expecting that. I thought maybe she wouldn't remember me due to the dementia but that isn't what happened. I felt that we had been cheated, not having the best relationship, particularly with her, one of the nicest people on the planet. She was in a good care home and she was being well looked after; she wasn't there for very long, about four months, and then she had a massive heart attack and that was it."

There was such an obvious bond between Jane and Jilly, and I put this to her, and Jane said, "Oh, yes. Vic, my late husband, always said I laugh just like Jilly, which makes me feel nice. It's another connection. We definitely got on straight away. We didn't have to work at it. It just came very naturally and the whole family – her family – were so very supportive."

I asked Jane whether they discussed the fact that Jilly had been raped. Jane said she had never even guessed that could be the case. "I just assumed she'd maybe had a relationship and it hadn't worked out. In fact, she wrote me a card to tell me what it happened, and that she didn't really have a lot of choice and that she really did want to keep me. At the time it was really hard, and everyone would've known in the small town she lived in. I suppose she was protecting me. Anyway, I probably had a better life being adopted than I might have done if I'd stayed with her as a single mum. Her mother's partner had just left, so there was a lot going on. And there were other young people to look after."

Jane describes her parents as being working class, but in good jobs and that gave her a very solid foundation. Jane has always identified as being working class. "That's where I get a lot of my politics from, their ethics. From what they believed in; they were just good people. My dad was very encouraging. He always urged me to become educated because they didn't themselves have much of an education. They were very encouraging – not pushy."

Jane tells me that Jilly went into Woodside mother and baby home in Plymouth. "That's where my parents went to collect me. My mum did say that she saw somebody hovering around and she thought it might have been Jilly. You would do that, wouldn't you? After all, Jilly didn't know what my parents would be like, whether they would be decent people or not. You're just not told anything, it's unbelievably cruel."

We discussed how difficult it is to access files and paperwork, which is so vital to unravelling the past and understanding who you are, and the sequence of events that led her mother into the home and then into an adoption process. We reflected on the fact that it takes individuals a long time to get to the point where they can move forward – to get hold of information – *and* to be able to make sense of it.

"Everything feels like it's difficult," Jane says. "You've already had a battle internally with your own emotional self before you ever get as far as getting your files or getting in touch with an organisation or social workers. You want to do your best, but there are so many conflicts, and it throws up so many things. Will I want to know this? Is it a good idea? You just don't know, but in the end, for me, it became an overwhelming driving force. I thought, why don't I just do it, and just deal with whatever comes out of it, and luckily it was okay. There were issues with my mum obviously. But in terms of finding Jilly, it was one of the best things I ever did. I don't regret that at all and wish I had done it sooner. Life gets in the way, then you overthink it. Wondering if you're going to hurt a lot of people, but sometimes we just must act. And I felt better for knowing it, meeting my family. I've got my family tree and, in fact, my grandmother was a cockney, which is amazing because I had this huge pull for London, and ancestors that worked at Chatham on the Rope Walk. And you do feel like your jigsaw puzzle is complete. You know where all the bits go."

I offered Jane, as I offered to everybody, the opportunity to make the rendition of her story completely anonymous.

Jane said, "I don't want that, because I feel we have been anonymous for too long. It's not going to hurt anybody, Jilly is dead. My mother is dead. I just think it's so important. She was anonymous for so long and she felt guilty. There was no justice, of course, because he [her rapist] should have been in prison, and he's done this to a lot of other women. He was the most awful character and should have spent a lifetime in prison. He hasn't.

"Nothing happened to him and, in that respect, there was no justice, so having an apology is part of that justice. An apology for Jilly would be good."

I thanked Jane for her thoughtful insights, and her bravery in sharing this story, and went on to reassure her that I would seek a further meeting with the relevant shadow minister. I would use Jane's testimony and others to impress upon the minister, the need for an apology as soon as possible.

Jane shared my fear that an apology from the anticipated Labour government couldn't be relied upon and said, "It's not important enough – I don't mean to those of us that are involved – I mean to the political establishment."

As the interview was closing, Jane revealed something powerful. She told me her name was Sibson, not Pulford, and that she had changed her name to her mother's name when she gained her Equity card. She admitted that she had to change her name, in any case, and that this was an identity issue for her as well. I put it to Jane that by doing that (using her mother's name), she was really honouring Jilly.

Jane explained, "As an actress in improvisations, I would often use my mother's name as a character. I was making my mother part of me, in the only way I could at that time. It's almost like your life only begins when you're adopted and you're given a new name. Before that, you're in some sort of limbo, not existing." She then tells me her first name was actually Karen and that she has a special affinity with other Karens … Another connection. Finally, Jane said, "There's so many stories that need to be told; there's been so much repression." I couldn't agree more.

Nickie

"You're going to do what you're told to do,
especially if you're in trouble or in disgrace."

"I don't think they understand to be very honest, and I think they would take it very personally." Nickie was speaking about her adoptive parents and how she didn't want them to know she was contributing to this book. "I decided to write it all down, and I wrote and wrote; it was very therapeutic."

"Like a record for your own children?" I suggested.

"Yes, exactly, that's why I wrote it. I want them to know."

Nickie explains how her adoption journey unfolded for her. "I was fifty-two at the time. It was October 2020, during Covid. I received this lovely envelope, very posh, and inside there was a nice handwritten note and I thought it was a lovely wedding invitation, something nice. I opened it up and inside I saw 'Adoption Tracing and Intermediaries Services.' I thought what on earth is this? It contained a letter that said someone was looking for me and asked me to call a number … It said it was genuine. I didn't know what to do with it.

"I wanted to know about my past; I had thought about looking … but it has always been a secret. We never talked about it. Never talked to anyone. My husband knew, but we didn't discuss it. I felt guilty for even reading the letter. I put it in a drawer. But I was curious and I took it out on the rare occasions I was alone in the house – difficult during Covid.

I sat in a corner where nobody could see me and I phoned the number. They said, 'You know what this is about?' I said, 'Yes, I'm adopted,' and they explained, 'It's about your birth mother. She's looking for you.' I was dumbstruck but also pleased. They said there's a letter for you from her and they emailed it to me, and it was the loveliest letter.

"She explained she was sixteen when she became pregnant, and living in Singapore with her mother and father, her father being in the RAF. She was sent back to the UK in disgrace; she had me and then had to give me away. She wrote, 'I never wanted to give you away, but I had no choice,' and said she'd regretted it ever since, and she wanted to make it up to me. I wrote back to her and sent a few more letters. But I didn't hear anything back and I thought she doesn't want to know me after all. But then the agency contacted me, and it turned out that she'd had a stroke, and had also suffered a stroke years previously and she was no longer able to write.

"She was living in north Scotland. Eventually, we spoke on the phone several times and discussed meeting up in the summer once the restrictions for Covid were lifted. We made our plans. I had so many questions about her and her family. She said, 'Don't worry, I'll tell you everything when I see you,' adding, 'I'm going to work hard on my physio to make sure I can get out and about with you.' We had such lovely telephone conversations.

"In March 2021, I had a phone call from one of her friends who told me she was extremely ill, in hospital, with hours to live. Of course, we still had all the Covid restrictions in place. There were no flights to Scotland. I said to myself you know what I'm going to do? I'm going to get in the car and I'm going to drive. I was in flight or fight mode. As I live in southern England, I drove through the night. It was illegal due to the Covid restrictions, and I did get stopped and asked why I was in breach of the restrictions. I explained I was travelling to see my dying mother and no action was taken. An hour before I arrived, I received a call saying that she passed away."

Nickie explained that her own family, her children of fourteen, fifteen and seventeen, had no idea what was going on. "My departure up to Scotland was the first thing they knew about my background. Of course, I had been talking to my mother – Chris – on the phone. But I didn't know enough about her and I wanted to wait until I'd got a clearer picture before talking to them about my mother, and suddenly there was no more time left. My husband was left to explain where I'd gone – and why. They were really moved by it. My youngest was very upset that she never met her grandmother.

"I continued my journey and went to her house, and from there, I pieced together her story through meeting her stepdaughter, my cousins, and my uncle who had married her sister. He knew the full story. So, I was able, little by little, to piece the story together. What had happened was, she was sent back to stay with relatives, and her father refused to ever let her return to Singapore because he was awaiting a promotion, which he wouldn't get if she returned. Obviously, the promotion was far more important than anything else.

"She was sent to stay with family, one of her mother's seventeen siblings near to or on RAF Holton, which had a big hospital. She had explained to me in her letters that she was passed around from a social worker to an adoption counsellor, back to a welfare officer, and then to a social worker. She was told that she would be able to nurse me in the hospital, but her parents decided this wasn't a good idea, because she might get too attached to the baby, so she wasn't allowed to. I remember her telling me that she was told that she could nurse me, but she was only allowed to hold me for a few seconds, then I was taken away from her.

"She said, 'I never saw you again and I didn't even know this was going to happen and this was all arranged without my knowledge.' It's awful. She was sent away to a country that she didn't know. It must've been horrendous for her. Back in Singapore, her sister who is three years older than her became pregnant two months later, and she was also sent back to the UK, but when she was leaving the family home, there were two cars waiting for her, one was our father's, the other was her boyfriend's parents' car. She got into her boyfriend's parents' car. My mother's sister went to live with them, and she ended up marrying and keeping her baby. Whereas my poor mother didn't have that option. All her life, she was reminded of me by this other child who was almost identical in age."

Nickie provides some context about life in Singapore. She explained to me that at the time there were thousands and thousands of soldiers. "They weren't allowed to mix with the locals, so there were very few western women that they were allowed to mix with, so my mother and sister were easy targets. The weirdest thing is my adoptive parents were also in Singapore when I was conceived; they've got no idea about this. It's bizarre. I have tried to figure out if they might have known each other.

"It turned out that my birth father was also in the army. He would've been driving officers around and I guess their paths may have crossed. I think my grandfather pulled strings and had him returned to the UK in disgrace. When he returned to the UK, he got married very quickly, and within a couple of months they had a baby, six months after I was born – my half-sister.

"I have three siblings on my natural father's side. I'm just getting to know them.

"My adoptive parents went to the Oxford Diocese for 'moral welfare' – I think it was called. It blows my mind that! How moral is it to take a baby from its mother? The agency tried to match us as closely as possible. Mum – Chris – told me they tried to match by looks. She had red-golden hair, and my mother would say you've got red highlights in your hair and your birth mother did too. Also, the forces liked the fact that my mother was a very good swimmer and so was my birth mother. She never said that they were from Singapore. I don't think she knew that, nor that I would sneak into my dad's study and look at my records.

"I was about twelve when I discovered my original name and my birth mother's name on the documents, and some of the letters from the adoption agency to my parents. My mother had been asked to send a photograph of me to the agency so they could send it on to my birth mother, who had requested one. I don't know what my adoptive mother wrote back, but then there was another letter from the adoption agency, which said, we know that you don't feel happy about sending us a photograph, but it would really help.

"My mum obviously didn't want to send this photograph and I never knew if my mother sent one or not until I got up to Scotland, and it was there, my natural mum had the photograph and kept it all her life.

"The matching process is strange: it is as if you're just going to be able to settle down and settle in and carry on with your life. I never felt that I fitted in. I had a brother who was also adopted. All my life I wanted to look *like someone*. It was so important to me and now I'm finding people that I do look like. This September, I went to my birth cousin's wedding, and they were all saying, 'Oh, you look so much like your mother and your grandmother.' It was so nice to hear and they were so easy to get along with. We have the same sense of humour."

Nickie mentions that she's just received some photographs from her birth father's sister and "her daughter looks just like my daughter! That's really nice to see."

The shared traits go beyond looks. Nickie explains, "My mother apparently was a good writer and I have always liked writing too. And my children also are very good at it. Also, cooking. My birth mum was a great cook and that's what I love doing. It was great to go to her house and see all of her cookery books."

I asked Nickie what an apology would mean to her. She replied, "I think it's important for Chris, even though she's not here anymore. It's really for her. She said she wanted more children, but she never had another child. I think it altered her life hugely and for me, but I never knew my family ..."

Nickie is upset at this point, and it's hard not to feel tearful with her as the emotions are so strong, so raw and the injustice is so great. "I didn't know any of my family. I didn't grow up with any of them. I don't know any of the family stories. I don't have that heritage. I'm not really part of that family, and I'm not really part of my adopted family, do you know?"

I asked Nickie how her adoption experience might have impacted the development of her own family. "I wanted a big family. The thing that really impacted me was that I was sent to boarding school, so I was absolutely adamant that I was going to be at home with my children and they were not going to be sent anywhere. I was going to be there for them because I always felt nobody was there for me. I felt abandoned twice. I was going to be the mum that was there when they needed me."

I asked Nickie if the lack of a family had left her feeling less grounded? "I found the beginning very difficult," she tells me. "For instance, I had postnatal depression with all of my children. I don't know why. I really struggled at the beginning."

I wondered if Nickie had told her children that she was adopted. "I did tell them when they were very little, and then I didn't talk about it anymore. There was a time before I was in touch with Chris, when we were sitting around having Sunday lunch and the issue of adoption came up in conversation, and I said, 'Well, you know I'm adopted?' And they said, 'What!' They had completely forgotten; it had gone out of their minds and they were completely shocked. And I felt awful because I replicated exactly the pattern my adoptive parents had set and not talked about it. But not intentionally to keep it secret, but just because we didn't talk about it.

"I knew I was adopted. I was told as a small child, but then after a while, it was never mentioned again until I was around the age of ten. We never talked about it anymore. It then became uncomfortable, and I felt I couldn't talk about it."

I asked about Nickie's brother. She told me they discussed it recently. "He said, 'Do you ever remember having a conversation about being adopted?' and I said, 'Yes, I remember one conversation when I was in the bath, and that was when my mum told me about Chris's hair, my hair, and the swimming and why I was chosen, and he said he'd had a very similar conversation when they were in the car, Mum told him a little bit. A little bit like a sex talk – you do it once and then you never mention it again.

"My brother's adoption was organised privately through my mother's doctor. She'd visited her doctor due to difficulty conceiving, although they'd only been married for two years. He said to her, 'I know someone who is about to have a baby, who doesn't want it and you can have that one.' Isn't that terrible? Isn't that awful? That was 1965. That doctor became my brother's godfather."

I was shocked by this disclosure of the private arrangement, appalled at the idea of handing a baby over from its birth mother to a set of parents, who a doctor decided was suitable. Who knows what the real motive was? I wondered what record-keeping was required at that time and what safeguarding protocols were in place both for the baby but also for the mother.

I also found the quasi-eugenic presumptions that were at work within Nickie's adoption shocking. The attempt at matching physical features, especially hair colour and aptitude – such as swimming – and of course the idea that they were all 'service' families. As if this might make the whole family work and somehow gel. It seems faintly hysterical in today's climate.

Nickie concluded by saying how she looked at her own teenage daughters now and saw how easy it would be to make them do what a responsible adult thought was best for them. She couldn't imagine that they would be able to stick up for themselves if they were in that sort of situation. She says, "Of course, you're going to do what you're told to do, especially if you're in trouble or in disgrace." Which is exactly how coercive control works, exploiting the imbalance of power.

Wendy

"It's well recognised in America that adoption attracts narcissists."

Wendy was born in the early 1970s and is now in her early fifties. Wendy began our discussion by asking to remain anonymous.

"I'm still dealing with a shedload of shame, and this is very much a secret." She explains, "I didn't have a good adoption. I was, in fact, adopted by very coercive and very controlling parents. I realise now this isn't unusual – I've had to educate myself. Both of my adoptive parents have now died. I nursed both of them right until the end.

"I reached a stage in my life as an adult, when you think someone else's behaviour is just not right, and it cannot always be my fault. I cannot always be such a bad person, surely? With that in mind, I googled my adoptive mother's behaviour – if you start googling someone else's behaviour, you know instinctively that that behaviour is wrong. So, basically, in my late forties, I used the web to research my late adoptive mother's behaviour, and straight away, it revealed that she was a narcissist. I didn't even know what a narcissist was … I read everything – it was like reading my life. Then I found a blog by Lynn Grubb, called *Narcissism and Adoption*. It's well recognised in America that adoption attracts narcissists."

"What do you mean?" I asked.

"Think about it. If you're going to take somebody else's child, you've got to not care about the birth mother; you are going to want to create this fairy tale of what this child is going to be. You're going to *make* this child; you're going to *mould* it. It's going to be what you want it to be. It's called magical thinking. When I read this, I was like, my God, this has been my entire life!

"I don't believe in adoption at all now. I think guardianship is better, so the child always has the option of turning to its birth mother and father. Nor do I believe that a child should have to change identity. A narcissistic adopter person wants to change all those things."

Thinking about narcissism and adoption, Wendy continues, "They – my parents – couldn't have their own children, which is why they decided to adopt. Because a narcissist lives a fantasy life – that's part of the syndrome – they have a clear idea of what you – the adoptee – should be like. But the ideal is something that you can never attain because it's magical, mythical, and you're going to be this perfect thing. Well, nobody is perfect, are they? So, you are basically a constant disappointment …

"Unfortunately for me, I had two narcissistic parents. What I've learnt about narcissists is that they need what's called a 'flying monkey', that is the person who the narcissist relies on to support their behaviour. In my case, the 'flying monkey' was my adoptive father, and although my mother's behaviour was completely unreasonable, and as I became older, I would say so, he would say, 'I don't care! You go along with what she says. Do as you're told, be a grateful little girl, after all that we've done for you and how we've saved you.' What they did was they weaponised my adoption, to make me more compliant.

"I would always be scared. When I was little, I distinctly remember my adoptive mother telling me 'a lady in a suit came to see me today and told me if you don't behave she will come back and take you away!' The sheer terror that came over me, that I was going to be taken away again, was just horrific."

Wendy gives me another example. "For instance, one of my work colleagues was adopting and although I deliberated about telling her that

I was adopted, in the end, I told her, 'I am an adopted adult,' and she responded, 'That's fantastic. Can you tell me how I can stop this child from making enquiries about her birth mother when she gets older?' I was horrified by her approach.

"For adoption to work in our society, you've got to have people that are prepared to take somebody else's child. If the person that takes these children has got no accountability, doesn't care about the birth mother, doesn't even want you to speak about your birth family, you're not going to be able to know yourself. Even now most people adopting are narcissists. Organisations like *Adoption UK* don't want to hear about it.

"I think that social services should only encourage the sort of people to adopt that will actively support adopted children to find their birth mother and parents. Because that's your right: it's your actual identity, but we are still encouraging the wrong sort of people to adopt – those who want to stop you from fully knowing your identity and heritage."

Wendy was also very concerned about practices currently in place at adoption agencies. These concerns include safeguarding and data breaches. "You are being given a new identity which you own until you want to relinquish it, but what I've seen in some circumstances are breaches of that process. I've also raised this with others, the difficulty of being adopted by a narcissist and they appear to agree with me. I am not the only one who feels and thinks this way. One adopted adult told me that her adoptive mother shamed her and gave her the silent treatment – that is so familiar to me.

"I know pressure is still being applied to young mothers today. They're still told, 'You're not good enough, you're not worthy, give your baby up to better parents.' This is especially true when a woman might have a mental health crisis." Wendy explained to me about a young mother she'd seen on TikTok who'd had her baby removed from her because she suffered a mental health setback. Wendy makes it clear to me that only the baby was taken and put up for adoption; the other older children were left with their mother.

Wendy continued, "This young woman went to social services and asked if they could help her with her child while she got better, which she should be congratulated for, but instead, it cost her baby. They took her child. She also has other children but they didn't take those. Only the baby. The baby is at a premium. My question would be why, if she's got several children, have they only taken the baby? Because the baby is easier for adoption purposes. It's scandalous." It's hard not to disagree.

We moved on to the topic of counselling, which Wendy said she would like, but "there was an Ofsted ruling that means I can only use a counsellor that has extra training in adoption. I understand that decision and it's great to have the specialism, but unfortunately, very few people have undertaken the training. I'd have to travel impossibly long distances to take up counselling. But if I had a crack cocaine habit, I could walk into counselling tomorrow! Because I'm adopted, I'm not allowed any, because the number of counsellors with adoption training is so few it effectively serves as a barrier."

During my interviews with adopted people, it was very evident that counselling and therapy were needed and often sought. Usually, the individual bore the cost. One woman I interviewed, who is a similar age to Wendy, was offered counselling, but only if she would state explicitly that she was feeling suicidal. She was unable to 'tick that box' and so has forgone access to any therapeutic process and much-needed support.

Wendy points out that adopted adults are four times more likely to kill themselves. Other adopted people I have spoken with have claimed psychiatric wards have a disproportionate number of adopted adults on them. I feel sure that might be the same case amongst the mothers forced to surrender their babies. I can't imagine the trauma that they go through being forced into giving up a baby. There are, as we have seen, suicides and suicide ideation, amongst women in this cohort.

"This whole thing is driven by shame," Wendy says. "I was massively shamed throughout my childhood. And I still feel it now even though it isn't my shame to carry. And I recognise that but getting it off my shoulders is easier said than done. I have started taking baby steps and approached certain people – it's why I've reached out to you for this interview. It's not the sort of thing I've done before. I'm not here to educate people; I want to talk to people who are already switched on.

"We really need that apology because it will validate us. Most of us have been hugely gaslit – often by professionals. What I want them to say is, 'You're right that is what happened, and it wasn't right.'

"Adoption is the only trauma that is celebrated by society. If you tell someone that you've been adopted, they say, 'Oh, how lucky for you. I bet you've had a wonderful life?' I think to myself what if I told somebody my parents are dead, then they would say, 'Oh, how terrible.' But it's the same thing – you're still separated from your parents. Whether they're gone voluntarily or not, you've still been taken from them as a baby. I've witnessed this when I was on a work Zoom call with colleagues and one said, 'Don't mind my little one. I've just adopted him.' And everybody joined in, 'Oh, that's wonderful' and 'You're such an amazing person for doing that.' All I could think of was how this child had been stripped from its own mother! It's not an okay thing to be celebrating. There will be some cases, where there is no option other than adoption, but that still doesn't make it a cause for celebration. In my opinion.

"I think there have to be really extenuating circumstances where a baby or young one is taken away from its family and given a new identity, such as imminent danger, which I think would be rare. I don't think adoption should still be going on."

Wendy referred me to an article in *The Sun* newspaper, 'ADOPTION HELL. We adopted two brothers, but 8 years later we gave one back.' 23 January 2024. The report had caused Wendy distress and she felt sure the mother at the centre of the story was a narcissist.

Whilst I am not a fan of diagnosing others, and I have no psychology qualifications, I could see her point. The article highlighted the adoption of two children aged four and eight, and explained that the adoptive parents were unable to cope with the behaviour of the eldest boy and he was returned at sixteen to care. But that is the thing about children – they can be extremely badly behaved; adolescence is often a particularly turbulent time, and most parents know, understand and tolerate this. And frankly, have to put up with it, because they cannot send their own children away. Children at all ages and 'stages' can be extremely difficult and challenging. There should be no shying away from that fact.

Wendy, clearly shaken by the story, continues her analysis. "They've got the *scapegoat* and the *golden child* in the story. The scapegoat is always bad, always trouble, and the mother makes a point that the older child took a video of her naked in the shower, and then shared it with other children. What wasn't taken into account by the mother was that when children are adopted, they are quite often not at their chronological age, but at an earlier developmental stage. So maybe this child was developmentally younger and he would find the circumstances funny. The adoptive mother seems not to have taken account of that. She's clearly been giving him the vibes that he's not wanted, he's not welcome and he is, in return, misbehaving. Now, she has given him back and he is sitting in a care home. The authorities should have been asking the mother why she wasn't bonding with the child."

Wendy provides examples of children from different parts of the world who were apparently picked out for adoption and didn't even have their own birth certificates. There is a certain sort of zeal around this issue of rescuing children – a sort of colonial approach which, mixed with the possible narcissism of the adoptive parents, renders life toxic for the adoptee. The opposite of the popular narrative.

Wendy continues, "Like most other adult adoptees, I didn't really start to look at the issue of adoption until I was older. And even where some adoptive parents are open about the adoption, it's often with the caveat that the child never speaks about it again, which isn't useful to the child. The average age a grown-up child starts to trace their birth parent is 48."

Wendy tells me she had a non-biological adopted sibling who is three years older than her. "My take on the situation is that he wasn't the ideal child. Developmentally, he was younger than his age because of trauma and therefore they then adopted me because I was a baby, and they had a lot more control – he then became the scapegoat.

"There's also triangulation to contend with. My adoptive mother did that throughout my life. We were pitted against each other. He would hit me and I would run to her crying to say he'd hit me, and she would then feel powerful. He was treated very badly. They actually asked him to leave home at fifteen. He was a child, and he was forced to live on the street. They had money – that wasn't an issue. I didn't really have a relationship with him at all – he spent a lot of time in his bedroom. He had behavioural issues. They didn't address these issues because they weren't really interested … and they didn't really want me to have a relationship with him. After they kicked him out, I was told that I couldn't have a relationship with him at all and, if I did, they said they would disown me too. I was ten or eleven and that fear was enormous. *I didn't want to be thrown out as well.* I was just a child."

Wendy describes how she established contact with her sibling later in life and that it wasn't wholly successful. Like her, he had finally traced his birth mother, only to find that she had committed suicide. Wendy described her adoptive brother as an eight-year-old trapped inside a big guy. "It's an odd relationship. He is very much a stranger to me. I was hoping that we could connect, but we can't. The gulf between us is just too huge to bridge.

"My adoptive mother was also somewhat of a sadist, not in a physical way, but she liked to cause emotional pain. She was also partly a psychopath and a sociopath. When I first researched these personality traits, it was like a light bulb going on. I suddenly realised what the hell went on: the gaslighting, you're difficult, you're this, you're that, you should be grateful and so on.

"In fact, she coerced me into my first marriage; I didn't want to get married, because I had aspirations. I wanted to go to sixth form and on to university. If I'd done that, then I would've left home and that wasn't what she wanted, because I was there in case they needed me. When I was in my mid-thirties, I asked her, 'Why did you have children?' She replied, 'Because when we get old, we're going to need somebody to look after us.' It made me feel like a possession and that was how I was treated. She would've looked at me like I was a chair – so long as I was useful, I was wanted. I don't believe she regarded me with any empathy.

"People like my adoptive mother don't want to know about 'issues'. They're not going to give you the information, attention, the love you crave and need.

"How are we going to get across to people what went on then and what's going on now?" Wendy asks. "I think about my work colleague. I asked her if she'd had any psychological assessment and she said, 'Oh, we've been to a couple of sessions to hear from people who have gone through the process of adoption.' I asked her if she'd spoken to any people that had actually been adopted. No, she said. She explained they couldn't get an adopted person to participate. I know that's rubbish because I have approached various organisations offering to do exactly that. I have offered to tell prospective adoptive parents what adoption is like first-hand. They said no. I wonder why that was?"

Could it be true that these organisations only want people involved in the adoption process that stay on script? Only want people who say the least controversial things? That adoption was the best thing that ever happened to them? About how grateful and lucky they are?

Wendy resumes her story, "As children, we can't verbalise or necessarily understand everything we see, but as a child, I knew I didn't like what was going on around me. I knew that I had to mirror her behaviour or I would be in trouble! For instance, if she walked into a room, I'd be looking to read her facial expressions to make sure that if she was looking like she was sad, then I knew I would have to say, 'Are you okay?' That's parentification – when the child becomes the parent – that's basically what I did to survive.

"It breaks my heart. I had to marry who she told me to marry, and it took me a long time to get out of that relationship because of all my problems with attachment. It was very difficult for me to walk away. Many of the adopted people I've spoken with know that dealing with the impact of being adopted is like opening Pandora's box – you know there's going to be so many difficult issues to address. You need a very strong support network around you. In my case, that came from my husband. If you haven't got support, you're on an island on your own."

I wondered how Wendy had gone about tracing her birth mother. She informed me an adoption agency she approached charged £3,000 to start the tracing process. Wendy wryly points out, "It seems as though somebody is making money from the adoption industry at every stage.

"When we started looking for my biological parents, we were expecting a scenario of a young person. But in fact, my birth parents were twenty-four years old when they gave me up and they married shortly after. They didn't come back for me. I have been in contact with them, it didn't go well … I was in contact with my birth father, first of all. I received such a curt response to my carefully worded email seeking confirmation that he may be my biological father. It more or less said, 'Yeah, that's me. What do you want?' I sent more emails; I really wanted to understand more about my adoption and why I was given away … Then I received a very blunt email. 'By the way, you've got half-brothers and sisters and you can contact them on Facebook if you want.' I found this so inappropriate; I didn't feel able to contact anybody like that on Facebook. I thought it was clear that he really didn't want to connect with me.

"I left my search for a couple of years. Then I found an uncle and made contact. He was very judgmental, asking, 'Why are you making contact now, having left it so late?' He also said he was glad that I'd been in touch because he was getting quite old and would need somebody to take care of him! I didn't pursue that relationship.

"I left it another year, and then I approached my birth mother. This didn't go well … She essentially said that I needed to send her a photograph and that she *might* then send me something. It felt very transactional and blunt. I didn't like that degree of control. I didn't *owe* her anything and I didn't have to give her something to get something back.

"I've been abandoned by both my adoptive parents and my birth parents, which isn't something that's spoken about in society today, but also I lost out on broader family connections. On one occasion more than forty years ago, I recall going to an uncle's house. He said, 'We will welcome you in part of the family – for today.' It was a temporary situation and it was made clear that I wasn't really part of the family."

Wendy believes this vindictive statement was reinforced by a vindictive act many years later. As Wendy explains, "When my adoptive mother was in hospital terminally ill, they [her adoptive mother's family] sent a solicitor to her bedside to change her will, to ensure they were made beneficiaries … She abandoned me again after a lifetime of servitude to her. They didn't care about the impact on me. The impact on me was dreadful. I was so hurt I suffered from suicide ideation and my husband effectively saved my life. I dropped into a chasm of hopelessness, feeling that I couldn't live with this horrible realisation. Gradually, I came through it, but I really do feel that if he hadn't been there then – one hundred percent, I would've killed myself.

"I did everything I could for them, and when she died, I didn't feel a thing. But I had the satisfaction of knowing I'd been true to my own moral code and done the right thing. I can put my head on my pillow at night and sleep.

"My mother always used to say to me, 'I'm not surprised you were given away, you nasty child,' and even later on, in my thirties, my adoptive father said to me, 'What sort of a cunt gave birth to a woman like you!' Overall, I can only conclude that they didn't really like me, and it was my misfortune to be passed from one set of parents, who obviously didn't care too much about me to another set of parents who were narcissists, and who failed to care for me emotionally. And the State failed to notice that lack of care."

Wendy's experience is alarming; after our conversation my determination to challenge the stereotype was affirmed. Adoption isn't always successful. I wonder what care was taken to ensure prospective adoptive parents were suitable for the most demanding role of being a parent, and what support was available to them.

Anna

"My mother was looking for a perfect daughter, but I could never be that because I wasn't from her ..."

Anna's experience is as complex as it is shocking – dreadful by today's standards where young women are more self-aware and cognisant of their rights. It's hard to imagine how only a few decades ago, society was so indifferent to the rights of the individual. The way Anna was treated, the way she was manipulated, and the way in which she had no voice is appalling. Anna was utterly unable to raise the questions she desperately wanted to ask.

In common with many of the young women dispatched by their families, or their church, social workers and moral welfare officers, Anna and her baby were reduced to a problem to be hidden and disposed of. She was expected to comply, and after the trauma of birth and forced separation, Anna and the others in her cohort were expected to resume their lives as if nothing had happened. For most, decades of traumatic silence passed before they could speak out.

Over recent years, and perhaps with time, Anna has gained confidence and become successfully engaged in writing her life history, partly as a therapeutic process and partly because her story, like all of those on these pages, is a story that needs to be told. More than that, it needs to be heard.

Anna is seventy and was adopted at six weeks herself. She, like many young girls, fell pregnant and was sent away to a mother and baby home without choice, to endure and be blighted by the shame-inducing practices prevalent at that time. It was 1971 and she was sixteen years old. At just twenty-four, Anna had to have a full hysterectomy, which meant she was unable to have more children. The baby she had been forced to surrender was the only child she gave birth to – something she could never have foreseen. She, in turn, became an adoptive mother. If anybody understands adoption from a 360-degree perspective, it's Anna. I'm very grateful for her time and our conversations.

Anna and I really connected during our call and, immediately afterwards, I wanted to read the book that she'd written. Only then did I google her; here's what I found on her website, annaandersonbooks.com:

Survival Without Roots – Memoir of an Adopted Englishwoman

'Is there anyone out there who looks like me, talks like me or thinks like me?' This is a question that has plagued Anna throughout her life as she seeks to unearth the answers. Adopted as a baby in the 1950s, she grows up knowing she is an 'imperfect fit' for the 'mum' who raised her. Years of criticism, control and complete withdrawal of love, destroy Anna's self-esteem and affect her journey through life. Join her as she careers and swerves through the first eighteen years of searching for somewhere to belong. Will she find the resilience to survive her upbringing and the tragedies encountered along the way? Difficult roads often lead to beautiful destinations … or so they say. A story of fighting against the odds and hanging onto hope, resilience and determination.

Anna talked about her writing journey and how, when she started to write, her life became littered with notes, papers and scribbles. "As I started typing, the tears just kept spilling out of me. I kept my feelings locked in for all those years." She started to write because of her childhood, and the fact that she was adopted, realising as a child she wasn't the perfect fit for the mum who raised her. "She was just a cold, calculating, manipulative person. She controlled me completely, whereas my dad was lovely. He died when I was fourteen and then I turned into a rebel overnight. I'd had enough of the control … And I had been left with this woman who was not nice … All my life I have searched for a place to belong to and to be loved; she didn't offer that and I ended up making choices that were wrong.

"So, my first love and I were together for two years, and he was the father of my baby. I had kept this all inside of me for sixty-seven years. I haven't really spoken to anybody about it. When my adoptive mum died twelve years ago, it just hit me and I started writing … because I knew it was time to let it all out. And then I could start to heal.

"It was a lightbulb moment after that when I realised that my book would help other people as well. I developed a sense of pride about being able to help other adoptees, birth parents and adoptive parents.

"It's also put me in touch with other people who read my Facebook and I'm still in contact with them."

Anna and I acknowledge the power of writing, not only for catharsis but also as a process, which can assist in removing the memory blocks. As Anna says, "You're moving it from your heart onto the page … You don't understand at the time you're doing it, that it's going to help. When I was writing my book, the emotions were so strong. It was like I was writing about yesterday, not all those decades ago.

"I don't know the circumstances that led my birth mother to give me up for adoption. I was told two conflicting stories: one being that my mother had conceived me outside of her marriage, that she already had three children, and she was told that she had to have me adopted or she would be divorced. I don't know if this is true or not. I did meet her before she died, and she told me a different story. So, I don't know what led to my adoption, where I was adopted from, and I don't know who my father is. I don't have any information about what happened to me when I was a baby until I was adopted."

Anna tells me within her adoptive family she was the only child. She continues, "My mother was looking for a perfect daughter, but I could never be that because I wasn't from her. I was such a different person and we didn't get on from day one. I tried *so* hard, I just wanted her to be proud of me and love me, but nothing I did was good enough. It was always wrong; everything I said was wrong. If we were in company, she would introduce me, 'This is my Anna – my *adopted* daughter.' She would always pull me down. It was dreadful as if I wasn't good enough to be called her daughter. I realise now this has had a significant impact on the way I've developed. I just know the way she brought me up isn't really me. For instance, she was very much a 'social climber', aspiring to be middle class. I just knew I could never be like that. It just wasn't me. Mum's aspirations meant she liked to be on local community committees and her and my dad ran a greengrocers together.

"I hated the way she treated me. She slapped me every day and I used to wonder to myself, 'What have I done? I just walked past you!' Anyway, I've survived, which is why my book is called *Survival Without Roots*. I can still hear her voice in my head when I go to do something, I think to myself, oh, she wouldn't approve of this! But I'm a seventy-year-old woman and I'm going to do what the hell I like now." Anna sounds determined. She concludes by saying, 'I was manipulated, controlled and moulded into being a pink girl, and even though I was in a fluffy, frilly dress, I was a tomboy. She tried to manipulate me into something I could never be."

I found it very interesting that Anna had an innate character that could not be controlled or smothered. Anna agrees, telling me she was happiest when she was with her dad mending a puncture or washing the car. Whenever her mother asked her to write a Santa list, Anna always asked for boys' toys. None of these toys ever materialised, and her bedroom was full of dolls, which she had no interest in. Instead, she used the dolls to create a pretend family, the sort of family she really wanted to be in.

Anna's adoptive father died when she was fourteen, and her mother used this event – it appears – to exert a different level of control over her. Anna was not allowed to attend the funeral. She was denied the opportunity to say goodbye to him. Other children, contemporaries of Anna's, also lost parents around the same age and she recalls they were allowed the opportunity to attend the funerals, so Anna does conclude this was her mother exerting control. It's an example of different treatment – different, Anna believes, because she was an adopted child.

Anna elaborates, "It was pure power. She wanted another way to control me. There were instances where I thought she was jealous of my relationship with my father. I'm sure she didn't understand why I loved my dad. That turned me into a rebel. With my dad now gone, I was intent on finding love. Which is how came to meet my first love.

"It was an exciting time. I was introduced to the world of pubs and alcohol, which I enjoyed. I kept our relationship a secret, but after six months she found out about it. And she forbid me to see him, but that didn't work. Then I became pregnant but didn't tell anyone, not even my boyfriend, and for six months I just carried on as normal because I didn't believe it was happening to me. I still walked two miles to school and back.

"Eventually, I told him and he then volunteered to tell my mother while I hid around the corner. I didn't see him again after that. *She* took over. She took time off work and we went away to Leeds to stay with her sister who was as cold as my mother was. I stayed there for a couple of months until three weeks before my due date. I was taken into a mother and baby home called Fallodon Nursing Home."

An online search yields Alan Foster's entry on the Secret Leeds Facebook page:

Fallodon Nursing Home, 4 Allerton Park Leeds. These residences for unmarried mothers were humanitarian but experienced by the women living in the Homes as punitive. For some it was refuge, others imprisonment, and their only hope or a last resort. They are remembered with fondness, with horror, with pain, with distance. Most frequently the women who resided in these Homes arrived around six-weeks before their due date and remained about six-weeks after. Leaving after their babies had been adopted, whether they personally desired such a permanent separation. They were run by voluntary organizations, local authorities, and a range of religious groups including the Salvation Army, the Church of England, the Catholic Church, and more. The home no longer exists and flats now occupy this site.

Another entry states: "The cost of staying there in the late 1960s was twenty-two pounds a week." A sizeable amount back then. Anna's inheritance left to her by her father would have lasted around eleven weeks. Less, if you assume that she, like others, would have also provided a fee for fostering until the baby was adopted and a layette. She had no choice but to use this money.

Anna continues to describe what happened to her, "During this time, I managed to have some contact with my boyfriend on and off. He would call me at a public phone box at a pre-arranged time and I would wait outside for his call. On occasion, I would meet him at the library in Leeds. One day when I was expecting to see him, he didn't come on the day and it absolutely broke my heart. I didn't see him again for ages."

During this time Anna also studied for O-levels, and she says, "I had taken them in the dining room of my auntie's house with my aunt and mother invigilating. There was no social worker in the home I was in, in 1971. Twenty years later, I found out that I could have had financial support. Back then, you did as you were told. You had no choice.

"I went into the home with no money. My mother told me that my father had left me £250 for my twenty-first birthday, but I wasn't going to get that now because I'd been a bad girl and I had to cover the costs of being in the mother and baby home.

"There was an unmarried mothers' quarter in Fallodon, a well-to-do married mothers' quarter, and an abortion clinic. I was put into a room with three other girls. It was a godsend because we supported each other. We had physical chores to do from morning till night." Anna continues describing Fallodon, "It wasn't a prison. The door wasn't locked, but I knew I couldn't leave. I had to do manual work whilst I was there and I was asked to do things that I didn't feel safe and comfortable to do.

"Anna Anderson, nurse Anna – which is why I write under her name as a tribute to her – got me through the experience basically and she delivered my baby. She also gave me pain relief, gas and air, which she wasn't supposed to do because we were supposed to suffer. My baby exploded out of me, face upwards and came out and kind of sat up and faced me. It was quite extraordinary really. Then I was wheeled back into the room and I already knew that I was expected to start breastfeeding. But not my own baby, the other women's babies. You were never given your own baby to feed. We had to do that for about five days. At the time, it seemed unbelievable, but it wasn't unbelievable because we just had to do what we were told to do. And at that age and stage, I wasn't analysing what I was going through.

"The staff were cruel. They looked down on us and they told us how bad we were and that we should be ashamed of ourselves, and they would say, 'If you want the best for your baby, then you will give her up so she can have the life she deserves.' They just went on and on. Nurse Anna Anderson was the only decent one.

"There was no antenatal preparation; I didn't have a clue what was going to happen and, in fact, when my waters broke, I didn't dare to look under the covers to see if I'd actually had the baby, and Nurse Anna came and told me, 'No, it's not that easy,' and she explained about my waters breaking. That was the first time anybody explained anything to me. I didn't dare to ask any questions, I just put my head down and got on with it.

"After I'd given birth, my baby was taken straight to the nursery, and Anna broke the nursery rules for me so that I could say goodbye to her before she was taken. I went to the toilet and she came by and gave a secret knock, meaning the coast was clear for me to go into the nursery to hold my baby and to say goodbye. For that, I am forever grateful. There are no words to describe how it devastates your life.

"When I returned to my hometown, I was allowed to see my boyfriend – but I had to go onto the pill – I was made to wait five weeks, until the contraceptive was effective, before seeing him! He never mentioned our baby, and I couldn't believe that he could carry on as if nothing had happened. The relationship only lasted for one year more because I couldn't believe he never mentioned her. I came to hate him for that.

"After a week at home, I went back to school and, of course, the people that weren't supposed to know, did know. In class, one girl said, 'Oh, so was it twins then?' And I stood up in front of the whole class and said, 'No, it was triplets!' That was the first time I stuck up for myself."

Eventually, Anna settled down and perhaps because of her earlier experiences with both her mother, and in the mother and baby home, and being forced to surrender her baby, Anna found herself in relationships that were less than ideal. Through a set of coincidences using Friends Reunited, she contacted her first love and she also saw on the screen a person that she was convinced was her daughter. She described the experience of seeing this person as "a complete physical shiver. I just knew it was her."

Anna had been searching, but until the law changed in 1974 it was extremely difficult for a mother to track and find an adopted child. It transpires that Anna's daughter had also been trying to find her mother, but at that time, with what was a common surname, tracking and tracing were extremely difficult. Whereas her father – Anna's first love – had a much more unusual name and so that's how contact had initially been established between him and their daughter.

As is common in these situations, reunion is often far from straightforward. In many cases, parents of adopted children went forward into new relationships and many decades passed. And in keeping with the trend, and the advice of the time, parents quite often did not disclose the fact that they had previously had a child, nor that the child had been adopted. No one really anticipated the pull to be reunited, nor the occasionally explosive impact it had on families that were formed after.

For Anna, finding her long-lost baby gave her strength. It brought her a sense of self-belief and self-confidence that had previously eluded her.

Eddie

"Since I was three weeks old, I'd never actually looked at anybody else that shared any of my features."

I met Eddie in his local pub. He is clearly a man at ease with himself and the world. To all intents and purposes, Eddie is a very successful guy; he is well-regarded and well-respected in his local community. He's made a name for himself. To look at a man like Eddie, you would automatically assume he's had a joyfully uncomplicated life.

But life has been anything but easy for Eddie. As he congenially apologised for the likely disturbance and background noise – the ukulele band was just starting their weekly practice in the adjoining room – he gently told me his story. And what a story …

Our conversations started with Eddie explaining to me how much an adoption apology would mean to his mother, Christine. "She has told me many times over the years since we've been in reunion that she feels guilty. It's the guilt that's eating away at her and corroding her life. The irony is, if she'd been in Ireland, I would still have been taken from her and, I guess, she would've had a different kind of guilt. But in England, she *signed the papers*, she signed me away. In the correspondence, you can see that there is no record of her fighting to keep me."

Eddie went on to explain how his mother and father were together, but that both sets of parents didn't like the other because "Mum was from

Birmingham and Dad was from Portsmouth and Mum's parents were a bit sniffy about southerners."

Eddie continues, "Mum was seventeen and Dad was eighteen. She just turned eighteen when she had me, but they had this prejudice, and my mum's older brother, who was eleven years older, had got his girlfriend pregnant and brought her home. Their mum and dad said right, you're going to get married. There was a shotgun wedding, and they then sold the house and moved away to another part of Birmingham, so the neighbours couldn't work out the child was illegitimate. That was the level of shame we are dealing with. After that, her dad would say to her throughout her teenage years, 'Don't you ever dare shame us like your brother. Don't you ever dare do that.' Which, of course, is exactly what she did."

Eddie explained how his mum and dad met at Dudley teacher training school. "They had a mad love affair. Then rumours began to circulate around the college that she was pregnant, and inevitably she got called into the principal's office. She was asked if she was pregnant and she flatly denied it. Summer comes along, and Mum is relieved; she believes she can sort the situation out during the break from college. She knows she won't get any support from her own parents. And she's scared. She hitch-hiked to Yugoslavia with a friend." Eddie refers to a photograph of his mother sitting on the back of a hay-wain seven-and-a-half-months pregnant. He says his mother told him her plan was to give birth to him in Yugoslavia and to maybe leave him there ... "And that way nobody would know she'd had a child. Apparently, her friend knew someone who might be able to help them." Eddie pondered how somebody from Blackburn could have those kinds of connections.

Eddie's mum's plan didn't quite work out and with the end of the summer holidays, and September term-time beckoning, Eddie's mum, now heavily pregnant, and her friend hitch-hike back to the UK. She goes to see Brian, his dad. He spent the summer working on the roads in Portsmouth, trying to earn money because he wants to marry Christine and to look after them both. At this point, Eddie leans in towards me to tell me, "My dad is a really good man, a solid and honest, decent bloke. He was training to be a PE teacher, which eventually he did become. In the meantime, he was saving up money, playing football, hoping to marry my mum. In the meantime, Christine turns up, and Brian puts her up in an old pillbox – a fortification from the Second World War – hardly a place for a pregnant woman, or anyone, really! Dad was sneaking food out of his family kitchen to give to my mother who was staying in the pillbox – and his sister knows about this but is sworn to secrecy. They still don't know what to do, so she and her friend hitch-hike back to Blackburn. At this stage, Christine goes into a mother and baby home in Blackburn; the home is called The Grange; it's just outside Wilpshire on the A666."

Eddie tells me, "I later found out that The Grange mother and baby home was supported financially by a local brewery, Thwaites." Eddie, being a successful brewer himself, writes to Thwaites and thanks them for sponsoring his first home. He tried to make it jocular by saying he was sure that their accountant would be pleased they had supported a major competitor. He never received a response.

Eddie continues mapping out what happened. "That's how my mum ended up in The Grange. Then social workers were assigned (they were Church of England) and they persuaded Mum that she needed to go and see her parents. She went to Birmingham one Sunday night because she knows on Sunday nights all the curtains will be drawn. It's an early night for everyone; she's heavily pregnant and people in the street won't see her. She knocks on the door; her dad answers and slams it shut in her face! She must go back to The Grange. From then on, the writing is on the wall. With her parents turning their back on her, she can't legally get married, and she's got no support network.

"The correspondence that I've got details that Christine is a lovely girl; she's got her A-levels and she's got a place at teacher-training college. It also says she's beginning to understand that this is the best thing for baby. My mum remembers the staff at the mother and baby home as being lovely. She felt very secure there, and the other girls were great. The mothers were taught how to breastfeed – but then they weren't allowed to. She went to the Queen Alexandra Hospital, which is now no longer there. She remembers the shame and hiding under the covers, and all the other women 'tut-tutting' at her. The nursing staff were the same. She felt utterly isolated and shamed, to the extent that she hid herself away.

"She doesn't remember anything at all about my birth. Nothing, not even if it was painful or not. She couldn't even tell you what time of the day. She does remember afterwards not being allowed to breastfeed and I was only brought to her at feeding times. She was required to bottle-feed me and then I was taken away – that went on for three or four days. Then she returned to The Grange but not for very long. I was then sent away to a foster home and my foster mother, Mrs Green."

Eddie then tells me that he was adopted three or four months later. He explains, "I've only today looked at my file for the first time in almost ten years." He was conscious that it would make him emotional, possibly too emotional for our meeting, and although the tempo of our meeting was bubbly and jovial, and Eddie is a great raconteur, underlying the recounting of his mother's journey and his own baby days, there is deep sorrow and pain.

"The adoption agency that looked after me was based in Liverpool. The adoption worker who had been involved from the beginning instructed my mum to bring clothes for me – ready for the adoption. She hadn't seen me for three or four months, and *she must go out and provide me with the clothes* … Then, she has to come to the offices in Liverpool. The social worker then collects me from my foster mother in Lancashire and brings me to Liverpool, and my new mum and dad travel to Liverpool."

Picture the scene: in the room are the new mum and dad, George and Betty, Christine and the social worker, and presumably somebody from the adoption society. The social worker brings baby Eddie into the room and hands him to his new mum in front of his old mum. *Old* mum – birth mum – must then hand over the baby clothes. Then the birth mother gets up and leaves, catches a train and returns to Birmingham.

Eddie adds, "There's only one reason to do that and that is to ramp up the punishment. There's no legal reason to do it. It's just a horribly punishing thing to do to somebody …"

I asked what happened to Christine next. "She lost her place at teacher-training college, so the social worker's assertion that surrendering her baby for adoption would be better for her and better for the baby was completely wrong. The claims that she could carry on with her life and career came to nothing. More punishment in a way.

"Christine had a variety of jobs after that and did clerical work, probationary work, and she went into social work, and became a Labour city councillor. When I met her, she was a social worker with a brief on addiction and adoption – almost as if she's repeating a trauma cycle." Eddie thinks it's obvious that his mother is suffering from PTSD; she doesn't remember his birth, and she self-medicates with alcohol.

We talked about the impact of being adopted on Eddie. Even though he was on home turf, looking comfortable and talking about Christine very fluently, I knew this was going to be difficult. He'd already spent considerable years thinking – and feeling – his situation. He'd invested his time and energy in coming to terms with the impact on him. Even so, describing a perception of another person's experience is one thing – detailing your own visceral, often painful version, is quite another.

"I do remember my new mum, Betty, telling me that she wasn't my real mum. I can't remember where we were, what she was wearing, what I was wearing, or any details at all, not even my age."

He breaks off, "Look, if you asked me this question twenty-five years ago, I would've said I couldn't remember anything at all, but that was because I was in the business of not remembering. But I do clearly remember the utter horror of what she was telling me. It was the most horrifying thing anybody has ever told me. The next question was obviously going to be why? I remember thinking to myself. I am definitely not going to ask that question. And I never asked. That was it. I shut it down. Until I was thirty-nine.

"My new parents also sent me to boarding school in Blackpool, which compounded everything that I knew. I was good at school. Pretty quickly, it suited me. I became self-sufficient at boarding school and I stayed self-sufficient ever since. I also had an older brother and a younger sister – they were also adopted. My new parents were naïve and ill-informed as most adoptive parents were. There was no training for them and no support. I know that they were doing their very best for me.

"Betty would say, 'We chose you because you're special,' and even as a youngster, I would think that sounded really iffy. It was a very strange upbringing, and I knew it was very weird that these people I was growing up with were alien to me. There was no connection between us. There wasn't a huge amount of love in the house, but to be fair there was no abuse. My dad could be quite warm and loving but he wasn't around a lot, and we 'siblings' were also very different from each other. Mum and Dad weren't getting on, they adopted because they couldn't have children of their own. Dad hung around with my mum until the youngest of us was eighteen and then he left my mum.

"In my late teens, if I'd been a bit wild at university, I lost the plot as a young man. I didn't know who I was, as I clearly had an identity crisis. I thought the rest of the world was crazy, but it wasn't. It was me. I was the crazy one. I had every expectation of dying by the time I was thirty, and it would be either drink, drugs, or killed at work – and I was a mining engineer in one of the most dangerous professions you could do, and I had chosen it! Why had I chosen that?

"Then I met somebody who understood me a lot better than I understood myself. She kept me alive long enough to get me back on my feet. When she met me, I was at the nadir of my life. A few days before I met her, I was literally lying in the road in Holloway, covered in my own puke. And, also, I remember that my passions in life until that time had been football, cricket, and climbing mountains. I knew during that period of my life that I would never do any of those things again. There was a real sadness to me. I'd lost touch with my dad because he'd separated from my mum after twenty years.

"It wasn't until I did a lot of therapy that I realised I wasn't cool about the situation in the slightest. In fact, I was born with anxiety and I have lived with it every moment of every day of my entire life, but it's all relative because when everybody else gets stressed out, I stay the same. One of my ambitions is to learn how to relax. What has helped enormously is finding my mum and her family. The most relaxed I get is if my kids are around at home, or if I'm with my brother and sister, then I'm more relaxed. I think it's about connection and belonging.

"I was with my partner for nearly twenty years. I don't know why she chose me. She pulled me out of the gutter and got me back upright just with the force of her personality, just with her love. Sometimes I think she must've thought, 'Bloody hell, I've bitten off more than I can chew.'

"It goes back to that moment I was born and then taken away, and then brought back and taken away, and then brought back and taken away multiple times … And then finally, just taken away and given to somebody else, and then sent away to school.

"So, when Betty said I'm not your real mum, I thought, oh no, I'm not having that, so I just shut down. It was something I buried inside myself that was just too horrific for me to ever look at. I've visualised it as a box inside and I thought I'm not opening it, no way. And nobody else is either.

"And then, I had my first child, which I never expected, but it was what my partner really wanted. I had my daughter, and the moment I looked into her eyes – I don't know, everybody does this – and the world just disappeared, but for me, there was that extra special bit – she had my eyes! Since I was three weeks old, I've never actually looked at anybody else that shared any of my features. It's incredibly powerful.

"I used to think humanity was a family tree and that I was a leaf wobbling around mid-air unattached to any branch, and then suddenly I was attached to my daughter and my partner. It was profound. Now I had a connection to one who was connected to another and I was connected to them both. Five years later, we had a boy and he was also the apple of my eye."

I said I thought it must have been a beautiful experience, enhanced by the fact that he'd never seen anybody that he was related to before. If you stop and think about that, it's almost unimaginable, beyond the grasp of my imagination anyway, having been one of those 'ordinary' people who simply grew up in a family and took the notion of seeing yourself reflected in others for granted.

I wondered how Eddie started his journey to find his mother.

He said, "My partner never pushed me, but I was always conscious that if I ever wanted to go and find my mum and my roots, the support would be there for me, and she would be pleased that I'd made that decision. But I was always like … no, I'm fine! I've got my doctors here," Eddie indicates his pint. "But then, quite by chance, I read an article in *The Guardian* about the experience of a woman who had given a child up for adoption, detailed the circumstances, and her sadness and regret for the rest of her life, and the frustration that she can't do anything, and her longing for him to try to contact her. I started crying, and I wrote an email to this woman care of *The Guardian* straightaway and I said I'm very touched by your story. I could've been that boy, but I'm not as the years are wrong, and although I'm very touched, I don't think I will be going to look for my mum, but I was very moved. I went and told my partner about this and then said, right I'm going out for a pint. I walked twenty feet up the street; I was thirty-nine and I was about to climb Mont Blanc for my fortieth birthday. And I just changed my mind, I thought no, I'm going to find my mum. I went from denial into U-turn. I'd clearly been working through things in the background without recognising that.

"Then I threw myself at it one hundred percent. Years earlier my mum, Betty, had told me my name but I was drunk. My younger sister had gone to find her real parents and Mum was worried about her, and I reassured her she would be alright, and in that conversation, Mum asked me, 'Don't you wonder about yourself? I can tell you what your name was if you like.' I said yes and because I was drunk, in the morning the name was gone. I never asked again because it was symbolic of starting to open that box. I thought to myself, I'm not going to ask, I don't want to know, because I know what happens after that … I have to open the box if I start asking questions.

"After making that decision, the first thing I did was to call my dad George, and he said, 'All right, son, you've got a hundred percent support from me.' I said, 'Do you know what my name was?' and he said, 'It was Simon Bell.' I started a blog called *My Name is Simon Bell*. That was the moment everything changed. Life went from being huge turmoil, created by trying to avoid the turmoil created by avoidance turmoil.

"All shades of heaven and hell were let loose, and now it's kind of calmed down. That was sixteen emotional years ago." Our conversation deepens, and Eddie tells me he's "not the biggest emotional risk-taker," and that on some levels, he is still emotionally stunted. He clarifies, "I can't form a normal relationship. For some people that's okay – some people can understand that – but for most people, it's actually a nightmare, because if you're spending your life with someone who won't attach – who can't attach – that individual has to be pretty damn secure in themselves."

Eddie and his long-term partner, and mother of his children, separated. He tells me, now "the waters have calmed" and the process is complete, he is in an entirely different place, living with a new partner, with his grown-up kids all over the place and new family scattered everywhere.

He details his new family: "My mum's family, her husband, half-brother, half-sister, stepbrother, stepsister, my dad's two sons, and cousins. So, I've gone from being family-less to family all over the place. My kids at one stage had eleven grandparents, so they refuse to write them thank-you letters!"

We discussed trauma. "My early life trauma led me to having issues that made it very difficult to have any sort of stable existence. The only way I made it was through this incredibly stable and understanding person. The irony was, when I got to address my own problems, the relationship fell apart. We knew at the time that this happened to quite a lot of people going through what I went through. It was the last thing in the world I expected. It's a process of opening. Those boxes you go through, with these ridiculous waves of emotion, you're opening and looking at the stuff that you shut out years ago. And in those boxes are emotions and feelings. By letting them out and dealing with them, you become a different person. And when you're a different person you do different things. Especially if you go from being a person that never did emotion, to doing emotion. You are in a very vulnerable position and you have to open yourself up. When you're that vulnerable, it's a very exposing and dangerous place to be. I would fall in love four times a week. When you've got no training and no experience at being in this emotionally vulnerable position, it's really choppy waters. We'd buy books and read them and think about what was happening to me and how it impacted us, but in the end, it was like trying to teach astrophysics to a not particularly bright eleven-year-old."

I nod in agreement and say, "It's one thing reading books and understanding theories in your head. It's another thing feeling it."

Eddie tells me how he set about finding his birth mother. He started the blog, and he had a community of followers who came with him on his journey, from all around the world.

"I had to apply to the Office of National Statistics and I was like, for goodness' sake, I have finally come to this place in my life, have I not been through enough hardship? I thought to myself, can I not just ring somebody up and get answers – but no. You must apply to the ONS. Now, I thought I'm a statistic, not a person. I was told it would be six weeks before they would be back in touch. I was in turmoil. I was on the floor. I had kept everything bottled for thirty-nine years because that's what society expected me to do, and now I'm expected to wait even longer. That was the system. Six weeks was so long. It was three or four months before I got my birth certificate that showed my mother's name. Then I had to hunt for my mother's birth certificate so that I knew her age, so I could identify her, so I went through birth, deaths and marriages, and my partner helped a lot. After a number of months, she said I think I've got a photo of your mum. I was staggered. I went to look at the computer. I thought I was having an out-of-body experience.

"The emotional turmoil was mad. I never had a conversation with anybody about this, but as a kid, obviously, my real mum was an absolute angel. I think every adopted kid who doesn't know their mum thinks their mum is an angel. They kind of know it on a very deep level. A pre-1975 adoption process meant seeing a counsellor who tries to prepare you for the experience. You could find out horrible things about your ancestry, you could be rejected again, also your contact with your parents could be difficult for them.

"I had a good relationship with my social worker. I would go to see her and put my feet up on the couch as if she was a shrink, and she would say, 'Look, I'm not your psychotherapist,' and would laugh. But I really had to work hard to unravel some of the mess, as well as getting my records. When I finally got my records, when we knew where Christine Bell lived, my social worker wrote to my mum. I wanted to do it properly. Two weeks passed and I heard nothing and I was in a terrible state waiting. Then the next day, I received a letter. We talked on the telephone a couple of times before finally, I went to meet her. By this stage, I had a photograph of her and she wasn't the same as the angel in the photograph album in my head. I could tell she'd already had a glass of wine; she cried a lot. We walked around and we talked. I came home feeling sad. However, I'd had enough warnings. I understood about the process. This was to be expected. Then we planned to meet my brother and sister and they, funnily enough, had always known about me because Mum told my sister one night about making a mistake earlier on in her life and, of course, the two of them did talk about it to each other, but not to Mum, so they always knew I was out there.

"I always knew I couldn't be unhappier at the end of this process than I was at the start. I've been so unhappy, not knowing who I was, not knowing anything about myself, and feeling rejected. I wasn't a great father. I wasn't a great person because I wasn't secure in myself. So, I expected the worst, and I actually got the best."

I asked Eddie what his children thought about his situation now that it was all out in the open. He told me that they were lovely about it.

"Very interested. Very supportive. I talk to them about the 'damage cascade' and how one of the ways in which the damage cascaded was in the separation between me and their mother. They think they're going to be fine and I think they are.

"I gave evidence to Harriet Harman's Parliamentary Inquiry. There were only two blokes in the room. We gave evidence to a particular MP. She said, 'How far have you come?' and I said, 'Fifty-five years', then she asked the person next to me and she said 'Fifty-six years', and we went around the table like that. We've all become friends. We are the 'Ungrateful Little Bastards'. It was a very emotional occasion and I was completely drained – we were all completely drained – and I said, does anybody fancy a drink? We were laughing and crying and having the finest of times. And all the adoption jokes were there and it was great fun.

"It's the primal wound being wrenched away from your mother. The layers upon layers of pain, the secrecy, the lies, the loss of identity, but nobody wants to talk about it, so in the end you say to yourself, 'I'm here, this is me'. I was handed over in an office and my dad George said, 'All right, son, I think I'm going to call you …' and he reeled off a list of names before deciding on George Edward and I wondered how in retrospect. Wasn't my name, Simon Bell – the name the midwife gave to me because my mother couldn't think of a name – good enough? Apart from wiping everything out, did I really have to have another name? So, I'm going to change my name to plain Eddie. I can't go back to being Simon Bell – it would be so difficult professionally.

"Funnily enough, when I went to boarding school, one of the first things that happened was that I dropped my identity and said no, I'm not Edward, I'm Eddie. Every adopted person I know hates the renaming process, even if they like the new name, they still hate the process. For God's sake, if you bought a boat you wouldn't rename the boat, and if you bought a dog, you wouldn't rename the dog …

"I don't blame my adoptive parents for anything; they were doing everything by the playbook, the best way they could, but seriously you don't send adopted children to boarding school. It's very common for the babies of the working classes to be adopted into the middle classes, and into that middle-class aspiration. I wasn't the only adopted kid in my boarding school."

As our conversation concluded, Eddie again gave heartfelt thanks to the one special person who pulled him through and reflected on the irony of having had a partner who saw him, for who he was, who held out her hands to hold him up. Who was there through the thick and thin of it, whilst he went through the necessary, unavoidable pain. Ironically, it was that process in the end, that pulled them apart.

As Eddie frames it, "You've met each other and you form this relationship based on who you are – who you are right there and then

– before you know who *you really are.* It was eighteen years that we were together whilst I was going through this process and you come out of it changed. It's a really tough ask. We didn't see it. We didn't recognise it. We are both happy now, and the kids are fine and happy."

Judy

"How many babies died of neglect in those homes as Judy's did? It's never been investigated."

Stephen's contribution is a testament to his late wife, Judy, and her baby, also named Stephen, who was born in 1964 at St Monica's mother and baby home, a Church of England home run by the Diocese of Carlisle in Kendal. Judy was seventeen when she went into the home. Like all women in this book, she had no choice.

Stephen and I exchanged several emails before finally speaking at length on the phone. We've been in regular contact ever since. As I prepared for our conversation, I felt a strong sense of trepidation and, indeed, responsibility to share Judy's experience accurately and powerfully. From the background we had exchanged, I fully anticipated the details he was going to reveal to be emotionally charged and possibly difficult to process. How right I was.

Stephen has been fighting for justice since Judy's untimely death in 2006 and to expose the truth about what happened to Judy, and her baby who died of neglect in St Monica's. He's had great success, persuading both BBC Northwest and ITV News to make and air several news reports and programmes. He has been redoubtable, strenuous and persistent in his attempts to expose what he believes – as I and many others do – to be a great injustice.

It has taken a significant toll on his health. He explains, "I had my heart attack on the very day the first BBC broadcast went out on 17 October 2023." The broadcast in question was a hard-hitting and thorough investigation into Judy's circumstances and the death of her baby. It's a calibre of journalism that I fear we don't see often enough. It's also an ample illustration of cruel and inhumane practices at St Monica's mother and baby home. It begs the question: why isn't a more forensic investigation into the issues raised now being undertaken? Exactly how widespread was this sort of treatment and malpractice?

Stephen continued, "I was so nervous about getting the details right – after all the hard work we and the BBC had done. I felt this huge pain like a rheumatic ache across my chest; my wonderful son and daughter-in-law, who live close by, knew something was seriously wrong with me. I went into hospital and had a stent fitted. I was told I was a lucky boy! My artery was ninety percent blocked. It was a culmination of the hard fight to try to be heard.

"The whole concept of what happened to Judy's baby, and possibly other babies dying in those homes, hasn't yet been thoroughly investigated. Public concern has been focused on babies that were stolen from their mums. I say 'stolen' because they were all young and vulnerable and they were forced into this process. How many babies died of neglect in those homes as Judy's clearly did? It requires robust investigation."

Stephen explains Judy's baby was born in April 1964 with hydrocephalus and spina bifida. He clarifies his understanding of what happened. "The nun running the home declined to either bring in appropriate medical care for the baby or to take him to a hospital, despite Judy begging them to give her baby proper treatment. All these years on, it's clear that baby Stephen, not only may have had an increased chance of survival but also would have suffered pain caused by these conditions. Judy wasn't allowed to hold or nurse him; she would have heard him crying in pain and would have wanted to respond. It was anguish for her to know her baby was in distress and that she could not go to him to offer comfort." Judy's experience viscerally amplifies the amount of coercion and control exercised in mother and baby homes.

Stephen's voice drops as he says, "How many other babies requiring medical attention weren't allowed to go to hospital? I just felt so angry the little mite was born with hydrocephalus and spina bifida, and in 1964 that was treatable. I accept he might have died, but he would have received decent treatment and pain relief, but the home simply wouldn't allow him to go to the hospital. I believe the home wanted to hide it. So, he was kept 'in house'. He died eleven weeks later."

I wondered how much longer and how much better the survival rate might have been for Judy's baby if he'd been allowed medical treatment?

Stephen continues, "He was kept in the on-site nursery, and Judy was only allowed to visit twice a day for short periods; she was only allowed to look at him from a distance. She wasn't permitted to touch or hold him. Then, finally, when he was – bless his little soul – passing away, she was allowed to hold him for the last hour of his life and use a pipette to drop water on his lips. He died in her arms. In my opinion, that's criminal neglect. I would like the police to investigate.

"When Judy was alive, she wouldn't let me investigate because it was too painful for her, and I promised her that I wouldn't. But after her death, I was determined to find out as much as I could."

Stephen pauses, then tells me what happened to his wife. "In 2006 after a lifetime of struggling with her mental health, Judy took her own life in a lonely lane, only 400 yards from where baby Stephen was buried. As close as she could get to him. His loss lived with Judy all her life, and you could not convince her that it wasn't her fault. She always felt guilty. She lived a life of guilt. She tried to kill herself nearly a hundred times and a lot of those times we dealt with her distress together. In the seventies, eighties and nineties, she was banged into mental institutions, which were also abusive. Her mental illness meant she lived her life in a black pit of despair most of the time. We fought it on our own because I loved her."

Shortly after their marriage, they moved to London where Judy trained as a nurse and eventually became a well-respected paediatric nurse specialising in end-of-life care. After her first suicide attempt, she was transferred from her local hospital in North London into Napsbury Hospital mental institution in St Albans.

This reference to a mental health institution piques my interest. An internet search reveals a website for Napsbury and thousands of entries. One is particularly revealing:

> I was admitted for a two-week period, around 1992. I had no idea what horrific scenes i would witness; even now it still haunts me. My father made me promise never to tell my mother what it was like. Horrific, does not express what i endured or saw by staff. I know that i was not well, very underweight. To be subjected to the treatment i received, was brutal. To see how other patients were treated, the ones with no family or support. Those people that had a duty of care. I really hope they find it hard to sleep at night. What i witnessed, even now i find it so distressing to write.
>
> Imogen Wing, *Hertfordshire's Community Archive Network*, 27/12/2018

Judy, a patient in the early 1970s, was unlikely to have experienced better treatment. Thankfully, many psychiatric hospitals have improved in recent decades, but it's depressing and rather sickening to envisage Judy in an institution that has been described in such harrowing terms, especially after she had been captive previously in another nightmarish institution.

Stephen presses on describing Judy's story. He is measured, calm even, and utterly believable.

"Karen, if I could just prove what happened in there, and I can't, I only have Judy's word for it, and she only told me twenty years later because she didn't want me causing trouble. She was sexually and physically abused in Napsbury – by the staff. She was also put in a padded cell, straitjacketed, and force-fed. She was trying her best to get out of the place, and they wouldn't let me visit her because she was sectioned under several orders. In the seventies and eighties, those orders were draconian. They said to me, your wife is in one of the severe wards, you cannot visit, but you can phone the office once a day at nine o'clock. That was their treatment of me! And by then I had our baby to look after. It came as a shock."

Stephen laughs and says, "I know that's what you ladies have to do in any case." I know he means looking after the baby and how difficult that can be, especially in those first weeks and months of adjustment. I am amazed that his humour and empathy, and natural warmth, shine through what is objectively a horror story.

"Our little one went into a nursery run by Brent Council, who were amazing and had so many facilities for mothers and babies at that time. It was also where Judy was a staff nurse. There I was, with no one helping me and that's how it's been throughout. The doctors and psychiatrists just wanted to issue medication; no one ever wanted to delve into Judy's past."

This wasn't a surprise to me, as I've heard from many adult adoptees that when they require treatment, and especially in relation to mental health, no one asks any questions about their upbringing, or explores the fact that they were adopted.

"She had nineteen psychiatrists over forty years. It wasn't a great experience. I wouldn't say any of them were very good. I always wanted to protect her. It's been my raison d'être. I think what a wonderful woman she was and that she did not deserve this. She had such a lack of support."

Clearly, the trauma of losing a loved one (however they die) will leave deep scars on those left behind. But suicide is more complex to process as the following quote illustrates:

> Losing a loved one to suicide is one of life's most painful experiences. The feelings of loss, sadness, and loneliness experienced after any death of a loved one are often magnified in suicide survivors by feelings of guilt, confusion, rejection, shame, anger, and the effects of stigma and trauma. Furthermore, survivors of suicide loss are at higher risk of developing major depression, post-traumatic stress disorder, and suicidal behaviors, as well as a prolonged form of grief called complicated grief. Added to the burden is the substantial stigma, which can keep survivors away from much needed support and healing resources.
>
> (*Suicide bereavement and complicated grief, Dialogues Clinical Neuroscience*, 2012;14:177-186)

Stephen continues, "I always told her she had nothing to be ashamed of, and that she was guilty of nothing. Other people are the guilty ones, but Judy would say, 'No, I'm the guilty one.' She believed she caused his death by her actions, even though it was others who had power and took all the decisions. My mission is to get this message out, to get it into the public arena and that has now started to happen. That's why I'm talking to you. I'm looking for any opportunity to tell Judy's story.

"Just four weeks before Judy died, and six months after her father had passed away, she told me something truly shocking: 'Do you know, Steve, when I was a young girl, I was sexually abused?' I was absolutely blown away. She changed the subject, and I didn't go back to this topic."

Stephen is very collected whilst he conveys this impactful information to me. It is not said with any note of hyperbole, rather it's exactly as he describes, "a puzzle where the last piece finally reveals the full picture". Stephen is careful to caveat his theory, cautioning, "None of this is provable. But I am certain that what happened to Judy in St Monica's did cause her mental ill health. It was called the 'slut house'. On the occasions where the girls were allowed out, passers-by would say, 'Oh, there's one of those sluts.' They were all dreadful places, Karen," Stephen says grimly, "But Dr Michael Lambert of Lancaster University seems to think that St Monica's was particularly dreadful. Girls were put into those homes first and foremost as a punishment. Judy was made to work, cleaning and scrubbing. I never pushed her for information, just taking snippets whenever she gave them to me. She was a good person and a great nurse, and I don't want her to be buried and be forgotten. I want to do something in her name to recognise all the other Judys."

I couldn't agree more with Stephen, and so I put it to him, "That's exactly the question: how many more Judys and baby Stephens are there?"

He goes on to tell me that when he bought baby Stephen's plot, one of many unmarked baby graves in Parkside Road Cemetery, Kendal, he met a local council employee "who said, 'There are other bodies in this grave, but this plot is yours, and you have the right to put a headstone in there', which of course I did. I had a proper Christian ceremony, and I placed Judy's ashes with her little baby, and I promised her, 'I'm not giving up, love. I want justice for you, and I want justice for all the other girls.' Because how many did die, Karen, because of losing their babies? All these others unmarked infant graves? This hasn't been looked at properly."

It's a very pertinent question: how many other babies are buried at Parkside, how many mothers and babies died in homes in England, and how many women took their own lives after being in a mother and baby home and having their babies taken from them? I've certainly interviewed one person who had discovered his mother had died by suicide after he was taken and adopted. Another interviewee spoke of two girls she knew that killed themselves after having their babies taken. The question remains, when will the suicides of mothers whose babies have been taken be properly researched?

"I'm being brutal," Stephen says, "but I think this government want them all to die off, to see the back of them. Our local MP, Liberal Democrat Tim Farron, stated on TV that what Judy went through needs to be thoroughly investigated."

Stephen uses his life experience with Judy as the basis for lectures at a local university. He tells me how many of the students have been directly touched in similar ways. "It could have been their mother or grandmother that went into one of these homes. Our discussions generate real emotion and improve understanding about the impact of mental health." Stephen thinks it's important that he does this. In fact, his ambition is to give a speech at a major NHS conference, so that many more people understand what women in mother and baby homes and their children experienced.

"I want people in authority to come and to listen. I want to make sure I can get the message through. The Diocese of Carlisle have expressed an interest in my talk about Judy's life and have asked me if I would be willing to do one for them and, of course, I've said yes. Just give these women some peace of mind and tell them none of this was their fault. It's painful what these women go through. They remember the birthdays, and Christmas time will bring it all back. It's a long-lasting torture and it is the greatest social injustice this country has ever seen. I think the government are concerned about possible compensation. But it's not about money, it's about the apology.

"My way of dealing with grief is to fight for Judy," Stephen says, and he also states how much admiration he has for the MAA's late Veronica Smith, and Diana Defries who now runs the MAA.

In the weeks and months after our conversation, we exchange further emails. Stephen met again with Dr Michael Lambert who confirmed the worst fears about baby Stephen's death, and stated his concerns in an email to Stephen in February 2024:

We cannot know from the scant information the extent or severity of baby Stephen's condition and the way such a decision was taken. Nevertheless, the protocol at that time for babies born with significant congenital malformities – mainly spina bifida and hydrocephalus – was early surgery at a specialist regional centre (Pendlebury, or possibly Alder Hey which had a surgeon with nationally recognised expertise in such operations) to increase their chances of survival and improved quality of life. The consultant obstetrician would have known that, as would their pediatrician. Did Stephen have a chance to see them? Was it intentional, or was it down to key staff nearing retirement and being unaware of the latest practice? Given how staff at St Monica's were connected to local medical networks and developments, especially those concerning childbirth, I find it hard to believe.

The Medical Officer for Cumberland did not want to renew the contractual agreement because he said maternity care was persistently substandard, as was well known and documented in the records. Young, teenage pregnant women having their first children were considered a high-risk group according to the 1959 Cranbrook Report which recommended hospitalisation according to certain markers.

The Medical Officer for Cumberland said that deliveries from St Monica's should be transferred to Helme Chase (Kendal, an NHS maternity hospital), who had capacity to deal with them. This was also in a context of a rising number of women with complications as mentioned before, questions being raised about the ability of existing staff to deal with these issues because they were not properly trained and exposed to enough deliveries to learn, and more reported problems among mothers and babies in annual reports. Although other deaths were mentioned in report statistics, Stephen's was not. In the annual report covering his period at the Home, health was documented as 'good'. St Monica's remained a maternity home mainly in the interests of secrecy, and their preference for confinement over ten days to have the child fostered and adopted, rather than the seven-day (or shorter for easier deliveries) trend which was pursued at Helme Chase in line with standard medical practice.

I don't know what the withheld and closed material from the Diocese of Carlisle does or does not say. Nor do I know whether the police or any legal team would see the material gathered – in face of the odds – as sufficient evidence for criminal prosecution. Nevertheless, it presents a clear picture of St Monica's being problematic across a range of areas, which were known about by the authorities involved, but unwilling to change. These clearly contributed to Stephen's untimely death. By 1966 the landscape had changed as there were more 'illegitimate' births as a proportion nationally, and more adoptions by societies outside of children born in mother and baby homes alone. This meant greater pressure from the sponsoring local authorities to get value for money for their 'service' (cheaper nursing costs for the home, and they invoked the 'economy' of Coledale Hall, at Carlisle, as a comparator for a home which was previously a maternity one but now sent deliveries to the hospital). St Monica's closed not long after in 1970 like so many other homes after running into deeper financial, staffing and services crises.

Dr Lambert continues at length, amplifying the lack of care in St Monica's; his expert research is damning. Little wonder both the BBC and ITV quote his concerns about St Monica's as one of the worst homes he has come across. He adds:

Even by the standards of the day, it was completely substandard. Its unique arrangement – being funded exclusively by local authorities – meant there wasn't enough money to go around. There were regular complaints about the standard of care – no trained midwives, and a lack of trained support.

Thanks to years of tireless campaigning, Stephen has had significant impact. In particular, BBC North West Tonight have featured his campaign several times along with ITV News, where journalist Sarah Corker has worked determinedly to uncover key facts. Following Dr Lambert's recent access to the Church's archives, it is now a matter of public record that more than forty-four babies, the youngest surviving for just forty-five minutes, the oldest eleven weeks, were born in St Monica's and were buried near to baby Stephen in the unmarked graves in Parkside. Dr Lambert concludes that the forty-four babies were also denied the medical treatment that they should have received, according to the clinical standards in place at the time. Dr Lambert believes that these babies were disposable because the prospective adoptive families wanted only able-bodied children. A further fifty stillborn babies have been recorded, no-one yet knows what happened to their remains.

Unsurprisingly, Stephen has again demanded police action. Tim Farron is also calling for an investigation. Speaking on 19 July 2024, Farron said, "Those that were desirable for adoption were given the modern care available at the time, and those that were not – were not. That is unspeakably awful ... They [the babies] should be afforded the dignity they have been robbed of."

Speaking to ITV News about their latest research on 17 October 2024, the acting Bishop of Carlisle, Rt Rev Rob Saner-Haigh said, "The Church of England should do all it can to support people who have lived with the trauma. We need to listen and give them a choice in decision-making so they can tell us what they need, and as an organisation we show them the love and dignity that they weren't shown before."

Following the same ITV News investigation, these newly discovered facts about St Monica's were also put to Education Secretary Bridget Phillipson who said, "What happened there was completely and utterly unacceptable," and that her department was urgently looking at the findings of the report and hopes to say more soon.

When pressed to answer if the government would issue a formal apology given that the Scottish and Welsh governments have done so, Minister Phillipson responded, "As a new government there are a range of issues that we need to consider, this is one such issue where I have sought advice on … how we should proceed, but I do recognise a grave injustice that was done to far too many women."

It would seem the victims of historical forced adoptions are inching towards a formal apology. This is in large part due to Stephen's tenacity in working with the media to bring this into the spotlight, not without great personal cost. When we last spoke in October 2024, Stephen had been advised by Carlisle Council that arrangements are now being made to discuss the practicalities of giving the babies in Parkside a proper headstone and the Diocese of Carlisle will provide a dedicated service. He anticipates this will happen in spring 2025.

A service, a memorial stone and a formal apology would be a fitting tribute to Judy and baby Stephen, and to her husband's determined efforts to seek justice on their behalf. I can't see either Stephen or MAA accepting less.

Jill

"Even though I had a lovely life, I looked in the mirror and I thought to myself, who am I?"

Following our energetic exchange of emails and rapid-fire WhatsApps, I started following Jill on Facebook prior to our conversation and our eventual meeting some months later at her home. Her tag, 'Champion Pasty Maker' intrigued me, along with her tempting thrice-daily updates such as: 'Luscious lemon orange Cointreau pancakes,' which popped up on Shrove Tuesday. These were the dishes she was cooking, photographing and promoting on social media to sell in her business, The Town Cook, located in her hometown of Deal, Kent. I wondered incorrectly if the pasty maker was a reference to a Cornish connection. In fact, Jill is simply an exuberant foodie businesswoman with a strong community focus, who loves to create great food and has transferred her passion into a successful venture.

She gave me a potted history of her life. "I'm Jill Martin. I was born 8 October 1950. I was born Susan Jones. I was adopted – apparently at four weeks old." Jill smiles at me. "My mother, Mary Matilda Matthew, was in a workhouse, 145 Belvedere Road, Burton-on-Trent before she was transferred into a mother and baby home run by the church and the Burton-on-Trent Association For The Protection of Girls shortly before my birth."

I couldn't resist looking up the workhouse, which was an austere, prison-like building described on a local history website:

> Conditions were harsh so as to deter the able-bodied idle poor from relying on them. Discipline was strictly enforced with typical punishments being a beating on the open hand or rear.

This workhouse too was designed to shame poor people and to provide a plentiful supply of cheap labour to local businesses. My research also revealed great details about the diet in the workhouse.

> The diet was also deliberately poor quality because it was not intended to attract inmates. An early breakfast in separate sittings consisted of a piece of bread and bowl of gruel. No second helpings were permitted except on Christmas Day. Lunch was a rationed bowl of poor-quality vegetable soup though this was a luxury not seen in most workhouses. Dinners were dull, predictable & tasteless and supper usually took the form of a crust of bread and cheese. Members of the workhouse generally suffered from malnutrition. All meals were eaten in observed silence and, in the early days, no cutlery was provided.
>
> Burton on Trent Local History, *Belvedere Workhouse – General History*

I imagined Jill's mother pregnant and hungry – how she must have craved sustenance.

Jill continues to outline her early life. "I was brought up by wonderful people, Mary and Arthur Hobbs. They were very loving and kind. Unfortunately, I lost them when I was very young – I was just twenty-four years old. Mum had an accident and died, then Dad passed away suddenly. I've been married for fifty-four years. I started my own family. I've got three children and I adore my family."

I don't doubt this; her voice is sincere and full of warmth. When I meet her in person a few weeks later, she points from her sofa across the rooftops and explains that's where her daughter lives.

"She is doing us roast beef this afternoon," Jill beams, "before we go on our holiday." Her excitement is palpable. "It's our first holiday since lockdown …" Jeff appears with two mugs of coffee and says he'll leave us to our conversation.

"Just before Dad Arthur died, he asked me if I wanted to see my birth mum and dad, but two weeks later he had passed away, and sadly we didn't have an opportunity to have a further conversation. They never kept my adoption a secret. I can remember Dad Arthur, sitting by my bed, telling me the story of how they came to choose me. 'Tell me that story again,' I'd ask. I was always asking him to repeat the story. They never hid anything from me and I've got all the paperwork and a receipt of twelve shillings from Deal Town Hall. That's what they paid for me, to *adopt* me." Jill has the file ready for me to read on the coffee table. There are a large number of documents. I know I'll need a considerable amount of time to go through them.

"You must've heard this from other adoptees," Jill says, "even though I had a lovely life, I looked in the mirror and I thought to myself, who am I? Who do I look like? Where do I get my funny ways from? And I searched a lifetime, but when your surname is Jones, that's like searching for a needle in a haystack." She laughs, and I agree, searching for the right Jones – or Smith – would indeed be difficult, especially so before the internet.

"When I was in my early sixties, we were on holiday in Greece, and we had a phone call from my daughter. She was very excited and said they had some news for us – I thought perhaps they were having a baby – but on our return, it transpired my son-in-law, who was also adopted, had found his birth father. We were all delighted, of course, but I wanted to know how they'd managed to make the connections. He explained to me that a site called Missing You had been very useful.

"I already knew that my supposed adoption had taken place at Deal Town Hall in February 1951. And I suddenly thought to myself, there must be records about me somewhere. It hadn't struck me before, partly because I was so busy, bringing up my own family, working, and managing day-to-day life. But I was spurred into contacting the adoption department at Dover District Council. Subsequently, I met with someone who explained the various steps and potential outcomes, and I was prepared to go ahead. I had to wait several months, then a couple came to see me with a book, which was a little bit like *This Is Your Life* with Eamonn Andrews. They said, 'You better sit down. This doesn't make great reading.' They had found all my adoption records.

"For the first time in my life, I saw my father's name and my mother's birth date. They took me through everything, but I didn't really examine the documents in detail. I never gave it a thought that it could've been unlawful or illegal … Whenever my Dad Arthur told me 'the story', they were at the courtroom in Deal. He'd say, 'You were already in Deal at four months old and we had fallen in love with you.'"

Jill had assumed her adoption was a straightforward legal process. She explained to me, that somehow both her birth mother and her adoptive mother came across each other in a corridor adjacent to the court – and they were both in what she describes as "a terrible state. My birth mother stood up in court to oppose the adoption, informing the magistrates, 'He is going to marry me,' referring to my birth father. This puts absolute fear into my adoptive parents because at that stage I was already 'their' baby and they had taken care of me for four months. They had not foreseen the surfacing of the birth mother, let alone with a claim to have me returned to her!"

Jill continues, "My dad, Arthur, being *my dad,* went to find my birth dad to speak to him and he told me repeatedly as I was growing up, 'He was the nicest bloke I'd ever met.' He was right, as I found out when I finally met my birth father decades later. My birth father explained to Dad Arthur that he was only twenty-four and he wasn't yet ready to marry, nor was he quite certain. My birth mother was twenty-seven and she had been married before and already had a young daughter. She was now separated for more than two years and was desperately trying to get her *Decree Nisi* so that they could legally remarry. Just eight months after the so-called adoption took place on 28 of February 1951, my birth parents did marry. Years later, my birth father blamed himself for not being clear enough in the court by standing up and stating that he 'was going to marry her.'"

I also wondered, as a young man beginning a relationship with a soon-to-be-divorced woman, who already had a child, if Jill's father had perhaps come under pressure from family and peers.

"The whole thing was a mess and Deaconess Fairburn from the mother and baby home was responsible, with the State's backing." Jill tells me, "The more I research this the better I understand it. Deaconess Fairburn was hell-bent against my birth mother and she did not want me to be brought up by her, preferring instead to have me adopted. She clearly disliked my mother; she wrote several times to the court to confirm she wasn't suitable to be a mother, that she wasn't fit to be a mother."

Jill reads the following, "The heading is Burton-on-Trent Association For The Protection of Girls:

Dear Madam, re baby Susan Jones, care of Mrs Hobbs, Deal.

We are having a bit of trouble with the mother of this child and feel it would be wisest if you could get her to agree to face up to things at once, by either getting her to sign the consent form, or refusing to, then we should just know where we stand … The worker rang me in despair a week ago, but I have not heard a further word and I am hoping it was a spasm on the part of the mother. Anyway, I do not want the Hobbs to break their hearts if the girl does decide to keep the baby.

Jill remarks, "The girl! My mother was twenty-seven at the time," before continuing:

… if the girl does demand the child back, although I must say it would not be in the child's interests to let her have it.

The hostility towards Jill's birth mother is transparent. The documents portray her as 'juvenile', as 'a girl' and 'not suitable', and by implication that she is reckless and unable to make clear decisions, the value-laden judgment that 'it would not be in the best interests of the baby', is clearly based on prejudice. Or so it seems to both Jill and me. Indeed, if somebody is employed by the Association For The Protection Of Girls, it stands to reason that they must be seen to be active in the business of adjudicating who should be protected and actively shield those deemed requiring such attention. Or else what are they there for? Their vested self-interest would be best served by demonstrating the need for protection; in this case, that Jill's birth mum was both in need of protection from herself *and* that a further intervention was required to *protect* her newborn baby from her. This way, the objective of the Association For The Protection Of Girls was demonstrated and met. However, no concern was expressed about the older daughter.

Jill continues, "It's Deaconess Fairburn's evidence that ensures I was adopted." She shows a letter to me dated 3 February 1951, Deaconess Fairburn writes:

If you think it's advisable, I will gladly attend the court. The mother says she is now going to court to ask for the child back.

The court then write back to Deaconess Fairburn saying they would 'very much appreciate her attendance. The letter details that the adoption was 'private' and adds *if* an adoption society was used that the court should be notified.

"Deaconess Fairburn," Jill explains, "stayed close friends with my adoptive parents, all their lives. When mum died, she sent a lovely letter referring to my mother as a butterfly."

Referring to other letters, Jill points out there are no signed consent forms, no official adoption, and no placement orders in her file. It's clear that the Deaconess's evidence carries a great deal of weight and effectively ensures the adoption is carried out. Deaconess Fairburn's letters and opinions carry more weight than the birth mother's claims that she is about to marry and that she and the birth father can bring Jill up.

Jill sums up her thoughts, "The judge said obviously 'that's it then' – even though they travel to the Court to inform them that they are going to marry. When I did find my dad, I felt an absolutely instant connection. I had a full brother, but my full sister had died years earlier. Dad broke down and said he was only twenty-four at the time and that it was all his fault. He said, 'I told them I was going to marry her.' He broke down in tears. I did forgive him."

It seemed so sad that this couple, who were so close to being able to get married were prevented from doing so and, in that legal grey area, prior to the issue of the *Decree Nisi*, the moral maelstrom snared the innocent baby; the prevalent social mores dictating that the baby should go to someone of better character, less burdened with shame and more deserving. The mother had ended up in a workhouse and it transpired that her boyfriend, who was working, paid fees for both the workhouse and the mother and baby home. In the late 1950s, living together would have been very frowned upon, as divorce was. Perhaps if this nascent family had any chance of being together, they had to toe the line, be pragmatic and look to the future.

I asked Jill how she found her father. Encouraged by her son-in-law, she explained, "I used the same website as he did: the General Register Office, which is a GOV.UK free site and I found out that they were married in December 1951. Although it was after midnight, I rushed to tell Jeff that I had found them and that they did indeed marry."

At this stage, it's worth reiterating that Jill didn't know what had actually happened to her birth parents, after the court ruling; she thought they may have drifted apart after the trauma that they had both been through.

With the additional information on the marriage certificate, Jill was then able to trace phone numbers. "I knew my birth father was by then in his eighties, and after I dialled a very gruff, grumpy voice answered the phone. I thought that really could be him. I said, 'I hope you don't mind Mr Dickens, but I'm trying to trace my family.' I found out then that my mum had died two years prior and my younger sister had passed away in her early thirties with a rare cancer. Without revealing who I was, I asked him questions about my mother, which he was able to answer. Only then when I was certain, I said to him, 'Mr Dickens, I think you're my father.' His first words to me were, 'I always thought this day would come, and you are welcome in my home any time.' He then told me, 'We have a son.' I couldn't believe I had a brother."

It then transpired that her parents had kept Jill's existence a secret from him. Jill is animated as she continues, "It was better than winning the lottery. I found the most amazing family, including my brother, after they had explained everything to him that day. We are in contact every day, my cousins, my aunts, my nieces and my nephews. We go to see them. I see my aunt Joan who is ninety-six. She's such a lovely lady."

"My birth mother was originally married to a Jones, hence my surname. She married young and I have now met my half-sister who is wonderful. We clicked immediately, and there is a strong resemblance between us. We even sign our names in a similar fashion. She shared with me my birth mother's correspondence regarding her divorce from Mr Jones, her first husband. It is clear that even though they had technically divorced in 1948, two years prior to my birth, she was still waiting for the final document and doing all she could to obtain it so she could remarry."

Jill shows me other letters. "Deaconess Fairburn writes after the court case that she's 'so grateful that the little scrap is now safe with the parents who adore her.' She also writes that my mother didn't take good care of me, 'She … sticks a bottle in her mouth, wakes her too early, and mixes the feeds incorrectly. I feel it is definitely in the interest of this child to be adopted as I do not consider Mary sufficiently responsible to be a mother.' Although, she was already a mother and both my parents went on to have a very successful marriage and build a loving family. It was a breach of my right to family life, and although I was lucky to be brought up by very good people, I never played with my sister, I never hugged my mum, she never read me a bedtime story. I didn't have the life I should've had … It's just so extremely wrong. My adoptive mother and father bought me for twelve shillings. Dad never hid anything."

Jill then says, "I didn't realise that it – my adoption – was unlawful. It never sat right with me, but I never, ever, thought that it shouldn't have happened the way it did."

Jill passes me a photo of her mother and father at their wedding, which is just a few months after Jill's birth. Jill's mum is in a two-piece suit; for divorcees, the wearing of wedding dresses was frowned on. Anyone looking at the photo at the time may have easily discerned her status. They look a happy handsome couple, flanked by close family members. I peer and peer at the blurred figures, I think I can see Jill. I wonder what conversation they must have had between the two of them, and with their wider family. Post-war, I imagine they were encouraged to be pragmatic and to put the past behind them, to make the best of it.

Jill asks me if there is a campaign to get the Government to now say sorry to mothers who lost their babies and to those who were adopted.

She quotes Harriet Harman MP, who she heard on the radio, "'It was wrong then and it is wrong now.'"

"The injustice is overwhelming. I get emotional, I get angry, I get upset. It's so damn wrong. It's this thing that will never go away. I am a very positive-thinking person, and I've got a great life and a very loving family, but this will not go away. I am at the age where the truth should be told. I was told that what happened to me would never stand up in court today. It's like bashing your head against a great big mountain in front of you.

"I'm seventy-four this year; something needs to happen soon before it's too late. I will fight until the bitter end. Women have been discriminated against for so long. Why should having babies leave us so vulnerable for so long."

Jill's story doesn't end there. When her brother died, Jill was his only surviving relative. "He didn't leave a will. I sorted everything out for him – funeral and all of that. I am not interested in his money, but, when another more distantly related relative claimed I'd been *adopted out of the family*, I really wasn't happy. I was deeply hurt. I am *family* and I am his next of kin." Jill is now engaged in a difficult probate issue and it turns out that not having properly registered adoption papers is a problem. Deaconess Fairburn has a great deal to answer for.

Jill, like many others I have interviewed, needs more than an apology. She needs urgent practical help to resolve a complex costly probate problem.

This is the reality of forced adoptions.

Susie

"It's a lie that the parents who are not your natural parents are going to be better for you than your own parents. It's just not true. It's a crime against nature."

Susie and I spoke at length. Like many others, she expressed the clear sentiment that she didn't want to cause anybody, even inadvertently, any pain or discomfort. She said she had people on her birth parents' side that she didn't really know and she didn't want to risk upsetting them.

That has been a theme throughout the interviews. Susie's care and concern for others was palpable and had evidently guided her working life into the caring industry – she is currently training to be a psychotherapist. She said other adopted people were also working within her field and that this didn't surprise her.

We began our discussion by focusing on the increasingly urgent need for the adoption apology to be issued. She said, "There are two things: one, it's quite ageist not to because we are getting on, and it happened in a different era. Perhaps the policy makers think we won't be around for much longer and that makes us not very important. And secondly, it's the importance of learning from us, those of us with the lived experience of being adopted, and from survivors, learning from what we've been through. We could be helping those people being adopted now. I think the whole area of adoption needs to be exposed. All the difficulties that children being adopted now are experiencing, require exposure. How many of those children require psychological help now? How many of them are maladjusted as they get older? How many of them are suffering now? How many siblings are being separated now? We are a resource for those people, for these children.

"But instead, it's like we don't exist and that these negative things simply didn't happen to us. I know that's not going to be very popular politically. They don't want to be concerned about adoption because it serves the need to provide kids to parents who want them."

We agreed that governments had turned a blind eye to the difficulties connected to adoption for both the mothers and the children and babies concerned. Susie continues, "It's a social justice issue and nobody wants to address the issue of mass mistreatment of hundreds of thousands of people. Nor do they want to learn from it or apply that learning to what's happening in families now, to children and birth mothers now. Because that's too expensive. Because to support those mothers properly to keep their babies, to prevent the psychological damage that happens, is enormous, and we adult adoptees are testament to that."

Is Susie overstating the psychological damage that happens during the process of adoption? Was she an unlucky individual? I put this to her. Firstly, Susie says that she had very good adoptive parents – she only had positive things to say about them. But nonetheless, she admits, "I felt like I'd been dropped from outer space like I wasn't born, that I'd come out from this terrifying void, this darkness. I felt like I was superhuman, I felt like I wasn't part of the human race. And I felt that from very young – from being alone in my bedroom as a little girl, I just felt really scared. I wondered where did I belong. I wasn't like anybody else." Susie is crying, and this is clearly very distressing for her.

"I was carrying huge shame, which is not acknowledged. You feel different and you don't know why. You behave in a certain way, and of course, your adoptive parents don't understand why, so they assume it's bad character. For instance, when I was bad-tempered, my parents didn't attribute that to my adoption, didn't think it could be caused through the trauma. That I'd been separated from my birth mother.

"In fact, my parents lived opposite a children's home. So, I was a little girl watching these children outside the great big gates opposite our house, and that just terrified me. I was absolutely petrified of them. I believed if they found out I was adopted they would kidnap me because they would know that I really belonged to them. That I wasn't where I was supposed to be. I told my mum this when she suggested that I play with these kids. I explained to her I was scared of them and that they might kidnap me. Of course, she told me I was being silly, that they were poor kids and I had to be kind to them. She had no comprehension."

Susie was particularly keen to explain that she understood her adoptive parents had been given no support or insight and that they were doing their best.

Susie's experience of psychotherapy has been life-changing. In fact, she's found a therapist who is also an adult adoptee, and she described how she has experienced more learning with this one individual in a few sessions than in years of therapy with other practitioners who didn't share the same lived experience.

Susie revealed that she had asked her therapist how she had found peace and she told me it was through the training she'd undertaken. "I decided to put myself through it because I felt it was going to be so helpful, and it really has been. I feel passionate about changing the narrative. There are so many assumptions around from the adoption point of view. For birth mothers too, the fact that there is an assumption that they gave their babies away, that it was supposedly a voluntary thing. That needs to be challenged."

We talked about Susie's experiences and she explained, "I've got a thing about identity, lots of issues are about identity. For instance, I always had this kind of fear of being found, so as a little girl I developed a defence mechanism. The way I coped was to be in denial about adoption and to be really fearful about my birth family coming to find me, and it's still frightening for me. It's deep in my subconscious. Even though it's illogical and it doesn't make sense anymore, it's very deep; it's at my core, and it's just fear. In fact, it's the trauma of being taken as a baby. My younger brother, on the other hand, used to send messages in his head to his birth mother saying come and get me, come and get me. But for me it was the opposite – leave me alone, leave me alone – and fear.

"I was adopted at four weeks old; my birth parents were Irish, and my mother Maria came over to the UK to have me. I was born in Sheffield and was adopted through Catholic Care. I have met Maria. She died a few years ago, but my relationship with her was difficult and we didn't have an ongoing relationship. I don't have a huge amount of detail about what happened to her at that time, but I do know that Maria was nineteen and going out with my father, Paddy who was twenty-seven. She had an awful time; she was staying with people she knew and she was working. I assume she came to England early in the pregnancy. When she did give birth, she was treated inhumanely. She was left all on her own; she was in agony and was told this was her punishment. She told me this when I met her in Dublin. She told me that her parents were also not married. She was brought up with her father and paternal grandmother and her mother was not in the picture at all. I remember her saying there were difficulties because her father was Catholic and her mother was Protestant, so she had a double trauma. She was abandoned by her mother. She was very traumatised, then she became pregnant with me, and her grandmother told her she couldn't keep the baby. She couldn't stay at home; she had to go and get rid of the baby. She was in therapy and had so many unresolved issues, matched with tremendous unresolved need. I think she expected me to be able to deal with this. In a way, I think she wanted me to be the parent and for her to be the child. I think this degree of trauma is probably common with birth mothers who have had to relinquish their babies, and have unresolved issues and unresolved pain; there was an enormous need for me to heal her. They're looking for you, the adopted child, to do that. This baby, that they were forced to give up, is what they need to feel whole again. My birth mother felt it in a really overpowering way because she had also lost her own mother and then she lost me. So, she was pushed out of her home and pushed into another country. She came over here I assume, as part of the effort to cover it all up. I wonder if people in Ireland knew at that time how awful the mother and baby homes here were. I think they were even worse than those in Ireland.

"I had a really lovely girlhood. My mum and dad were really lovely people. Other people that I know had awful experiences growing up. I'm not grateful, but I am lucky. However, they had no clue about the psychological impact of adoption. They weren't given any background knowledge to help them. Other than being told 'Baby is a blank slate and you two,' (a GP and another professional) 'will provide a much better home for this baby than the young working-class girl, who is feckless and immoral.' They have the moral high ground, don't they? Nor would they have realised that the whole thing was a great big lie. Because it was a lie that Maria wanted to give up her baby. It's a lie that the parents who are not your natural parents are going to be better for you than your own parents. It's just not true – it's a crime against nature, a terrible thing for a baby to be torn away from its mother.

In utero, the baby knows its mother, it anticipates meeting her, being with that one mother. That is what we are supposed to do and the baby knows. As somebody put it: 'It's not that baby doesn't know, it's that baby can't forget.' You are born in trauma. This trauma occurs very young. Then, there's the whole identity thing.

"I am informed by a really excellent therapist, Paul Sunderland, who is an addiction therapist who has developed an interest in adoption and its impact. He noticed that adopted people were over-represented in his service, and also over-represented in terms of the people working in his service. He looked at the in-utero impact, the way in which we physically develop; all of that neurological stuff that happens and, more importantly, that doesn't happen when you're taken away from your birth mother because you're still developing. Everything is still growing and developing, and everything is supposed to happen with that one mother. When that doesn't happen with that one mother, he contends that your brain doesn't develop as it should. You literally have a traumatised brain. There's a lot more information on this now than there was back in the sixties and seventies in fact.

Susie continues, "Then there's intergenerational trauma … I know I'll be passing this on to my kids. What's happened to me will be happening to them – in a way.

"I look at my youngest daughter, and I have no idea who she's like in my wider family, but I know that there are absolutely going to be characters on my birth side that she resembles, that I don't know them and she doesn't know. My daughter has the same laugh as me. As human beings that familiarity and similarity is what makes us feel safer in this very frightening world. If we don't have that deep unquestionable sense of belonging, the sort that no one can question that you do belong, then it's very disturbing when it's missing. I think that's what every adopted child and adult has experienced and feels: this sense, this challenge that *kept* people don't have. You have to find your peace with this thing that's missing. There's the *kept*, which is the majority, the *unkept*, which is us adopted people, and then there's the relinquished. So, adoption as a term doesn't really describe what's happened – it's more *relinquishment*. Adoption as a term is a cover-up. It's used to make palatable a process for the people who are getting a child. For instance, they may say we are adopting, but that doesn't describe what's happening to the child. What happened to the child? The child was relinquished. Nobody wants to hear that, nobody wanting to adopt a baby really wants to think about the pain and what actually happens, which is what I mean about a false narrative around adoption.

"Look at the websites of adoption organisations like Barnardo's: it's all about smiley families, getting a wonderful child and how you can go about it, and lots of photographs of lovely parents, but it's not focused from the child's perspective and what it actually means. Please can we have some honesty? People need to realise what the process actually is. Until they do, they shouldn't go into adoption. I hear it a lot – friends that say, 'Oh, we've got friends that have adopted children. Aren't they [the children] lucky?' No, it's the parents who are the lucky ones. It makes me very upset. I've got a friend who is a clinical psychologist and her brother adopted two children and she thinks they shouldn't have been allowed to adopt. Because they want to mould them. They want those children to grow up, reflecting the adoptive parents' personalities – how can that even happen?

"It's ignorance, people just do not want to face the reality. It's too difficult. It's painful. Contemporary organisations in the UK are still using that narrative. There is still no open acknowledgement or opportunity to read the experiences of the women whose babies were taken for adoption.

"I know that this is currently being done to individuals because the State says they've 'done everything they can for these mothers', that 'they've got abusive boyfriends' and all the rest, but my argument would be, how about giving this mother the genuine support she needs, the money she needs. How about doing everything you can financially, so she can *keep* the baby? I know that's not happening – we know that's not happening. Even today, I would argue they are still doing what they used to do, which is believing this child is going to be better off with parents who have got money, security and all the rest. So long as they are loving and nice to the child – then that will do. If you go onto these websites, you have to dig and dig to find out something about these adopted adults, and about the impact on them, and how they are coping with life – it's like we don't exist.

"Barnardo's do run support groups for teenagers, but I'm fifty-odd and I still need support myself. The only support I had, and I happened to be fortunate because I live in a particular area (therefore, I got lucky), I've got six sessions with PAC-UK, a private adoption organisation. If you live in another part of the country, you don't have access to that. But it's like asking someone who is traumatised by an institution to return to the institution to ask them for help for the problem they caused. When I went onto the Adoption UK website, I was expected to sign up as a member, which I really didn't want to do. I've already had my life taken over as a powerless baby by an institution, I don't want to repeat that. No way! Leave me alone.

"There's a lot more in the [United] States about adopted adults, but in the UK, there is nothing. This is a lifelong need that we are living with."

I asked Susie what she felt about the matter of an adoption apology for both adopted people and mothers who were coerced. She said she thought it was, "hugely important, because it is a public acknowledgement from my point of view as an adult adoptee, because the narrative in our society doesn't reflect the reality – it's more complicated. It's awful for a mother to be separated from her baby, but I don't think people understand. It's terrible for a baby to be separated from its mother. I really want it for the birth mothers – because I know they carry the shame.

"My mother-in-law pierces me a lot with her careless throwaway comments, but in fact, they are simply a reflection of views and values held by wider society. For instance, she would say to me, 'You were lucky to be rescued by your mum and dad,' like there was something wrong with my mother – not recognising my mother is part of me – so what does that make me feel like? And how might that feel for my birth mother? So, people assumed that she wasn't a fit person to become a mother, so the baby needed rescuing from her!

"She said, 'I could never have given up my baby!' And my birth mother must've heard this from people. She also said, 'Oh, I remember a friend who kept her baby,' thereby proving herself to be superior. It's desperately important that these women receive an apology. And it would be incredible if we adopted persons – those who were relinquished – were also acknowledged.

"I think our society is still invested in believing adoptions overall are a very good thing. They don't want to think about the fact that they are actually extremely damaging."

Susie recalls a visit to the London Foundling Museum. She found it a very emotional experience. "We owed it to those children to bear witness." She describes what she saw: "They have a foundling dressing-up box and you can dress up as a foundling. It's like the equivalent of having a dressing-up box at Auschwitz and saying you can dress up as one of the prisoners! One of the other visitors was giggling about this, and I really challenged her about her attitude towards such an important issue.

"There's a total ignorance, and lack of understanding and acceptance, of the truth all around us. We are wounded all the time by that, by those microaggressions; it puts me in mind of life before Black Lives Matter and the MeToo movement. People say things like 'Who are your real parents?' The kind of stuff that people say without realising the impact. It is hard. And there are an awful lot of adopted people – and I was one of them – who, for years, were in denial. They were suppressing it because it is too painful. As a little girl, my way of coping was just to pretend my adopted mum and dad were actually the only ones that I had and I kept that going. Yeah, I convinced myself that genetics don't matter and that my birth parents didn't matter at all. There are lots of adopted people who are like that, they find a way to live with it, but there is, in reality, so much that they are burdened with, that they carry. It puts me in mind of Michael Gove who is adopted, and he would say he is really grateful – he's a grateful adoptee. He says he had such a great life and he's not curious about all of this stuff, but that's mad and it's repressed in my opinion. What human being doesn't want to know where they came from? It's a crime against nature. He is one of many adopted people who think like that."

Our discussion touched on the fact that there is some sense of not wanting to dig around in your own difficult and possibly traumatic past. Because, really, who welcomes pain into their heart, and also society doesn't exactly make it an easy process. Susie says, "You form your fragile identity as a child and gradually build it up. You get adoptees that are very defensive. For instance, I read an article in *The Daily Mail* by a well-known adoptee who was saying that they thought it was outrageous that people like me were doing adoption down. They were saying they were so grateful it had happened to them and they didn't need to know anything else. But I think that's fear and survival speaking. Because for a baby to be taken, that's the biggest threat. Anna Freud said to separate a baby from its mother is worse than the trauma of war, and that's absolutely true because you are at your most vulnerable. *Your mother is your survival.* You live or die by your mother. And that is what happened. That is what they were and are doing."

We return to the topic of Susie's relationship with Maria. Susie takes up the story. "I think if she was alive today, at the point I have now reached, I would be able to cope. That's the tragedy because we haven't had specialist health care; not only were we separated, but when we did find each other, we just couldn't handle it. I honestly had a breakdown over this. I couldn't handle what she wanted from me. I spent the whole of my childhood and a good part of my adult years, trying to tell myself that I belonged to this other set of parents entirely, with this really deep-seated fear about my first family. When I finally met her, and she was in such great need of me, it was like my worst fears coming through. It challenged my entire self, my whole identity; it literally shattered my sense of self. I could not cope with it at all. Also, the timing was pretty awful because my adoptive mum had just died. I was grieving her, which was enormous for me.

"I am seeing a therapist about this and she thinks what happened was that I never separated from my adoptive mother who brought me up, so I've got this shadow of her. I don't have a complete sense of an independent self. So, when she died, it was enormous, and then this 'other' mother is desperate for me, desperate, desperate, desperate and putting me under immense pressure. I stopped sleeping. I went into therapy for the first time in my life.

"My mother was all over me, couldn't stop talking and it was all about her. She just couldn't help it. She barely asked me a question about myself. She just had such a great need for me to heal her, for me to parent her in a strange way. At that point, I couldn't provide everything she needed. I hadn't managed to come to terms with what was going on for me or to process it, so I was shattered.

"My mother had had no therapy at all, no support – bless her – she went through that! She had her baby taken from her – she couldn't keep her own child. She did write to me. Both her and my father had written to the adoption agency and there were letters waiting on my file. She'd been told it was the best thing for the baby and she told me she regretted it ever since. Of course, she did. Anybody that's had a child can tell you that. You would've had an abortion instead, wouldn't you? They didn't have that choice. But once you've had the baby come through to full term, then it's your baby. How would that feel? It's nature, isn't it? It's the most powerful force when you've held that baby in your arms. I mean, oh my God, it's bliss, isn't it? Every fibre of you wants that baby, wants to care for that baby and it's a part of you. It must be like giving up a part of yourself.

"So, ten years ago, I went to get my notes from Catholic Care. My birth father, Paddy, had been in touch with Maria because he wanted to find me. He instigated it, wanted to know where I was and if I was okay. It turns out, I'm not the only child he had outside of a marriage. He had another girlfriend and she had a baby. This was Ireland all those years ago. My sister had already been in touch with him and knows him better than I do, and I've only recently really started to develop a relationship with her. So, he wasn't like one of those fathers who didn't want to know, but then I think he didn't keep us either, and he didn't want to be with Maria. He does carry some responsibility, I would say. I think he had more agency, more financial independence, given that he was twenty-seven. It's difficult to reflect back on those times though. Presumably, he would've also felt that it would've been a benefit to the baby to have two parents. I sometimes think he could've been with Maria, but I don't really know; it's conjecture on my part. I'm grateful to him that he wrote the letter and my relationship with him is a lot easier than it was with my mother. I guess it would be because he hasn't invested in me in the same way as a mother does. He really listened to me and was sensitive to how I felt. I think as he matured there was a lot of guilt involved for him.

"It has to be remembered that the strongly held belief that people were doing the right thing, by encouraging women like Maria and others to give up their babies, was powerful and persuasive. Perhaps, to such an extent, those alternatives were difficult to envision, let alone consider?"

Perhaps also, the mothers of those women who were unmarried and pregnant also had a sense of how hard life could be for those who transgressed the robust moral code that was enforced in countries like Ireland and certainly within Catholic communities across the UK. Not just the being an outsider due to being an unmarried mother, but perhaps the hard work, the labour if you like, involved in rearing a child. Of course, the older women in the family would also factor in the potential for a future match with a man and the potential for happiness through marriage, and the economic advantages that it most certainly affords. Single motherhood was clearly a potential barrier to that. The impact on the child – *the little bastard* – would've also been factored in. In my own mind, I can imagine the apocryphal tales of those women who followed their hearts, and not the advice of their elders and the church, who simply said go into that home, give up your baby and everything will be fine, and that's what they really seemed to believe.

Susie concludes, "I'm on an ongoing journey. I'll continue to try and understand myself because I've been in the dark all my life. I'm sick of it and psychologically, it's damaging. So, for my own survival, I have to continue. I've got to build my resilience and the only way I can do that is by understanding myself more and more, and therapy will be good for that. Therapy is hard, but it's also hard to find a good therapist for an adoptee and, of course, it's expensive. I think the Government should pay for this. There is a movement now for adoptees, which is literally the people that attended the formal evidence gathering held by Harriet Harman MP. They have formed a group and they want acknowledgement that they have had to pay for their own therapy for all these years. We've had nothing: not a bean, no justice, and still no apology.

"I disagree with Nadhim Zahawi, former Secretary of State for Education, that the formal adoption apology wasn't a valid request because that was 'just the way it was at the time, and therefore it wasn't the Government's responsibility,' but Dr Michael Lambert from Lancaster University has really held the Government to account and explained powerfully and with clarity exactly why the Government is responsible for what happened to women and their babies during those decades.

"I would like BBC Radio Four's *Woman's Hour*, or some other organisation, to take up our case. They should be campaigning for this for goodness' sake – it's *Woman's Hour*! Why can't they do more?"

We concluded our discussion by focusing on the impact on the babies.

"It isn't something that has really been considered, but it has a major impact," Susie says, before adding, "It's because the alternative is too damn expensive. Instead, we force those mothers into adoption instead of supporting them properly, instead of helping them to keep their babies to stop the psychological damage to those babies, to end that damage, which is enormous and we, the adoptees, are testament to that."

Kenneth

"They had no idea that my birth mother had actually lived and that I wasn't an orphan ...
The church had told them a load of old toffee."

At the start of our long conversation, Kenneth said, "I saw what Harriet Harman wrote when she tried to put it through Parliament just before Covid, since then it's just blossomed." He was talking about how Harriet Harman had instigated a Parliamentary Inquiry into historic forced adoptions and added that he was pleased that this subject, which had been hidden and forgotten for so long, was being brought into the sunlight at last. I think this increased openness and the prospect of a formal apology from the Government was what perhaps assisted him in disclosing his story to me.

"Anyone who went into a mother and baby home connected to the Catholic Church (although the Anglican church in Northern Ireland and in Canada had nearly as bad a reputation as the Catholics), should realise it was all to do with money – and all those impacted deserve an apology," Kenneth said.

He explained he has been conducting his own research into this issue over the years. "All these mother and baby homes from Tuam, to Roscrea to Bessborough Castle in Ireland, and Saint Pelagia's in Highgate London, they were all run by part of the Catholic sisterhood. Tuam was run by the Bon Secours Sisters, which is now one of the biggest nursing agencies in America after they left England in 1912. The ones that took over were the

Sisters of the Sacred Heart of Jesus and Mary – and they were the ones that ran virtually every other mother and baby home. They advertised their mission on the banner over the gate – *This is a baby home for abandoned babies and destitute mothers.*"

But Kenneth continues, "Most of the mothers that went in there weren't destitute. They had jobs, they had support, but because they were PFI (Pregnant From Ireland), the church would take them in, reassuring them that they could go into a mother and baby home and everything would be fine. Then, they would have the baby and wake up the next morning and ask, 'Where's my baby?' The mother was often told, 'Oh, I'm very sorry to have to tell you she/he passed away in the evening.' Just as shown in the film, *Philomena.* Then they were shown a rectangular patch of earth in the home or hospital garden and told that was their baby's grave. Then the adoption agency, in my case the Crusade of Rescue, would tell the prospective adoptive parents that they were going to take on an orphan who had no support, no relatives, and that the mother had passed away. That's exactly what happened to me and my mother.

"After I was adopted, I was told every other year at two, six and eight years old that I was adopted. When I was two and four, it just washed over me. It didn't mean anything. Then when I got to about ten years old, one Christmas time, we were at the dining table saying prayers, and they reminded me that I wasn't their child, but that I must know that they 'love me to bits', that I was really loved. 'We're not your natural mummy and daddy. But we are your mummy and daddy, and we really love you.' And I was overwhelmed with joy and thinking, 'Thank God, somebody loved me.'

"When I got to sixteen, I started going to work, I saw the world, and I stopped being a Catholic and going to church. I started reading a great deal and thought, hang on, what's going on? I started to read about the Highgate area of London. I knew there was something wrong there, something to do with the church.

"At that time, my life took off. I became a union representative, a magistrate, and held a seat on industrial tribunals. Just before Covid, my mum – my adoptive mum – passed away in Ireland. She was desperately ill and although I tried to get there in time, I missed her. I then did all the things that I, as her son, had to do. But when I came back to England, I thought to myself, I want to know … I want to know … I couldn't stop that thought. I reasoned there's no one left alive now. No one can interfere now or feel aggrieved; there's no one now who can get upset. So, I set about understanding and unravelling my adoption history. I wouldn't have looked while my mum and dad were alive because I would not have wanted to upset them. They had no idea that my birth mother had actually lived and that I wasn't an orphan … The church had told them a load of old toffee. My cousins in Ireland, all twenty of them, didn't know I was adopted, and they didn't know that their sister had adopted an orphan that wasn't an orphan at all.

"Around 2020, I started the process. I was told I couldn't obtain my papers without going through social services, which I did. I went to Milton Keynes to talk to somebody in social services who was very helpful. I knew I had rights to my documents, and I asked them to search for my paperwork so I could understand how I came to be adopted. Having started the process, I talked to my wife and daughter, and they agreed to buy me a DNA test.

"About two months later, seven documents turned up with a letter. There was my baptism certificate. It listed my name, my mother's name and my godmother's name. It turned out that my godmother was a 'Sister' and I assume she was a godmother to many, taking on the title without performing the duties. She was a nun from Clonmel, from the convent of the Sacred Heart of Jesus and Mary in Harrow, London. She probably did them like a conveyor belt, promising to look after my immortal soul – but on the following day, I was listed for sale! Turns out I was baptised within ten hours of birth. I doubt if my mother was even there. I imagine she would still be in bed following my birth. So, I was carried across the road and dipped in the font. 'You're now a Catholic. Thank you very much.'

"And then two weeks later, I didn't exist. They routinely told mothers that their babies had passed away. Maybe they said that we had diphtheria or whatever … I believe my mother was told I had died after birth. The home I was in, St Pelagia's, was investigated before it was burnt down in 1965; it backed directly onto Highgate Cemetery.

"I know that small black-and-white photographs were given to the agency, the Crusade of Rescue, who worked for the Catholic Church. They would have put these photographs up in churches, and on the walls of their office in Ladbroke Grove, London, so people who were unable to have a child for whatever reason, who wanted to adopt a child, preferably an orphan, could find one through the agency. They would choose a child from these little photographs, and that image was in my file from social services.

"The adoption paperwork showed my mother but incorrectly identified her as Mary Bridget Mahony. My DNA showed me that my mother was, in fact, Eileen O'Mahoney, born in 1930 in Clonmel, County Tipperary. Without the DNA test, I would not have been able to unravel the puzzle, as the paperwork for both my mother and me was badly wrong, perhaps deliberately so.

"It turns out Eileen O'Mahoney had a twin sister who went to America, and now I know I have loads of cousins in the States, but my mother's sister, my aunty, also assumed I was dead.

"When a couple, who became my adopted parents, came into the church and said they wanted to adopt an orphan, they looked at my photo and said, 'Ain't he lovely – we'll take him,' or something like that I imagine. Anyway, they then took me to their home also in Clonmel. In fact, they lived very near to my birth mother who, later I realised, lived just four streets away. So, when I was a little kid until I was four and we returned to England, I was running around the fields, playing with loads of children, any of whom could've been one of my eight brothers and sisters or my cousins."

Kenneth carries on, "Eileen, my birth mother's story continues very strangely. She was working as a spectacle technician. I guess that's how she met my real father because he was a glasses-wearing GI, who was billeted in Hendon. In 1949, just before he knew about me – because if he had known about me, he might have done something different – he left the UK. Then Eileen finds out she's pregnant and the rest is history as they say.

"My dad goes back to America. He's already got one child called Saul Anthony and later he has another son called Michael. By this time, my birth mum is married to a Kenneth Bradley. His sister is named Lillian Rose Bradley, and she falls in love with Richard Anstey, who was born in Ireland and they emigrated to New York. They had a daughter called Dora Lee Anstey; she married a guy called Michael, the son of my father. My mother's husband's sister's daughter married my father's son. So, she becomes my first cousin, my sister-in-law and her son is also my nephew."

"That's wild!" I say to Ken. It's tricky to understand the family relationships but easy to understand how a fluke could bring them together across time and continents. I ask Kenneth for clarification. "So, somehow your family are dispersed across the globe but become deeply connected?"

"Yes," he agrees and continues to explain the puzzle that he encountered. "Eileen then married in 1966 and had a daughter, that daughter had three children and I am now in touch with the three of them. I think that's brilliant and so do they."

Kenneth continues, "I often think what would've happened if I'd had my own page in the adoption literature, which said I was born to someone from Clonmel. If that had been clear when the prospective parents – my mum and dad – had walked in and said we wanted to adopt that little boy, maybe they wouldn't have chosen me, knowing that I would have been living so close to where my birth mother came from. All because they wanted to save one scrap of paper, they crossed out one name and inserted my name instead ..."

Kenneth sounded very jovial and measured about it all and I asked him how he felt. He told me, "I've been very lucky. I've been a union man for forty-seven years out of my fifty on the railway. I was very high up, working with people like Bob Crowe, Manuel Cortez and Mick Lynch. I've met a lot of politicians at Labour Party Conferences including Tony Blair. I've had a good life, serving on two union executives. I have won the union's gold medal for long service, supported Amnesty International for four years, then I became a magistrate and now I represent people at industrial tribunal. Yes, I've had a hell of a life and I say that because I kissed the Blarney Stone twice and I've got the gift of the gab. If I didn't get that from my mummy, I got it from somewhere.

"I've got my wife and daughter. And I'm really very happy and it could've been quite different, I realise that. I know other people from my circumstances had a more difficult time, including being used as slaves to work.

"I think it was a help that I knew that I was adopted from a very young age when they started to put the idea into my head that my mother was not my birth mother, but she was my mother. They really looked after me and they could not have done more for me. Even if they'd been my birth parents, they could not have done more. I think they did more for me, in fact, because I was adopted."

Kenneth revealed that his mother felt so much for him, as she was ageing, she actually asked him for permission to leave London to return to Ireland to spend the remaining years of her life with her brothers. Like him, she was deeply connected to Ireland, of course; he didn't stand in her way.

Kenneth also described that as a child living in London, his mother took on care for other children and at one point, there were three families living in one house and he saw the other children almost as if they were his brothers and sisters. So, although he was an only child, he had a special person in his life, one that he called he called 'little sis' who was, he believed, his mum's sister's child and her sister had returned to Ireland."

Kenneth expands on why the matter of an adoption apology is important to him. Firstly, he acknowledges that he was lucky to find helpful paperwork that ultimately gave him a trail to follow, and social services treated him well, so he was able to find out what happened to his birth mother. He knows she passed away in 2013 in Cambridgeshire and that she never knew he existed.

"She was told that I had passed away. What mother would not want to know? I mean, had I stayed with her, who knows what would've happened – she might have been terrible, she might have beaten me – who knows? But she did not deserve to get treated like that. She was, I believe, one of the mothers of 6,012 babies that were trafficked from St Joseph's in Highgate between 1946 and 1955. Trafficked, either back to Ireland, or to America. Most of them went to America. After the war, so many young American soldiers had died and their wives were at home with no husband and no child – but they had money. Each baby cost roughly one thousand pounds. Imagine that when you're earning thirteen quid a week! It's an enormous sum of money.

"My mother deserves an apology even though she's not here now. Someone needs to *give me* that apology."

We talked about the political change that we were anticipating – the move from the Conservative to a probable Labour government and agreed that an incoming Labour government needed to give a formal apology. Kenneth was very clear. He thought whoever gave the apology – whether it was Helen Hayes, Labour MP for Dulwich and West Norwood (at the time Shadow Education Minister) because "it might be more heartfelt coming from her", or the Children's Minister – "nonetheless, whoever gives it, it must be given."

Kenneth concludes that he believes British politicians knew that the survivors of mother and baby homes in Ireland, Canada, Australia, and Denmark had their lives altered, and knew some children were lost in the process. He contends that councils and government were aware of terrible practices within the homes. He says, "In my home, they even had a room staged, ready and photographed, that had six cots and toys so that when the inspector visited, they could show him a proper nursery. Everything was clean, and the babies there had been fed every three hours. But that was all window dressing."

Kenneth also told me what he knew about what had taken place in Tuam: "A nun with a trolley would go down between two rows of cots each containing two babies, one at the top and one at the bottom of a cot, and the nun would put into each cot two bottles of milk. What often happened was that the stronger baby took all the milk, and the weaker, possibly younger, less mobile baby would have none. So, in the end, one baby thrived while another starved to death, but the nuns could say, in all honesty, they had fed the babies, and during the official inquiry, the stenographer recorded that as a fact without context. The actual detail was greatly different – and deadly."

He talks about the paperwork that he received and, out of the six pages, only one, detailing the note of his baptism, was clear. These are common hurdles that adult adoptees face in piecing together their history, plus as Kenneth explained, "names are often changed – not necessarily by design – more due to errors and simple lack of care when transcribing a name onto a form. The spelling could end up quite different – especially with Irish names. This makes tracking down relatives difficult. Also, many details are redacted or covered, as was the case for me." All the more reason that slow, time-consuming and painstaking research is needed; he was much assisted by the use of DNA.

I hadn't realised how DNA could be so accurate, why would I? I've never had a reason to use DNA, let alone to check who my parents were.

Ken explains to me that as he understands it, "Each person has five hundred markers: half come from your mother's side, and the other half are an amalgam of your father, grandfather and great grandfather."

I was intrigued as to why someone called Eileen O'Mahoney had been registered as a Mary Bridget Mahony, and Kenneth explained to me that it was standard practice when you went into a mother and baby home to lose your name and to lose your identity. This was certainly the case in Ann Fessler's book *The Girls Who Went Away*. Similarly, the women that I interviewed for this book queried with me why they couldn't remember anybody's surname from the mother and baby homes that they had been in. This was because the use of surnames was frowned upon. In some homes, it was the nuns who would decide what the women in the homes were going to be known by whilst they were resident there. Partly Kenneth believes that this was so that when a woman left the home, it wasn't *her* that had given up the baby – because under Catholic practices, you were forgiven your sin following the baptism of the baby, when all sin was washed away, and so it was the person that carried the temporary name that had given away the child. The *fallen woman*, having surrendered her baby for adoption and doing the right thing in the eyes of the Church and of God, could then resume her previous life using her *real* name. It's an interesting theory.

Thinking of the babies, Kenneth emphasised that baby started out with one name, but once adopted that was routinely changed. There is no doubt there was a great deal of renaming happening as standard practice.

The matter of names is significant, and I asked Kenneth if I could use his name here in this book and he replied, "Yes, you can use my name. I have no problem with that at all because all of the people that matter are no longer with us. I am me. I know who I am and I have got my story. I've had a good life and if it helps someone else and they learn that it's better to tell an adopted person that they are adopted, that's great."

As our conversation drew to a close, Kenneth recalled a memory of a young girl he used to know when he lived in Clonmel, all those years ago. I found the recollection and sharing of this memory particularly poignant.

He explains, "I was in the kitchen listening to my granddad saying, 'It shouldn't have happened.' What had happened was this girl of eleven had overheard an argument between her parents, between the two people she believed were her mummy and daddy. The man says to the woman, 'She's not ours anyway.' This is how this particular young girl came to find out she was adopted. She realised her real mummy didn't want her and had surrendered her to this couple. She went down to the local river and threw herself in. That was the end of her. She didn't know the truth, she had never been told, and she only found out because of this terrible argument between the people that she thought were her parents, but who were, in fact, her adoptive parents."

I put to Kenneth that the truly sad thing was it wasn't only the words that would have had such a dreadful impact, but the fact that this child would have doubtlessly experienced behaviour towards her that made the words believable.

Tina

"There's someone out there that I need to connect with."

Over tea and biscuits, I interviewed Tina, who explained how close she was to her father, Tom, and that throughout his life, he was always very open about how being adopted had affected him. Tom was born in 1954 and passed away very suddenly in 2014. He was two weeks old when he was adopted. His adoptive mother had died when he was just fifteen years old. His adoptive father was much older than his wife and he died a few years later when Tom was just eighteen.

In common with many other adoptees, Tom was brought up in a family where he believed his siblings (who were the biological children of his parents) were his blood relatives. He was thirteen when he was informed he was adopted, and that had a huge impact on him.

Tina continues, "He went off the rails and he stopped going to school. Being adopted affected him all his life. Since his death, I have managed to trace his family. My dad couldn't do that; it was too much for him, although he always said to me, 'I'm not going to go and look for them because I promised my mum I wouldn't – but there's nothing to stop you looking.' That made me think something else was being hidden. The sad thing is, his birth mother who passed away in 1993, moved to Hastings in the 1980s, which is where we were living at the same time." Tina takes a deep breath and says to me, "All of those years she was living nearby; our paths must've crossed. Hastings was such a small town and one of those places where everybody knows everybody else. I wish my dad had been alive to even know that."

I wondered why the task of tracing her father's adoptive history had fallen on her shoulders. Tina explains that they did try to trace her father's mother years ago, before the internet.

"I sat down with him, going through his documents and then, when we got to a certain point, we found a frustrating dead end. I then left it, and it's only in the last few years that I started to look again and it's all there. It's all there now it's accessible on the internet. I found his mother – my grandmother – and cousins on her side of the family."

Whilst Tina is thrilled with the progress she's made, it's also painful, and she tells me she feels gutted.

"I had one nan and grandad, and all my other friends had two; the thought now of having a nan and grandad in my own town would've been brilliant. To think I could've had that!

"I have managed to make contact with some of my father's family, a cousin, and he has given me some photographs and spoken about my grandmother's personality, that she was an outgoing character, and that after she had my father adopted – which she had to do – she never went on to have any more children. Also, that she married three times, which made me wonder if that was due to the impact of losing her only child – my father. She was twenty-three then. Her father was particularly strict. He would not allow her to keep her baby and she was forced to give her baby up. Sadly, she died of cancer."

"What about your father's father?" I ask.

"The father's name is on the birth certificate and there was talk, family gossip, that he was a Canadian soldier who returned to Canada, but we don't really know who he was. We did find a photo of a man in uniform in the family collection, and nobody knew who he was, and there does appear to be a likeness between him and my dad. So maybe it's him, but we can't find out."

Tina said she would like to know exactly what happened, for instance, whether her grandmother went into a home to have her father and whether she looked after him for those two weeks prior to his adoption.

Tina continues sharing her experiences saying, "The scars of my father's adoption and his childhood, left him unable to maintain relationships. He was always jumping from one relationship to another, never feeling fulfilled in a relationship, always craving love. He married three times and had a fourth relationship and two more children. Even so, he was just always quite sad. There was a big void in his life, although there was so much love around him. He always felt something was missing. He loved the falling-in-love feeling. He ended up alone." Tina's love for her father is very evident.

I asked Tina if she and her father ever spoke about his relationship patterns. She explained, "I was very close to him and always felt his sadness. When I was much younger, I frequently asked him, where are your mum and dad? And of course, he had no answers. He felt he had been rejected by his own mother. I know now that if he could have understood that his mother was forced to give him up (I'm assuming that was the case) it would've been better for him. It would have made a big difference to him. He always felt that he had been unwanted and rejected.

Tina and I discussed how it's only in recent times that there's a wider understanding that unmarried women during the fifties, sixties and seventies who became pregnant, were subjected to significant shame, and had no real choice about whether they kept their own babies – that wasn't an option.

Tina summarises, "If he'd have known that, then perhaps he wouldn't have felt so angry and rejected.

"In the mid-nineties, he sent off for his adoption certificate and I sat with him to go through it. It was a big deal and Dad was really emotional about it. He didn't want to look at it at first, then when he did and he saw his mum and dad's names it was extremely emotional for him, seeing it in black and white. After that, he did seem to start dealing with his adoption a little better."

Tina, meanwhile, is now trying to track down his father, her grandfather. "There's a chance that he could still be alive." Given that Tina's father was dead, I wanted to know why she felt so compelled to piece together her father's history.

"Even when he was alive, I desperately wanted a greater understanding about my family background, and I'd had that feeling since I was a child. There's someone out there that I need to connect with. It's bizarre, it's hard to explain, it's a feeling inside. It would mean the finishing pieces of the jigsaw. Even meeting a distant relative would be amazing."

I wondered how far Tina would go to track down her family and with a laugh and a look of excitement, she pulled a DNA kit out of her handbag.

"I'm going to do this as soon as possible." Her excitement is palpable. Tina tells me her daughter is now helping with the tracing process using the web.

Our conversation turns to thoughts about what happened to the women to make them put their babies up for adoption.

Tina says, "It's increasingly being recognised by society that they didn't have a choice. How traumatised they must have been during pregnancy and after the birth, and throughout the rest of their lives. It would be so good if there was a platform where all this information was held and accessible, and where people could share examples of how they made progress understanding their own history."

Tina explained she was glad she'd found her father's cousins on his mother's side and that they had all done well for themselves.

"My dad didn't, although he was extremely clever, he suffered from depression all his life. I think that's the price he paid for being adopted."

Tina texts me an update on the results of the DNA kit test. "70% England and Northwestern Europe. 27% Scottish!!! Didn't see that coming. 2% German. 1% Eastern Europe and Russia. No Canadian. Back to the drawing board. I've got a feeling it's someone closer to home."

Whilst it is becoming more popular to use DNA kits, they don't tell the whole picture. In this case, there is an absence of indigenous or native Canadian ancestry, but for generations, English, Scottish, and European people have migrated and naturalised in Canada, so her grandfather could still be 'Canadian'. I have no doubt that Tina will continue her painstaking endeavours to uncover her family history, but the complexity and cost of her search merely underscores the need for the UK Government to assist in this process.

Is justice in sight?

The Movement for Adoption Apology has been been at the forefront of fighting for justice for everyone affected by the horrors of historic forced adoption. They, more than anyone, understand that it isn't enough for the UK Government to acknowledge responsibility for unjust, harmful historic practices, whilst failing to act. Other contemporary social justice campaigns: Windrush, Justice4Grenfell, Horizon Post Office, the infected blood scandal, and the Hillsborough Law campaign, to name but a few, are also clamouring and, in some cases, achieving action. They have actively engaged with the Government to seek remedy and reparations. In acknowledgement of those claims and the backlog within the social justice sector, the Labour Government included the following commitment to historic injustices in its 2024 Labour Party Manifesto:

> Under the Conservatives, too many victims of historical injustices have had insult added to injury by years of legal delays. Without justice and the truth, victims and their families cannot move forward. Labour will right this wrong, act on the findings of the Infected Blood Inquiry, and respond to the findings of the Grenfell Inquiry and the Covid-19 Inquiry, to ensure swift resolution.
>
> Labour will introduce a 'Hillsborough Law' which will place a legal duty of candour on public servants and authorities and provide legal aid for victims of disasters or state-related deaths. We will ensure the victims of the appalling Windrush scandal have their voices heard and the compensation scheme is run effectively, with a new Windrush Commissioner. Labour will also ensure, through an investigation or inquiry, that the truth about the events at Orgreave comes to light.

> Labour will stop the chaos that lets too many criminals act with impunity, turn the page with stronger policing, and rebuild our criminal justice system.

In January 2024 many people were engrossed by the ITV drama, *Mr Bates vs. The Post Office*. A powerful and moving account of injustice suffered by hundreds of Post Office employees. The drama brought the scandal to life and into people's living rooms. Under the weight of mounting public opinion, the then Prime Minister, Rishi Sunak, apologised to those involved and announced that a new law would be introduced so people wrongly convicted in the Horizon scandal were, "swiftly exonerated and compensated".

He stated, "This is one of the greatest miscarriages of justice in our nation's history. People who worked hard to serve their communities had their lives and their reputations destroyed through absolutely no fault of their own. The victims must get justice and compensation." Upfront payments of £75,000 were offered to some of those affected. Labour have taken that forward.

Just like those caught up in the Horizon scandal, the Movement for Adoption Apology women and adopted people affected by historic forced adoptions are inevitably reaching an age at which an apology and reparations are urgent. Just like those who endured the Horizon scandal, many women and adopted people had their lives scarred by trauma and in some cases ruined, through no fault of their own. And just like Horizon, when the pressure became unbearable, some people sadly took their own lives. However, we have yet to see 'swift exoneration and compensation' for historic forced adoptions.

On Monday 20 May 2024, a day which Rishi Sunak described as "a day of shame for the British state", he fulsomely (and correctly) apologised for the failures of successive governments over the infected blood scandal, and promised to pay whatever it takes to compensate the victims. In his speech, Rishi Sunak, highlighted the failures of the British Government, failures by ministers, civil servants, and the NHS. He concluded, "This is an apology from the state – to every single person impacted by this scandal. It did not have to be this way; it should never have been this way. And on behalf of this and every government stretching back to the 1970s, I am truly sorry."

By contrast, the Conservative government failed to issue a formal apology regarding forced adoption, even when instructed to do so by the Joint Committee on Human Rights. Nadhim Zahawi, the then Parliamentary Under-Secretary of State for Education stated "It is only right that this house acknowledges their unnecessary pain and suffering". This does not form an apology, rather, Zahawi states this is more to do with society's moral attitude to unmarried mothers at the time.

The stark contrast barely needs highlighting. How insulting for the women and adopted people whose wounds and claims have been disparaged and unheeded over the last seven decades. Disappointed but undaunted, MAA condemned the Government's failure to apologise and pledged to continue to campaign.

The JCHR expressed their dismay saying:

> It is disappointing that the Government has chosen not to issue a formal apology in recognition of the appalling treatment that unmarried mothers suffered during that time, and the lifelong consequences this had on them, on their children, now grown, and all those involved.

In the face of progress made by other social injustice campaigns, indomitable MAA activists wrote to me to highlight the following:

> We have been rebuffed many times and told that it was our 'decision' or that of our families so 'no apology is warranted'. Assertions which ignored a huge state-funded and sanctioned 'adoption machine' which facilitated the separation of infant from vulnerable young mother,

ensuring that the mother would be bullied to make certain that she could not fight back.

By way of a useful comparison with other social justice campaigns, whose aims MAA supports, the Post Office Horizon scandal impacts 900 people, plus family members. The Infected Blood Scandal impacts 30,000 people and their family members. By contrast MAA knows that 215,000 women (plus 215,000 children), so a total of 430,000 people, plus fathers and family members are impacted by this scandal. A realistic figure would be nearer to one million – though we suspect the number is actually higher.

Only two other U.K. campaign groups seek to represent a larger constituency of people. WASPI women, Women Against State Pension Inequality, who represent the 3.6 million women impacted by unfair pension changes and Excluded U.K. who represent 3.8 million U.K. taxpayers excluded from parity of government financial support during the Covid-19 crisis. Many of those affected by the issues on which MAA is campaigning also fall into one or both of those last two groups.

Assurances previously given to MAA by various prominent politicians are hollow, given the way we continue to be ignored and side-lined. It's difficult to trust politicians when progress is turgid and our campaign is seemingly unimportant. For instance, in 2018 Nadhim Zahawi, then the Education Secretary met with MAA following a debate on the topic of historic forced adoptions in Parliament. Six of us met with Nadhim Zahawi and two upper echelon Social Services staff. He promised he would look into it, he would help us, that he would follow up. He did nothing. We never heard from him, or the social service staff ever again.

Entire lives have been blighted by enforced separation of mother and new-born child, yet we have been treated as a group of women who are making an unnecessary fuss. Expert evidence provided at the Parliamentary Inquiry supports what we have been saying, yet still somehow, we are not entitled to a formal public apology and reparations, and recognition of the cruel injustices that robbed us of the lives we might have had.

The fairest way to deal with the entire matter would be a Public Inquiry. Yet we are told that we are less likely to obtain a Public Inquiry as we've already had a Parliamentary Inquiry.

Was that the intention, we wonder? Deny us further lines of inquiry by giving us something that will 'suffice' and still hadn't been completed?

We have had enough of empty promises. We are not specifically mentioned in the 2024 Labour Manifesto. Indicating this particular social injustice and human rights issue, which affects around one million people so fundamentally, is not deemed as important as others.

Unless we have a written assurance that our campaign will be dealt with properly by Labour, in a respectful, public and appropriate way, we hold no more hope of obtaining justice under a Labour government than we have had under the Conservative government.

The cost of historic forced adoptions has been significant to governments. The Tuam scandal in Ireland, assiduously researched and exposed by historian, Catherine Corless, forced the *2015 Final Report of the Commission of Investigation into Mother and Baby Homes*, which concluded that 56,000 women and about 57,000 children were placed or born in homes, mostly run by nuns between 1922 and 1998.

The Irish Government then began reparations for the 34,000 survivors of mother and baby homes in Ireland. In addition to the running costs, said to be €7 million per annum up to 2021, the additional bill for reparations cost €800 million, and was the largest of its type in the history of the state. Women who spent less than three months in a home were entitled to €5,000, with €10,000 payable to those who spent between three and six months in a home.

For adopted people born in the homes, who hadn't received compensation from another residential institution's redress scheme, the Irish Government offered between €1,500 and €60,000. The then

Taoiseach, Mícheál Martin, said the report described a "dark, difficult and shameful chapter" of Irish history. "As a nation, we must face up to the full truth of our past."

Further afield on 21 March 2013, Julia Gillard, the then Prime Minister of Australia apologised on behalf of the Australian Government to people affected by forced adoption or removal policies and practices and invested $11.5 million over four years to assist those affected. In 2017, additional funding of $5.7 million was found to continue the Forced Adoption Support Services to June 2021.

Based on the figures from Ireland or Australia, or compensation to other social injustice victims, it would be too crude and naïve to attempt to determine an aggregate 'per person' cost for those potentially eligible for compensation due to historic forced adoption practices in the UK. But, clearly, there's a need for *parity, transparency and urgent action* regarding support measures in the UK. How and when will that be achieved?

The UK seems a long way behind other comparable nations in addressing historic forced adoptions, despite the knowledge of approaches successfully implemented elsewhere. The UK has the benefit of these schemes in Australia and Ireland to use as a template – should it determine to do so.

It is vitally important to learn the lessons of historic forced adoption; not only for historical reasons, but due to a pressing need for a truthful narrative to address the current unmet needs of the mothers and the adopted people affected, and also deal with the potential issues and traumas prompted by new developments in reproduction such as surrogacy and donor conception. As donor conception grows, donor-conceived persons are now forming support groups around the world as they fight for their rights. HFEA, the Human Fertilisation & Embryology Authority regulate egg and sperm donation in the UK. The HFEA highlight that donor conception is responsible for 70,000 donor-conceived people born since 1991. This number will continue to grow.

This figure doesn't consider those who, for whatever reason, use informal and unregulated sperm donation and surrogacy. This can and has resulted in donor-conceived people with huge numbers of relatives. As Tory Shepherd points out in a Guardian article, "On top of the risks inherent in going outside the formal system is the potential trauma caused to donor-conceived people." Not to mention other risks. All sperm donors using clinics are checked for infectious diseases such as HIV, and carefully kept records can help further down the line with any inherited disease.

According to a Harvard Study, many donor-conceived people experienced a 'shift of self', when they found out how they are conceived, and half of those surveyed sought psychological help in order to cope, once they had learned about how they were conceived.

From 2023 donor-conceived people, aged 18, were able to apply to HFEA to access identifying information about their donor.

It is an *inescapable* conclusion that the lived experience of this unique group should inform and shape contemporary adoption policy and practice. The 'happy-ever-after' myth is surely exploded? What other social policy interventions can supersede or augment contemporary adoption practices, now that we understand the unavoidable damage that adoption – forced or otherwise – can and often inflicts?

MAA has struggled valiantly as an under-resourced, user-led, grassroots organisation – a Cinderella of the social justice world, hampered by, or maybe because of, the intersectionality of gender, age and class. As the Labour government finds its feet, within a landscape of fiercely competing demands, heightened expectations and inevitably constrained public finances, I hope they don't inadvertently facilitate what I would term a 'Hierarchy of Hurt'. Rather, use the challenge as an opportunity to reinforce the contract of confidence between state and citizen, to build back the value of trust as the currency between politician and voter. The cost of failure, with millions of people and their families now looking towards the social justice sector for action, seeking answers and solutions, is potentially extremely high. Voters will demand accountability and a high bar has been set. Labour would be wise to correctly calibrate the importance of these claims and act with decisive speed.

Far too many people are still keen to believe that what happened, happened in the swirling mists of time past and has no relevance today. Labour politicians, Stephen Twigg and Alison McGovern, along with Green Party MP, Dr Caroline Lucas, have pushed for action. Baroness Harriet Harman KC now sitting in the House of Lords and Ann Keen, both ex-MPs, are formidable figures who facilitated the Parliamentary Inquiry – no mean feat. In the past year, my meetings with Helen Hayes MP have been promising, but securing a formal apology has been a long time coming and is yet to be achieved. With a glacial rate of progress and few reliable political allies, it is little wonder MAA has adopted the disability rights activist slogan, "Nothing About Us Without Us". It's high time the survivors of historically forced adoptions were listened to, to formulate an apology, and to inform a survivor-centred approach to reparations.

These are MAA's most recent recommended measures to accompany a formal apology:

Nothing About Us Without Us

Recommended measures to accompany an Apology:

- Public formal apology which does not blame 'society' for what happened. The apology must accept full responsibility for the events and trauma and say sorry in an unqualified way.

- We must have a say in the wording of any apology, which must avoid any of the contemporary 'non-apology' terms, such as "I'm sorry you feel that way". That is not an apology, rather it seeks to avoid shouldering any blame by placing the blame elsewhere.

- We must have seat at the table when deciding policy and consultation on all matters prior to implementation.
- Fully funded trauma-informed and adoption-specific support for ALL those affected mothers, fathers, children and family members.
- Support with searching: optional fully funded assistance with searching, including the use of DNA.
- Optional fully funded intermediary assistance with making and sustaining contact for everyone affected. This must include guidance in relation to initial contact.
- Full access to records for ALL affected, including any information which will help with tracing a child or parent; identifying information including proof of status (alive or dead), family medical history for adoptees, and any other data or information which may be deemed appropriate or necessary.
- The option of integrated birth certificates following reunion.
- Adoptees to have the option to set aside/discharge adoption orders.
- The implementation and maintenance of an independent mechanism / database to ensure that parties on both sides of the adoption are informed should their relative become ill, be dying or die. This is particularly important if reunion has not been possible for any reason.
- Recognition of, and assistance with, issues around inheritance /probate and the right of a parent to bequeath to their child, even though (due to forced adoption) their heir is not legally recognised as a relative.
- All adoption records and related papers to be held in a central office or other suitable location that is free from all prior involvement with adoption. All historic records, dating from World War II up to the 1990s, to be made available by church organisations, secular organisations, and anyone else involved with historic adoption. This will ensure that searching does not involve contact with any organisation or agency which was responsible for the original trauma and loss. This will also ensure that documents and files are not 'accidentally' destroyed in a fire or flood, and remain safeguarded and made available as required, preferably in a digital format to avoid documents being further compromised.

- Claims that documents have been 'accidentally' destroyed must be fully investigated in a timely manner. If the records were intentionally damaged or destroyed, due legal process must ensure the person or persons responsible are held to account.

- No agency, organisation, group, or institution that is now, or has ever been involved with adoption is to be considered when arranging any support services. This includes the provision of help with searching or support. Contact with, and reliance upon, such organisations can be difficult and re-traumatising when searching or seeking assistance.

- Should full contact not be desired by one party, there must be the right to disclose identifying information, particularly medical data and determining a relative's status (see above). This must be made available to all adult parties, including descendants.

- A register to be available to anyone who specifies no contact, for which various parameters need to be considered, such as:

  - the conditions under which fresh medical information is to be conveyed.

  - whether any 'no contact stipulation' should be subject to a time limit, followed by a review; and

  - whether means of potential contact could be deferred in some way, so that both parties are in agreement.

- Peer support services and community groups (funded), to include opportunities to bring people together.

- One or more memorial style gardens, or similar, to raise public awareness and commemorate the injustices and the apology.

- A funded annual event / day to mark the anniversary of any apology, so that those who did not feel included (or were not aware it took place) can be included subsequently.

- The appointment of a forced surrender / adult adoption Tzar.

- Overarching political brief to be maintained by the Under-Secretary of State for Children and Families, or other, as appropriate.

- A commitment to funded research to identify and detail the impact of adoption on all affected, including intergenerational consequences.

The above list is neither complete nor final. As other issues are brought to our attention, we reserve the right to include them, so that this list reflects all experiences, views and requirements, to the best of our knowledge.

I can't agree more with MAA's list of requirements. After suffering unimaginable dimensions of trauma, including significant levels of suicide ideation, after waiting so many decades for justice, and believing a formal apology would be issued by the Government, the disappointment for those concerned is palpable. For my part as an informal interlocutor, I have done my best to seek at the very least, a round-table discussion between MAA and the Government, focusing on the apology and reparations. An open dialogue is vital. To date this meeting has not been forthcoming.

As a lifelong Labour activist, and someone significantly impacted by these historic practices, the tardy and seemingly uncaring attitude of my own party in government is distressing. However, I remain convinced that the Parliamentary Inquiry reached the only legitimate conclusion: this was a violation – in fact, an abnegation – of human rights. One that impacted hundreds of thousands of women, their babies, fathers and many more intergenerationally. Despite my personal disenchantment, I remain optimistic that the apology and reparations will be issued because the scale and illegality of this social injustice has caused untold suffering over decades, and a truly civil country, which cares about its most vulnerable people, would not allow such cruelty to be ignored.

From witches to suffragettes, history has illustrated the force of patriarchy in judging and controlling women's lives. Whilst undertaking my research, these lines from the conclusion of Alberta Guibord MD and Ida R Parker's study, *What Becomes of The Unmarried Mother? A Study Of Eighty-Two cases* (1922) stood out:

> Motherhood without marriage is such a frank departure from the social code of civilised peoples, it is so inevitably linked up with the idea of disgrace, we cannot wonder that the most compelling consideration of the girl who finds herself in this experience is to keep it secret.

As we have read, through the 1960s to the early 1980s, shame was weaponised by those running or otherwise invested in mother and baby homes, ensuring young mothers were so broken by shame that they were unable to cope. With no other choice or support, they caved into the coercion, providing a supply of desirable, adoptable and, preferably white and able-bodied babies. Most young, unmarried, mothers involuntarily learnt to assimilate shame as an integral part of their psychology in order to facilitate the practice. This systemic abuse of girls, women and their babies was patently barbaric, clearly traumatising, and profoundly shocking, yet it was fully accepted in everyday society. It's impossible to conclude otherwise.

We no longer talk about the sanctity of marriage – it seems anachronistic, wildly outdated – but for decades, it was a notion that both governed behaviour and acted as a standard against which a woman's morals, and thereby her worth were judged. (Note this standard only applied to women.) Yet throughout the 'baby scoop era' – after World War II into the early seventies – when pre-marital sex resulted in a high rate of newborn adoptions, it was precisely this breach of sanctity – this falling short by becoming pregnant outside marriage (and, by being pregnant, becoming a visible offender) – that allowed the system of forced adoption to be created. It is patriarchy in action.

Political remedy

Writing this book has allowed me a unique and unexpected opportunity to interrogate my own past, and to reflect on the complex trauma, which I heard about in every one of my interviews. My belief in the urgent need for political remedy has never been stronger.

In terms of the personal impact, although I was sent away into a mother and baby home, I was extremely fortunate to keep my son, but now realise that my reputation within my family never recovered. I could never set the record straight. Like Diana and others here, this reputational injury spurred me on career-wise to 'prove myself', attempting to offset the 'bad character' conferred by becoming pregnant outside of marriage at a young age, but ignoring the need for ease or comfort – mine, or anyone else's.

Other women I interviewed, also used their careers to absolve themselves, frequently following a particular career trajectory. For example, Judy, Linda and others who went into nursing and care work did so almost as an act of atonement. There's a sense of subconsciously attempting to recalibrate the narrative and rehabilitate their reputation. It's notable that so many women have also written their own books to set the record straight and to have a voice.

It was only though these interviews that I comprehended why I married (and divorced) at a very young age. Marriage appeared to be a way in which my reputation could potentially be restored. I was obliged to sit through the daily service in the mini church, located at the heart of St Paul's mother and baby home, and listen to the repetitive homily, combined with daily admonishments by the priest, that I had nothing to give my baby being a young single parent, whilst he coerced me to 'give my baby up' to a better family. That instruction hit its mark when I married at the first opportunity, wrongly anticipating that this would make me acceptable. I had digested the mother and baby home message. If I refused to 'give my baby up' to a *good* family – and instead, selfishly kept him in a *bad* one-parent family – it stood to reason that by marrying I could create better, socially approved circumstances. Of course, the reality was anything but.

Prior to conducting these interviews, I hadn't thought too much about intergenerational trauma and what I have inevitably passed on to my children and grandchildren. A BBC report on the topic stated that, "Our children and grandchildren are shaped by the genes they inherit from us, but new research is revealing that experiences of hardship or violence can leave their mark too." An epigenetic script is inherited by the child, along with the behaviours the child learns from its parents. In my case, I was never the joyful, carefree, natural mother I wanted to be. Rather, because of always deeply fearing negative judgment, my response, my mothering, could best be described as hypervigilant – a classic trauma response – I realise now. These insights were an epiphany. And to think, I was one of the lucky ones.

Consider the facts, which have emerged in my interviews, all of which could, and did, contribute to significant trauma. Thousands of women despatched into mother and baby homes, where they were forced into unpaid work, even though 'residential' fees were being paid by their family or claimed from the State. *Homes* where they were coerced, made to feel ashamed, broken, and had their babies taken, and even when they directly requested the support to keep their baby that they were entitled to, they were told it wasn't available.

The treatment of women – girls, as they most often were – during childbirth in mother and baby homes in this era was, by any measure, abhorrent – such torture a further breach of human rights. For instance, Pat was cut and stitched without anaesthetic. Ann had her legs slapped.

Diana, who was left in pain and fear as punishment, unable to reach her distressed newborn.

Lies were told about babies dying, when the reality was, they were alive and being adopted. *Babies were a lucrative trade.* Mothers were an obstacle to be manipulated; their health, well-being and lifelong complex trauma responses were tolerable collateral damage.

Think about the history of these babies, being chosen like cars in a showroom as Lin describes or picked the way most people choose a puppy. 'Even dogs,' one woman said to me, 'are usually allowed to keep their litter for a while.'

The women were falsely consoled that they could go on to have other children – yet it seems many were unable to do so. Society pretended that babies could be abruptly severed from their mothers without being damaged.

The institutional prejudice was astonishing. Record-keeping was shoddy, perhaps deliberately so, as Kenneth outlined, making tracing and reunion extremely difficult. Adoption records were sometimes falsified – presenting the women as deficient, or as morally degenerate. Little wonder that some adult adoptees don't seek out their mothers due to the manufactured and still prevailing myths that their mothers, were 'sluts' and 'slags'. Does anyone ever question the morality of the men involved? Also consider the adult adoptees who do instigate contact with their mothers, who due to lack of clarity about the circumstances of forced adoption, are unable to conceive of the severe coercion in play at the time, and still believe that they were abandoned.

It is a nuanced and difficult decision for any mother who has been through forced adoption to seek contact with her adult child. It proves extremely difficult and is often prohibitively costly, and indeed the adoption reunion process for this group appears to be broken. Whilst it sometimes worked in previous decades, now it fails. Perhaps due to workload strain on social service departments in the UK in 2024, it doesn't work for this cohort, and isn't fit for purpose.

Real life issues are magnified, such as accessing medical records to prevent illness, as we saw with Sally, who without a meeting with her mother at just the right time, would likely now be dead. Probate is another challenging area, where often wills are altered to exclude the adoptee. Consider the struggle of Gill and Wendy, both cut out of wills, because they were adopted into a family, and when it became a financial imperative, they were then told they were adopted out.

Aside from these serious issues, consider the impact of spending a lifetime wondering if you or your baby were sold, or if your own father made a profit from your teenage misery. Or carrying the trauma of not knowing how the child taken from you fared, or even whether they are alive or dead, the impact of which Jan spoke about most eloquently. We still have the unaddressed and appalling legacy of mysterious graveyards, and disabled babies denied the medical care they should have received, as Judy experienced with her baby, Stephen.

And indeed, what about women that took their own lives after their babies were taken? Have those women even been counted?

We know the trauma of this group has been frequently disregarded and has often gone untreated. The lamentable crisis in the NHS ensures there is no, or very little, trauma-informed support or therapy available. This must be addressed. It is not good enough for the government to hide behind the myth of mental health treatment being generally available via GPs, when it isn't. As we read, Wendy cannot obtain or afford the specialist help she needs. The consequences of forced adoption ricochet down the decades; the 'damage cascade' as Eddie refers to it.

So, to the political remedy. In a 2023 podcast with Joanna Cherry KC (a Scottish National Party MP until 2024), Baroness Harriet Harman KC, then MP, reflected on the lack of action since the conclusion of the Parliamentary Inquiry she instigated in 2021. "I think really, the Government need to step back and say, 'Was this a terrible wrong that was done? We are in the Government now. We can do a bit of good by officially saying that this was absolutely wrong. It will never happen again. It should never have happened, and we apologise …' And with that, recognise the horrific pain and lifelong trauma suffered by the birth mothers, and indeed, the problems and traumas for the children who were taken from them."

Harriet Harman is correct, a heinous wrong was perpetrated, resulting in lifelong trauma. She acknowledges that the Government are accountable, saying, "Ultimately, Government are in charge of all of these processes either by what they do or what they fail to do," and the fact that "it could never happen now … shows that it's the Government's responsibility."

There is a pressing obligation on the State to provide a genuine apology and meaningful reparations – starting with the practical support measures that MAA has collated from amongst its membership over the last decade, which have been supplied to the government. This requirement has now passed from one administration to another. The Labour government in power must end the prevarication.

The clock is ticking. Women and adult adoptees represented by MAA are dying. The need for the Government to uphold the JCHR-mandated formal apology is urgent. It cannot be made quickly enough if the thousands of women and children affected are going to receive the apology in their lifetimes.

Of course, all those involved with the adoption apology are wondering when that formal apology will come. Not just those directly impacted, but their children and now grandchildren. Many interviewees stated, "The government are hoping we'll die", but, as we know, trauma is often passed on.

In *Taken*, I have detailed women who have written to their MPs under the previous government, whose letters remain unanswered, or worse, they're informed that 'this sort of thing' isn't in the MP's department. These are the 'heroic' efforts of women trying to assert their human rights. Of course, the human rights agenda didn't apply in the 'baby scoop era', and until a formal apology and reparations are received, it seems the 1998 Human Rights Act including the 'right to family life' has been torn up and thrown away.

Even though what has happened in England has been firmly swept under the carpet, there's no doubting the human rights violations and on-going discrimination against women. It is useful to reflect on the important work underway in Northern Ireland where a Truth Recovery Process has been instigated, utilising an extensive legislative framework, as detailed in, *A Human Rights Framework: Background Research for The Truth Recovery Design Process*:

Overview of the UK and NI authorities' human rights law obligations.

The human rights treaties which applied to the UK (Great Britain and Northern Ireland) during the period of the institutions' operation include:

- The Forced Labour Convention 1930, which came into effect in 1932 and the UK ratified on 3 June 1931

- The European Convention on Human Rights (ECHR), which came into effect in 1953 and the UK ratified in 1951

- The Abolition of Forced Labour Convention 1957, which came into effect in 1959 and the UK ratified in 1957

- The Supplementary Convention on the Abolition of Slavery, the Slave Trade, and Institutions and Practices Similar to Slavery, which came into effect in 1957 and the UK ratified that same year and

- The International Covenant on Civil and Political Rights (ICCPR) and International Covenant on Economic, Social and Cultural Rights (ICESCR), both of which came into effect in 1976 and the UK ratified that same year.

In addition, the UK became bound by the Convention on the Elimination of All Forms of Discrimination Against Women (CEDAW) in 1986, and by the Convention Against Torture and Other Cruel, Inhuman or Degrading Treatment or Punishment (UNCAT) in 1988—shortly before the last Mother and Baby institution closed. Since the institutions closed, the UK has become party to the Convention on the Rights of the Child (UNCRC) (which entered into force in 1990, and the UK ratified in 1991) and the Convention on the Rights of Persons with Disabilities (which entered into force in 2008 and the UK ratified in 2009). The NI and UK state authorities must today treat victims and survivors and the relatives of those who experienced institutionalisation and family separation in a way that complies with these treaties also.

Set against this legislative framework, the continued lack of government action compounds the hurt, distress, and the pain caused by previous government policies, the churches and society at large. The on-going failure to formally apologise – which will only become more pressing – sadly hints at weak values and a lack of moral fibre at the heart of government. The case is so transparent, the government should apologise immediately without any further need for persuasion. The evidence and recommendations of the Parliamentary Inquiry are more than sufficient.

MAA have produced a very thorough and extensive list of recommendations for the apology. I believe these distil into three key areas, each of which has an important role in beginning the healing process:

An apology, which should be formal, sincere, remorseful, and genuine, informed by discussion and negotiation with MAA, and delivered in a public forum by the Prime Minister or other senior minister. Those impacted should be invited to bear witness to the apology. The apology would mean the burden of *the women's* decisions, often made as teenagers, decades ago, for example the signing of documents which resulted in their babies being taken, would be re-contextualised; the apology would effectively shift the burden from that being a wholly personal decision, which they had control over, to a powerful acknowledgement of the coercion and pressures they were deliberately subjected to – effectively meaning they had no choice. Their consent was manufactured. This is important to all those I interviewed and may even prompt 'reunion' where that hasn't yet happened. Also, a public apology is vital as women and adult adoptees do not always know of the existence of support groups, such as MAA, and a no doubt newsworthy public acknowledgement would help to make such support visible.

Reparation – or **support measures** – should result in the herculean assembling and reorganisation of complex personal files and records, including medical records, collated from several sources, and transferred from analogue to digital format, so that they are accessible, searchable, and form a permanent history. There should be professional, archivist-level support to access and understand them. Potential reunion should then be simplified, minimising waiting times and undertaken as a right belonging to both parties (whilst respecting the wishes and confidentiality of both parties). All impacted people should be able to access fully funded trauma-informed therapy, over and above any current NHS entitlement, and DNA tests. The government should consider offering a token amount for the pain and distress caused. Throughout my interviews it was clear that no-one I spoke to was actively seeking financial compensation. Indeed, there was a tacit understanding that *no amount* of money could compensate for the profound loss of a child and ensuing distress. But for some, a token would be welcomed. The issue of compensation should not impede urgent government action on issuing an apology.

Memorialisation is also essential. MAA feel a 'monument', which could be a sculpture, memorial garden, or other commemorative idea, should be decided in collaboration with them. Whatever is decided should be commissioned and installed without delay, and likewise a national Memorial Day should be established, so that across the UK people are encouraged to remember the women and families who suffered, and this time in recent history, when newborn babies were effectively a commodity. A shameful trade. It is important to respectfully honour the past but also educate future generations.

Many of the people I have interviewed expressed a *belief* and *hope* in the Labour Party, a certainty that they would pick up the baton and act where the previous government had failed.

Only the government can rectify these issues – firstly by telling the truth. That forced, coerced adoptions were commonplace, state-sanctioned, and for that they must offer a full and remorseful apology. MAA stand ready to assist and have been asking for a closer relationship since 2022. In the UK, we are witnessing other historic social injustices beginning to now be addressed. The government are coming under increasing pressure from both inside and outside the Labour Party. The union movement is now engaged and helping to promote MAA's struggle too.

After coming to grips with the loss of veteran campaigner, Veronica Smith, MAA have refocused their strategy, reinvigorated their communications, and are re-launching with an impressive campaign. They have adopted a targeted approach towards government which includes recently writing to PM Keir Starmer and are seeking meetings with relevant Ministers. They have a clear message and are energetically networking, deploying vibrant social media, promoting their e-petition, and have a new information leaflet. After years of patient and polite requests for an apology, their frustration has understandably increased.

Meanwhile, society can only contain its secrets for so long, and interest is mushrooming. Recently we have seen a fresh wave of interest in the topic of mother and baby homes in the media: Martin Sixsmith's groundbreaking 2013 film *Philomena*, and in the last year, *The Women in the Wall*, *The Fallen*, *Into the Fire*, *Small Things Like These*, *The Removed*, and *The Marian Hotel*. The issues depicted in these films and plays are as shocking as they are painful.

Any one of these could herald a potential *Mr Bates vs. The Post Office* moment: it's only a matter of time before someone emulates writer/director, Gwyneth Hughes' success and ignites the nation's outrage.

The media is effectively opening the can of worms that the Government so determinedly want to ignore, moving beyond the often-stereotypical trauma interest – the 'if it bleeds, it leads' approach – aligning the mothers' struggles with the broader public interest and human rights agenda.

Younger people are horrified when they hear of these terrible events in the recent past. They are aware of their human rights and believe in the same rights for others.

Older people, the generations impacted by historic forced adoption, have become more open, more understanding. At last, there is increased cultural acceptance and understanding about what happened. All of this is fertile ground to fuel a movement, or indeed, for a scandal.

A case in point is my interviewee, Judy, whose plight has been expertly amplified on the BBC and ITV News. The most recent story on 16 October 2024 has brought forward twenty more people who may be directly connected to the growing scandal of babies denied treatment at St Monica's. Forced by these events, Cumbria Police, who previously looked the other way, have capitulated, saying they "would welcome any new information which would assist them in relation to these premises."

Meanwhile, the Department for Education who are responsible for the apology, hold an increasingly fragile line. When asked to comment on the forty-five babies buried in Parkside Cemetery who died (due to lack of treatment, Dr Michael Lambert's research reveals), a nameless government spokesperson said, "We have the deepest sympathy with all of those who are affected. The practice was abhorrent and should never have taken place. While we will not be able to quickly make every change we would like, we will look at whether there is any more we could do to support those affected."

How long will that line last?

How long must these women and adult adoptees suffer?

The government must grasp the moment.

"Justice delayed is justice denied."
British Prime Minister, William Gladstone, Liberal, 1868

"Without justice and the truth, victims and their families cannot move forward. Labour will right this wrong."
Labour Party Manifesto, June 2024

Copyright acknowledgements

We are grateful for permission to reproduce the following material in this book:

Carrie Etter, *'A Birthmother's Catechism'* from *'Imagined Sons'* 2014 © Carrie Etter. Reprinted with kind permission of Seren Books.

Bibliography

Adoption UK, 'Adoption Barometer', *Adoption UK Charity*, 2024

Anderson, Anna, *Survival without Roots: Memoir of an Adopted Englishwoman: One* (Great Britain, 2022)

Barr, Heather, 'The Taliban and the Global Backlash against Women's Rights', *Human Rights Watch*, 2024

BBC iPlayer, 'BBC North West, St Monica's, Kendal, 19 July 2024', *YouTube* (2024)

Begum, Thaslima, '"I Was Told I Could Visit. Then She Went Missing": The Bangladeshi Mothers Who Say Their Children Were Adopted without Consent', *The Guardian*, 25 January 2024

Blanchfield, Theodora , 'The Layered Trauma of Losing My Adoptive Mother', *Verywell Mind*, 2022

Bouel, Shane, 'The Explicit Dominant Objectification of Adoption via Narcissism', *Medium*, 2023

Browne, Louise, and Sarah Reinhardt, 'Gregory: An Adoptee Gives Back. Adoption: The Making of Me. An Oral History of Adoptee Stories', 2023

Burke, Rennie, Yvette Ollada Lavery, Gali Katznelson, Joshua North, and J. Wesley Boyd, 'How Do Individuals Who Were Conceived through the Use of Donor Technologies Feel about the Nature of Their Conception?', *Bioethics.hms.harvard.edu*, 2021

Cahill, Fiona, 'BBC Piece Chris Page Did on Mums Forced Adoption and Forced "Repatriation" or Deportation to Ireland', *YouTube*, 2023

Cherieann, Gaynor, *An Adoptee's Journey: Letters of My Life*, 2022

Cherry, Joanna, 'Adoption of the Children of Unmarried Mothers from the 1940s-1970s', *UK Parliament*, 2023

Clark, Gillian, 'The Role of Mother and Baby Homes in the Adoption of Children Born Outside Marriage in Twentieth-Century England and Wales', *Family & Community History*, 11/1 (2008), 45–59

Cliff, Martha, 'Adoption Hell', *The Sun*, 23 January 2024

Cordeiro, Vanessa Cezarita, 'A Shameful Chapter of Irish History: Mother and Baby Homes', *Humanium*, 2022

Corker, Sarah, 'They just took the baby away', *ITV News*, 2024

Corsentino, Tony, 'Kinship after Severance', *Substack.com*, 2023

Dale, Jennifer, and Peggy Foster, *Feminists and State Welfare* (London, 1986)

Davis, Kingsley, 'Illegitimacy and the Social Structure', *American Journal of Sociology*, 45/2 (1939), 215–33

debyemm, 'Infertility and Narcissism', *Missing Mom* (2022)

Department of Children, Equality, Disability, Integration and Youth, *Final Report of the Commission of Investigation into Mother and Baby Homes*, (Ireland, 12 January 2021)

Diss, Kathryn, and Andrew Greaves, 'Ana and Elene Connected Online, But When They Met in Person, They Discovered a Dark Secret', *ABC News*, 1 March 2024

Dupont, Sophie, 'The Swiss Illegally Adopted Thousands of Children from Abroad', *SWI Swissinfo.ch*, 22 December 2023

Editor, 'Adoption Stories - the Pain of Giving up a Baby for Adoption - the Therapeutic Care Journal', *The Therapeutic Care Journal*, 2006

Etter, Carrie, *Imagined Sons* (Bridgend, Wales, 2014)

'FAQ on Hydrocephalus in Babies & Children(Causes, Treatment, Types, Diagnosis)', *Spina Bifida Resource Center*, 2022

Farmer, Jeannot, *No More Standing in the Shadows – Treating the Wounds of Historic Forced Adoption*

Fessler, Ann, *The Girls Who Went Away: The Hidden History of Women Who Surrendered Children for Adoption in the Decades before Roe v. Wade* (London, 2007)

First Minister, 'Apology for Historical Adoption Practices: First Minister's Speech - 22 March 2023', *www.gov.scot*, 2023

Foster, Alan, Fallondon Nursing Home, *SecretLeeds on Facebook.com*, 23 July 2018

Fox, Aine, 'Government "Sorry on Behalf of Society" for Treatment of Unmarried Mothers', *The Independent*, 3 March 2023

Frampton, Phil, *The Golly in the Cupboard* (2004)

Gallagher, Kevin, 'Burton on Trent Local History»Archive» Belvedere Workhouse – General History', *Burton-On-Trent.org.uk*

Gerhardt, Sue, *Why Love Matters: How Affection Shapes a Baby's Brain* (East Sussex, 2014)

Grubb, Lynn, 'Narcissism and Adoption -- Very Likely Bedfellows', *Blogspot.com* (2015)

Guibord, Alberta, and Ida R Parker, *What Becomes of the Unmarried Mother? A Study of 82 Cases* (USA, 1922)

Harman, Harriet, *Committee Hears from Mothers and Adopted People in Historic Adoption Inquiry, UK Parliament* (London, 16 March 2022)

Hayward, Chloe, and Hugh Pym, 'Infected Blood Scandal: Children Were Used as "Guinea Pigs" in Clinical Trials', *BBC News*, 18 April 2024

Henriques, Martha, 'Can the Legacy of Trauma Be Passed down the Generations?', *BBC.com* (2019)

HER, 'Sinead O'Connor Reveals How Her Time in a Magdalene Laundry as a Teenager Affected Her', *Her.ie*, 13 February 2013

Holmes, Jon, 'Jon Holmes, Generation Shame, BBC Radio 4', *BBC Sounds* (2023)

Howe, David, Phillida Sawbridge, and Diana Hinings, *Half a Million Women: Mothers Who Lose Their Children by Adoption* (London, 1992)

Into the Fire: The Lost Daughter Follows a Mother's Tireless Quest for the Truth, [documentary], (2024)

Ireland's Stolen Children Fight for Justice, [documentary], YouTube, 2023

Joint Committee on Human Rights, *Official Apology Sought in Recognition of Lasting Suffering Caused by Adoption Practices in 1950s-1970s Involving Unmarried Mothers - JCHR*, *Www.parliament.uk* (London, 15 July 2022)

———, *The Violation of Family Life: Adoption of Children of Unmarried Women 1949-1976 Third Report of Session 2022-23*, *Www.movementforanadoptionapology.org* (London, 15 July 2022)

———, *The Violation of Family Life: Adoption of Children of Unmarried Women 1949–1976: Government Response to the Committee's Third Report*, *Www.parliament.uk* (London, 3 March 2023)

Keating, Jenny, *A Child for Keeps: The History of Adoption in England 1918-45* (Basingstoke, 2009)

Keegan, Claire, *Small Things like These* (S.L., 2021)

Kiernan, Kathleen E, Jane Lewis, and Hilary Land, *Lone Motherhood in Twentieth-Century Britain: From Footnote to Front Page* (Oxford, 1998)

Kitova, Tanya T, and Anastasia V Bailey, 'Inbreeding as a Cause of Congenital Hydrocephalus', *International Journal of Infertility & Fetal Medicine*, 10/1 (2019), 4–7

Lambert, Michael, *A State Apology for Historic Forced Adoption in Britain*, (Lancaster University Medical School, September 2023)

———, 'Scotland Apologised in 2023 for Historic Forced Adoptions – but This Happened throughout the UK', *The Conversation*, 2024

———. Letter to Movement for an Adoption Apology, 'Letter from Dr. Michael Lambert', 6 March 2023

Langham, Rachel, 'Veronica Smith Obituary', *The Guardian* (2024)

Lewis, Jane, 'The Problem of Lone-Mother Families in Twentieth-Century Britain', *Journal of Social Welfare and Family Law*, 20/3 (1998), 251–83

————, *Women in Britain since 1945: Women, Family, Work and the State in the Post-War Years* (Oxford, 1992)

London Metropolitan Archives, 'Methodist Mother and Babies Home, Streatham', *LMA.gov.uk*, 1992

Marsden, Dennis, *Mothers Alone: Poverty and the Fatherless Family* (Harmondsworth, 1973)

Matthews, Helen Sarah, 'Illegitimacy and English Landed Society C.1285-c.1500' (2013)

McGovern, Alison, 'Forced Adoption in the UK - Hansard', *Hansard.parliament.uk*, 2018

Meredith, Robbie, 'Mother and Baby Home Survivors' Stories Published: "I Was Told I Was Going"', *BBC News*, 27 September 2022

Misra, Shivangi, 'Why Women's Rights Are Vulnerable in America', *Equality Now*, 2024

Mr Bates vs the Post Office, [television series], (2024)

Natasha, 'Adoptee Voices Amplified during National Adoption Week', *Researching Reform* (2023)

National Archives of Australia, *Without Consent: Australia's Past Adoption Practices* (Canberra, 2015)

Nicholson, Jill, and National Council, *Mother and Baby Homes: A Survey of Homes for Unmarried Mothers* (London, 1968)

Norris, Sian, and Sophia Alexandra Hall, 'How Privatisation of Foster Care Is Turning Vulnerable Children into Money-Making Commodities', *Big Issue* (16 February 2024)

O'Briain, Dara, 'So Where Were We?', *BBC iPlayer* (2023)

O'Rourke, Maeve, *A Human Rights Framework: Background Research for the Truth Recovery Design Process*, September 2021

Parravani, Christa, *Loved and Wanted: A Memoir of Choice, Children and Womanhood* (London, 2020)

Pearson, Michelle, and Eve Hatton, *Taken: A True Story of the Pain and Scandal of Forced Adoption (Stolen Lives)* (London, 2022)

Philomena, [film], (London, 2013)

Quarmby, Katharine, 'Hereditary Conditions Unknown: How the NHS Is Failing Adoptees', *Thelead.uk*, 2023

Robinson, Jane, *In the Family Way: Illegitimacy between the Great War and the Swinging Sixties* (London, 2015)

Rollings, Grant, '"Inside Wild Life of Rolling Stones" Brian Jones Who Slept with Bandmates' Lovers and Had 5 Kids before Shock Death at 27'.', *The Sun*, 15 May 2023

Scottish Government, '1. Introduction and Context', *www.gov.scot*, 2023

Shepherd, Tory, 'Strange but Ultimately Positive Genetic Discovery Reveals up to 1,000 Relatives Linked to Prolific Sperm Donor', *The Guardian* (2023)

Sherwood, Harriet, 'MPs to Demand Apology for Forced Adoptions in UK', *The Guardian*, 7 July 2018

Sissay, Lemn, *My Name Is Why* (Edinburgh, Scotland, 2019)

Small Things like These, [film], (London, 2024)

Thane, Pat, and Tanya Evans, *Sinners? Scroungers? Saints? : Unmarried Motherhood in Twentieth-Century England* (Oxford, 2012)

The Brussels Times with Belga, 'Catholic Church Put up 30,000 Children for Adoption without Mothers' Consent', *The Brussels Times*, 14 December 2023

The Fallen, [musical], (Glasgow, 2024)

The Labour Party, 'Labour Party Manifesto 2024: Our Plan to Change Britain', *Labour.org.uk*, 2024

The Magdalene Sisters, [film], (UK, Ireland, 2002)

The Marian Hotel, [play], (N. Ireland, 2024)

The Removed, [film], (UK, 2024)

The Woman in the Wall, [television series] (UK, 2023)

Tinggal, Theresa, *Against All Odds: A Life Changed Forever by Illegal Adoption in Ireland* (Milton Keynes, 2023)

Tofield, Sheila, *The Unmarried Mother* (London, 2013)

UK Parliament, 'Government Responds to JCHR Call for Adoption Apology', *UK Parliament*, 2023

van der Kolk, Bessel, *The Body Keeps the Score: Brain, Mind, and Body in the Healing of Trauma* (London, 2014)

Verrier, Nancy Newton, *The Primal Wound: Understanding the Adopted Child* (Maryland, 1993)

Walker, Marion L. (Jack), and Cathy Cartwright, 'Hydrocephalus in Infants and Children: Diagnosis & Treatment', *www.hydroassoc.org*, 2020

Welsh Government, 'People Affected by Historic Adoption Practices Welcomed to Senedd for Welsh Government Apology | *GOV.WALES*, 2023

Whiting, Kate, 'Jon Holmes: "I Have Never Looked for My Birth Mum, It Would Seem a Disservice to My Parents"', *BelfastTelegraph.co.uk* (8 August 2015)

Wing, Imogen, *Hertfordshire's Community Archive Network*, 27 December 2018

Winnicott, D W, *Babies and Their Mothers*, ed. by Ray Shepherd, Madeleine David, and Clare Winnicott (London, 1988)

Young, Dawn R, *Not Fade Away* (United States, 2013)

Further resources

MAA – Movement for an Adoption Apology

Movement for an Adoption Apology: Campaigning for a formal apology from the UK Government for everyone affected by historic forced adoption in the UK.

movementforanadoptionapology.org

Researching family history

UK Government resources:
gov.uk/adoption-records

FamilyConnect: A website to help adults who have been adopted or in care, find answers to questions about their origins.
familyconnect.org.uk

Adoptees' support organisations

Adult Adoptee Movement:
adultadoptee.org.uk/resources

PAC-UK | Adopted Adult Support:
pac-uk.org/our-services/adopted-adults

Adoption UK Charity: Information on adoption-related issues and campaigns for improvements to adoption policy and legislation. Helpline: 0300 666 0006.
adoptionuk.org

Mental health support

If you need help with your mental health, these services offer confidential support from trained volunteers. You can talk about anything that's troubling you, no matter how difficult.

NHS 111: Anyone in a mental health crisis can now call 111 and receive support from trained mental health professionals. The 24/7 service is available for all ages, including children, providing vital help through a single phone line.

Samaritans: Call 116 123 to talk to Samaritans,
or email: jo@samaritans.org for a reply within 24 hours.

Shout: Text "SHOUT" to 85258 to contact the Shout Crisis Text Line,
or text "YM" if you're under 19.

Childline: If you're under 19, you can also call 0800 1111 to talk to Childline. The number will not appear on your phone bill.